Microsoft® Word

2016
Level 1

Rutkosky • Roggenkamp • Rutkosky

PARADIGM
EDUCATION SOLUTIONS

St. Paul

Senior Vice President	Linda Hein
Editor in Chief	Christine Hurney
Director of Production	Timothy W. Larson
Production Editor	Jen Weaverling
Cover and Text Designer	Valerie King
Copy Editors	Communicáto, Ltd.; Page to Portal, LLC
Senior Design and Production Specialist	Jack Ross; PerfecType
Assistant Developmental Editors	Mamie Clark, Katie Werdick
Testers	Janet Blum, Fanshawe College; Traci Post
Instructional Support Writers	Janet Blum, Fanshawe College; Brienna McWade
Indexer	Terry Casey
Vice President Information Technology	Chuck Bratton
Digital Projects Manager	Tom Modl
Vice President Sales and Marketing	Scott Burns
Director of Marketing	Lara Weber McLellan

ISBN 978-0-76386-922-9 (print)
ISBN 978-0-76386-924-3 (digital)

© 2017 by Paradigm Publishing, Inc.
875 Montreal Way
St. Paul, MN 55102
Email: educate@emcp.com
Website: ParadigmCollege.com

Printed in the United States of America

23 22 21 20 19 18 17 16   1 2 3 4 5 6 7 8 9 10 11 12

Brief Contents

Contents

Benchmark Series: Microsoft® Word 2016 is designed for students who want to learn how to use this powerful word processing program to create professional-looking documents for school, work, and personal communication needs. No prior knowledge of word processing is required. After successfully completing a course using this textbook and digital courseware, students will be able to:

- Create and edit memos, letters, flyers, announcements, and reports of varying complexity
- Apply appropriate formatting elements and styles to a range of document types
- Add graphics and other visual elements to enhance written communication
- Plan, research, write, revise, and publish documents to meet specific information needs
- Given a workplace scenario requiring a written solution, assess the communication purpose and then prepare the materials that achieve the goal efficiently and effectively

Upon completing the text, students can expect to be proficient in using Word to organize, analyze, and present information.

Well-designed textbook pedagogy is important, but students learn technology skills through practice and problem solving. Technology provides opportunities for interactive learning as well as excellent ways to quickly and accurately assess student performance. To this end, this textbook is supported with SNAP 2016, Paradigm's web-based training and assessment learning management system. Details about SNAP as well as additional student courseware and instructor resources can be found on page xiv.

Achieving Proficiency in Word 2016

Since its inception several Office versions ago, the *Benchmark Series* has served as a standard of excellence in software instruction. Elements of the *Benchmark Series* function individually and collectively to create an inviting, comprehensive learning environment that produces successful computer users. The following visual tour highlights the structure and features that comprise the highly popular *Benchmark* model.

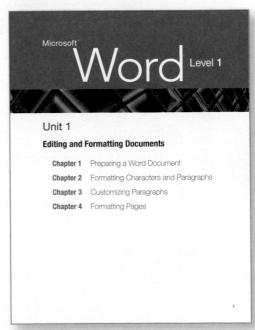

Unit Openers display the unit's four chapter titles. *Word Level 1* contains two units; each unit concludes with a comprehensive unit performance assessment.

Student Textbook and eBook

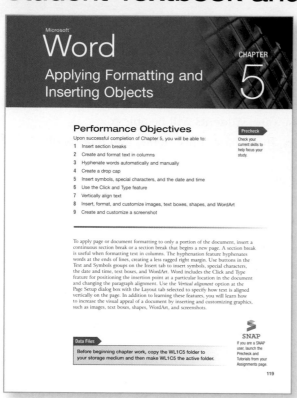

Chapter Openers present the performance objectives and an overview of the skills taught.

Precheck quizzes allow students to check their current skills before starting chapter work.

Data Files are provided for each chapter from the ebook. A prominent note reminds students to copy the appropriate chapter data folder and make it active.

Students with SNAP access are reminded to launch the Precheck quiz and chapter tutorials from their SNAP Assignments page.

Projects Build Skill Mastery within Realistic Context

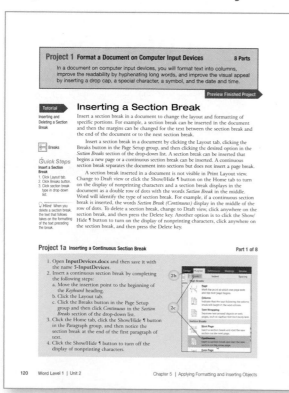

Multipart Projects provide a framework for instruction and practice on software features. A project overview identifies tasks to accomplish and key features to use in completing the work.

Preview Finished Project shows how the file will look after students complete the project.

Tutorials provide interactive, guided training and measured practice.

Quick Steps provide feature summaries for reference and review.

Hint margin notes offer useful tips on how to use features efficiently and effectively.

Typically, a file remains open throughout all parts of the project. Students save their work incrementally. At the end of the project, students save, print, and then close the file.

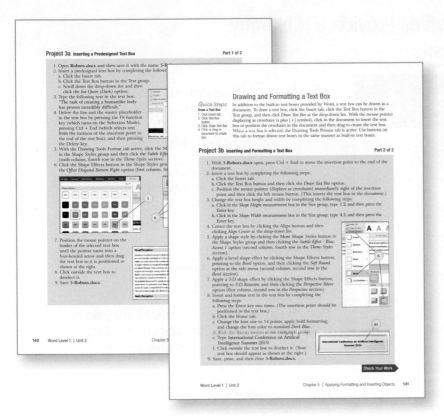

Step-by-Step Instructions guide students to the desired outcome for each project part. Screen captures illustrate what the screen should look like at key points.

Magenta Text identifies material to type.

Check Your Work allows students to confirm they have completed the project activity correctly.

Between project parts, the text presents instruction on the features and skills necessary to accomplish the next section of the project.

Chapter Review Tools Reinforce Learning

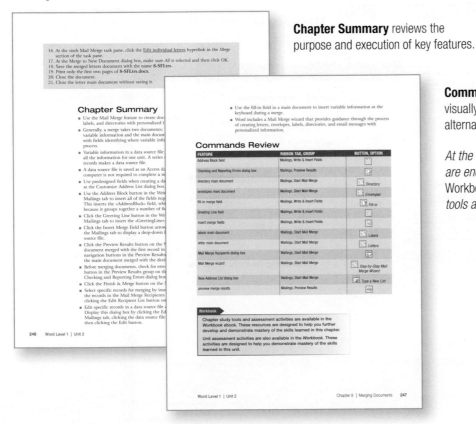

Chapter Summary reviews the purpose and execution of key features.

Commands Review summarizes visually the major features and alternative methods of access.

At the end of each chapter, students are encouraged to go to the Workbook ebook to access study tools and assessment activities.

Workbook eBook Activities Provide a Hierarchy of Learning Assessments

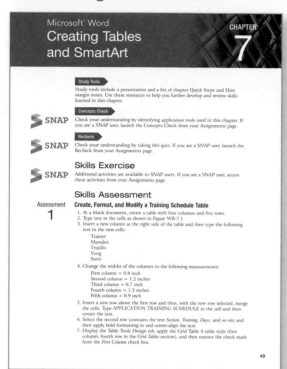

Study Tools are presentations with audio support and a list of chapter Quick Steps and Hint margin notes designed to help students further develop and review skills learned in the chapter.

Concepts Check is an objective completion exercise that allows students to assess their comprehension and recall of application features, terminology, and functions.

Recheck concept quizzes for each chapter enable students to check how their skills have improved after completing chapter work.

Skills Exercises are available to SNAP 2016 users. SNAP will automatically score student work, which is performed live in the application, and provide detailed feedback.

Skills Assessment exercises ask students to develop both standard and customized types of word processing documents without how-to directions.

Visual Benchmark assessments test problem-solving skills and mastery of application features.

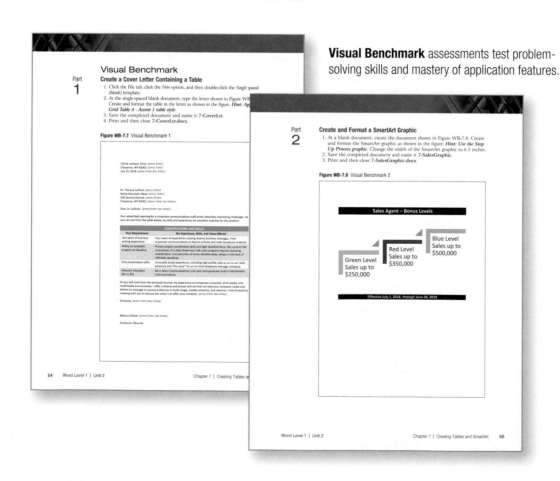

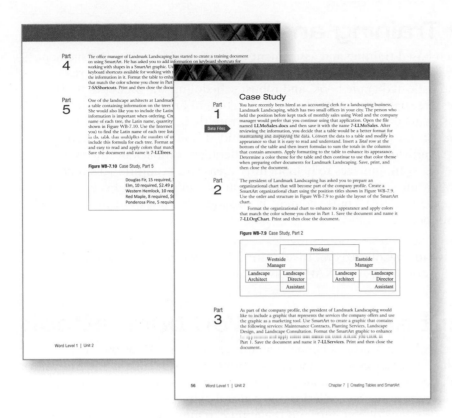

Case Study requires analyzing a workplace scenario and then planning and executing a multipart project.

Students search the web and/or use the program's Help feature to locate additional information required to complete the Case Study.

Unit Performance Assessments Deliver Cross-Disciplinary, Comprehensive Evaluation

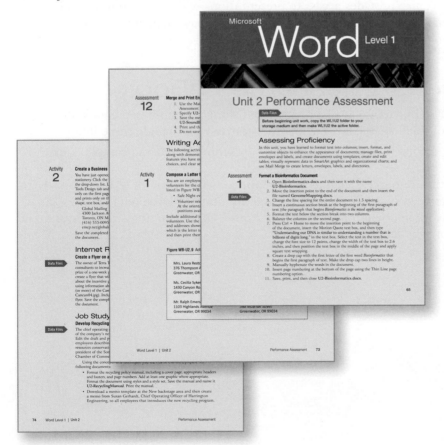

Assessing Proficiency exercises check mastery of features.

Writing Activities involve applying application skills in a communication context.

Internet Research projects reinforce research and information processing skills.

Job Study at the end of Unit 2 presents a capstone assessment requiring critical thinking and problem solving.

SNAP Training and Assessment

SNAP is a web-based training and assessment program and learning management system (LMS) for learning Microsoft Office 2016. SNAP is comprised of rich content, a sophisticated grade book, and robust scheduling and analytics tools. SNAP courseware supports the *Benchmark Series* content and delivers live-in-the-application assessments for students to demonstrate their skills mastery. Interactive tutorials increase skills-focused moments with guided training and measured practice. SNAP provides automatic scoring and detailed feedback on the many activities, exercises, and quizzes to help identify areas where additional support is needed, evaluating student performance both at an individual and course level. The *Benchmark Series* SNAP course content is also available to export into any LMS system that supports LTI tools.

Paradigm Education Solutions provides technical support for SNAP through 24-7 chat at ParadigmCollege.com. In addition, an online User Guide and other SNAP training tools for using SNAP are available.

Student eBook and *Workbook* eBook

The student ebook and *Workbook* ebook available through SNAP or online at Paradigm.bookshelf.emcp.com provide access to the *Benchmark Series* content from any device (desktop, tablet, and smartphone) anywhere, through a live Internet connection. The versatile ebook platform features dynamic navigation tools including a linked table of contents and the ability to jump to specific pages, search for terms, bookmark, highlight, and take notes. The ebooks offer live links to the interactive content and resources that support the print textbook, including the student data files, Precheck and Recheck quizzes, and interactive tutorials. The *Workbook* ebook also provides access to presentations with audio support and to end-of-section Concept Check, Skills Assessment, Visual Benchmark, Case Study, and end-of-unit Performance Assessment activities.

Instructor eResources eBook

All instructor resources are available digitally through a web-based ebook at Paradigm.bookshelf.emcp.com. The instructor materials include these items:

- Planning resources, such as lesson plans, teaching hints, and sample course syllabi
- Presentation resources, such as PowerPoint slide shows with lecture notes
- Assessment resources, including live and annotated PDF model answers for chapter work and workbook activities, rubrics for evaluating student work, and chapter-based exam banks

Microsoft®

Office

Getting Started in Office 2016

Several computer applications are combined to make the Microsoft Office 2016 application suite. The applications are known as *software*, and they contain instructions that tell the computer what to do. Some of the applications in the suite include Word, a word processing applicaton; Excel, a spreadsheet applicaton; Access, a database applicaton; and PowerPoint, a presentation applicaton.

Identifying Computer Hardware

The Microsoft Office suite can run on several types of computer equipment, referred to as *hardware*. You will need access to a laptop or a desktop computer system that includes a PC/tower, monitor, keyboard, printer, drives, and mouse. If you are not sure what equipment you will be operating, check with your instructor. The computer systems shown in Figure G.1 consists of six components. Each component is discussed separately in the material that follows.

Figure G.1 Computer System

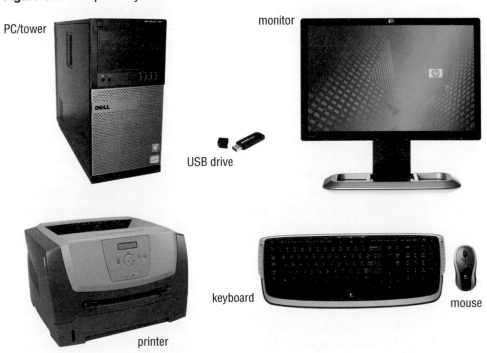

PC/tower

USB drive

monitor

printer

keyboard

mouse

Figure G.2 PC/Tower

PC/Tower

The PC, also known as the *tower*, is the brain of the computer and is where all processing occurs. A PC/tower consists of components such as the Central Processing Unit (CPU), hard drives, and video cards plugged into a motherboard. The motherboard is mounted inside the case, which includes input and output ports for attaching external peripherals (as shown in Figure G.2). When a user provides input through the use of peripherals, the PC/tower computes that input and outputs the results. Similar hardware is included in a laptop, but the design is more compact to allow for mobility.

Monitor

Hint Monitor size is measured diagonally. For example, the distance from the bottom left corner to the top right corner of the monitor.

A computer monitor looks like a television screen. It displays the visual information that the computer is outputting. The quality of display for monitors varies depending on the type of monitor and the level of resolution. Monitors can also vary in size—generally from 13 inches to 26 inches or larger.

Keyboard

The keyboard is used to input information into the computer. The number and location of the keys on a keyboard can vary. In addition to letters, numbers, and symbols, most computer keyboards contain function keys, arrow keys, and a numeric keypad. Figure G.3 shows an enhanced keyboard.

The 12 keys at the top of the keyboard, labeled with the letter F followed by a number, are called *function keys*. Use these keys to perform functions within each of the Office applications. To the right of the regular keys is a group of special or dedicated keys. These keys are labeled with specific functions that will be performed when you press the key. Below the special keys are arrow keys. Use these keys to move the insertion point in the document screen.

Some keyboards include mode indicator lights. When you select certain modes, a light appears on the keyboard. For example, if you press the Caps Lock key, which disables the lowercase alphabet, a light appears next to Caps Lock. Similarly, pressing the Num Lock key will disable the special functions on the numeric keypad, which is located at the right side of the keyboard.

Figure G.3 Keyboard

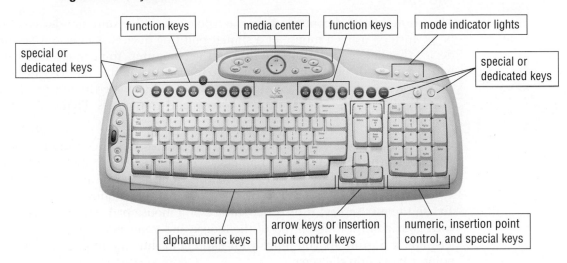

function keys

media center

function keys

mode indicator lights

special or dedicated keys

special or dedicated keys

alphanumeric keys

arrow keys or insertion point control keys

numeric, insertion point control, and special keys

Drives and Ports

A PC includes drives and ports that allow you to input and output data. For example, a hard drive is a disk drive inside of the PC that stores data that may have been inputted or outputted. Other drives may include CD, DVD and BluRay disc drives, although newer computers may not include these drives, because USB flash drives are becoming the preferred technology. Ports are the "plugs" on the PC, and are used to connect devices to the computer, such as the keyboard and mouse, the monitor, speakers, a USB flash drive and so on. Most PCs will have a few USB ports, at least one display port, an audio cable port, and possibly an ethernet port (used to physically connect to the Internet or a network).

Printer

An electronic version of a file is known as a *soft copy*. If you want to create a hard copy of a file, you need to print it. To print documents you will need to access a printer (as shown in Figure G.4), which will probably be either a laser printer or an ink-jet printer. A laser printer uses a laser beam combined with heat and pressure to print documents, while an ink-jet printer prints a document by spraying a fine mist of ink on the page.

Figure G.4 Printer

Mouse

Most functions and commands in the Microsoft Office suite are designed to be performed using a mouse or a similar pointing device. A mouse is an input device that sits on a flat surface next to the computer. You can operate a mouse with your left or right hand. Moving the mouse on the flat surface causes a corresponding pointer to move on the screen, and clicking the left or right mouse buttons allows you to select various objects and commands. Figure G.5 shows an example of a mouse.

Using the Mouse The applications in the Microsoft Office suite can be operated with the keyboard and a mouse. The mouse generally has two buttons on top, which you press to execute specific functions and commands. A mouse may also contain a wheel, which can be used to scroll in a window or as a third button. To use the mouse, rest it on a flat surface or a mouse pad. Put your hand over it with your palm resting on top of the mouse and your index finger resting on the left mouse button. As you move your hand, and thus the mouse, a corresponding pointer moves on the screen.

When using the mouse, you should understand four terms — point, click, double-click, and drag. When operating the mouse, you may need to point to a specific command, button, or icon. To *point* means to position the mouse pointer on the desired item. With the mouse pointer positioned on the item, you may need to click a button on the mouse to select the item. To *click* means to quickly tap a button on the mouse once. To complete two steps at one time, such as choosing and then executing a function, double-click the mouse button. To *double-click* means to tap the left mouse button twice in quick succession. The term *drag* means to click and hold down the left mouse button, move the mouse pointer to a specific location, and then release the button.

Hint This textbook will use the verb *click* to refer to the mouse and the verb press to refer to a key on the keyboard.

Using the Mouse Pointer The mouse pointer will look different depending on where you have positioned it and what function you are performing. The following are some of the ways the mouse pointer can appear when you are working in the Office suite:

- The mouse pointer appears as an I-beam (called the *I-beam pointer*) when you are inserting text in a file. The I-beam pointer can be used to move the insertion point or to select text.
- The mouse pointer appears as an arrow pointing up and to the left (called the *arrow pointer*) when it is moved to the Title bar, Quick Access Toolbar, ribbon, or an option in a dialog box, among other locations.
- The mouse pointer becomes a double-headed arrow (either pointing left and right, pointing up and down, or pointing diagonally) when you perform certain functions such as changing the size of an object.

Figure G.5 Mouse

- In certain situations, such as when you move an object or image, the mouse pointer displays with a four-headed arrow attached. The four-headed arrow means that you can move the object left, right, up, or down.

- When a request is being processed or when an application is being loaded, the mouse pointer may appear as a moving circle. The moving circle means "please wait." When the process is completed, the circle is replaced with a normal mouse pointer.

- When the mouse pointer displays as a hand with a pointing index finger, it indicates that more information is available about an item. The mouse pointer also displays as a hand with a pointing index finger when you hover the mouse over a hyperlink.

Touchpad

If you are working on a laptop computer, you may use a touchpad instead of a mouse. A *touchpad* allows you to move the mouse pointer by moving your finger across a surface at the base of the keyboard. You click and right-click by using your thumb to press the buttons located at the bottom of the touchpad. Some touchpads have special features such as scrolling or clicking something by tapping the surface of the touchpad instead of pressing a button with a thumb.

TouchScreen

Smartphones, tablets, and touch monitors all use TouchScreen technology (as shown in Figure G.6), which allows users to directly interact with the objects on the screen by touching them with fingers, thumbs, or a stylus. Multiple fingers or both thumbs can be used on most modern touchscreens, giving users the ability to zoom, rotate, and manipulate items on the screen. While a lot of activities in this textbook can be completed using a device with a touchscreen, a mouse or touchpad might be required to complete a few activities.

Figure G.6 Touchscreen

Choosing Commands

Once an application is open, you can use several methods in the application to choose commands. A command is an instruction that tells the application to do something. You can choose a command using the mouse or the keyboard. When an application such as Word or PowerPoint is open, the ribbon contains buttons and options for completing tasks, as well as tabs you can click to display additional buttons and options. To choose a button on the Quick Access Toolbar or on the ribbon, position the tip of the mouse arrow pointer on the button and then click the left mouse button.

The Office suite provides accelerator keys you can press to use a command in an application. Press the Alt key on the keyboard to display KeyTips that identify the accelerator key you can press to execute a command. For example, if you press the Alt key in a Word document with the Home tab active, KeyTips display as shown in Figure G.7. Continue pressing accelerator keys until you execute the desired command. For example, to begin checking the spelling in a document, press the Alt key, press the R key on the keyboard to display the Review tab, and then press the letter S on the keyboard.

Choosing Commands from Drop-Down Lists

To choose a command from a drop-down list with the mouse, position the mouse pointer on the option and then click the left mouse button. To make a selection from a drop-down list with the keyboard, type the underlined letter in the option.

Some options at a drop-down list may appear in gray (dimmed), indicating that the option is currently unavailable. If an option at a drop-down list displays preceded by a check mark, it means the option is currently active. If an option at a drop-down list displays followed by an ellipsis (...), clicking that option will display a dialog box.

Choosing Options from a Dialog Box

A dialog box contains options for applying formatting or otherwise modifying a file or data within a file. Some dialog boxes display with tabs along the top that provide additional options. For example, the Font dialog box shown in Figure G.8 contains two tabs—the Font tab and the Advanced tab. The tab that displays in the front is the active tab. To make a tab active using the mouse, position the arrow pointer on the tab and then click the left mouse button. If you are using the keyboard, press Ctrl + Tab or press Alt + the underlined letter on the tab.

To choose an option from a dialog box with the mouse, position the arrow pointer on the option and then click the left mouse button. If you are using the keyboard, press the Tab key to move the insertion point forward from option to option. Press Shift + Tab to move the insertion point backward from option to option. You can also press and hold down the Alt key and then press the

Figure G.7 Word Home Tab KeyTips

Figure G.8 Word Font Dialog Box

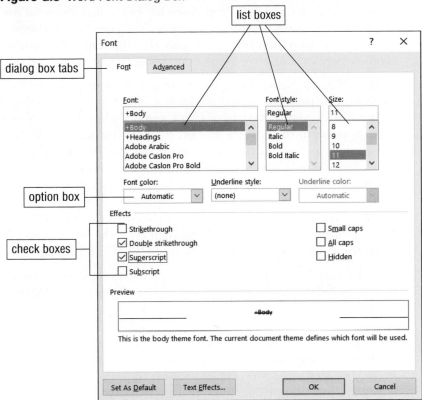

underlined letter of the option. When an option is selected, it displays with a blue background or surrounded by a dashed box called a *marquee*. A dialog box contains one or more of the following elements: list boxes, option boxes, check boxes, text boxes, option buttons, measurement boxes, and command buttons.

List Boxes and Option Boxes The fonts available in the Font dialog box, shown in Figure G.8, are contained in a list box. To make a selection from a list box with the mouse, move the arrow pointer to the option and then click the left mouse button.

Some list boxes may contain a scroll bar. This scroll bar will display at the right side of the list box (a vertical scroll bar) or at the bottom of the list box (a horizontal scroll bar). Use a vertical scroll bar or a horizontal scroll bar to move through the list if the list is longer (or wider) than the box. To move down a list using a vertical scroll bar, position the arrow pointer on the down arrow, and then click and hold down the left mouse button. To scroll up through the list, position the arrow pointer on the up arrow, and then click and hold down the left mouse button. You can also move the arrow pointer above the scroll box and click the left mouse button to scroll up the list or move the arrow pointer below the scroll box and click the left mouse button to move down the list. To navigate in a list with a horizontal scroll bar, click the left arrow to scroll to the left of the list or click the right arrow to scroll to the right of the list.

To use the keyboard to make a selection from a list box, move the insertion point into the box by holding down the Alt key and pressing the underlined letter of the desired option. Press the Up and/or Down Arrow keys on the keyboard to move through the list, and press the Enter key when the desired option is selected.

In some dialog boxes where there is not enough room for a list box, lists of options are contained in a drop-down list box called an *option box*. Option boxes display with a down arrow. For example, in Figure G.8, the font color options are contained in an option box. To display the different color options, click the *Font color* option box arrow. If you are using the keyboard, press Alt + C.

Check Boxes Some dialog boxes contain options preceded by a box. A check mark may or may not appear in the box. The Word Font dialog box shown in Figure G.8 displays a variety of check boxes within the *Effects* section. If a check mark appears in the box, the option is active (turned on). If the check box does not contain a check mark, the option is inactive (turned off). Any number of check boxes can be active. For example, in the Word Font dialog box, you can insert a check mark in several of the boxes in the *Effects* section to activate the options.

To make a check box active or inactive with the mouse, position the tip of the arrow pointer in the check box and then click the left mouse button. If you are using the keyboard, press Alt + the underlined letter of the option.

Text Boxes Some options in a dialog box require you to enter text. For example, the boxes below the *Find what* and *Replace with* options at the Excel Find and Replace dialog box shown in Figure G.9 are text boxes. In a text box, type text or edit existing text. Edit text in a text box in the same manner as normal text. Use the Left and Right Arrow keys on the keyboard to move the insertion point without deleting text and use the Delete key or Backspace key to delete text.

Command Buttons The buttons at the bottom of the Excel Find and Replace dialog box shown in Figure G.9 are called *command buttons*. Use a command button to execute or cancel a command. Some command buttons display with an ellipsis (...), which means another dialog box will open if you click that button. To choose a command button with the mouse, position the arrow pointer on the button and then click the left mouse button. To choose a command button with the keyboard, press the Tab key until the command button is surrounded by a marquee and then press the Enter key.

Option Buttons The Word Insert Table dialog box shown in Figure G.10 contains options in the *AutoFit behavior* section preceded by option buttons. Only one option button can be selected at any time. When an option button is selected, a blue or black circle displays in the button. To select an option button with the mouse, position the tip of the arrow pointer inside the option button or on the option and then click the left mouse button. To make a selection with the keyboard, press and hold down the Alt key, press the underlined letter of the option, and then release the Alt key.

Figure G.9 Excel Find and Replace Dialog Box

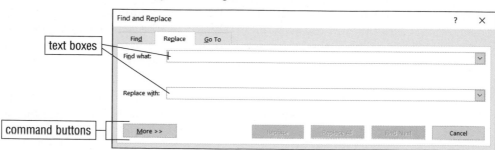

Figure G.10 Word Insert Table Dialog Box

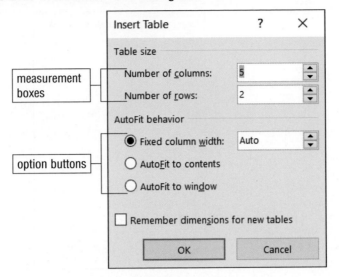

measurement boxes

option buttons

Measurement Boxes Some options in a dialog box contain measurements or amounts you can increase or decrease. These options are generally located in a measurement box. For example, the Word Insert Table dialog box shown in Figure G.10 contains the *Number of columns* and *Number of rows* measurement boxes. To increase a number in a measurement box, position the tip of the arrow pointer on the up arrow at the right of the measurement box and then click the left mouse button. To decrease the number, click the down arrow. If you are using the keyboard, press and hold down the Alt key and then press the underlined letter for the option, press the Up Arrow key to increase the number or the Down Arrow key to decrease the number, and then release the Alt key.

Choosing Commands with Keyboard Shortcuts

Applications in the Office suite offer a variety of keyboard shortcuts you can use to execute specific commands. Keyboard shortcuts generally require two or more keys. For example, the keyboard shortcut to display the Open dialog box in an application is Ctrl + F12. To use this keyboard shortcut, press and hold down the Ctrl key, press the F12 function on the keyboard, and then release the Ctrl key. For a list of keyboard shortcuts, refer to the Help files.

Choosing Commands with Shortcut Menus

The software applications in the Office suite include shortcut menus that contain commands related to different items. To display a shortcut menu, position the mouse pointer over the item for which you want to view more options, and then click the right mouse button or press Shift + F10. The shortcut menu will appear wherever the insertion point is positioned. For example, if the insertion point is positioned in a paragraph of text in a Word document, clicking the right mouse button or pressing Shift + F10 will cause the shortcut menu shown in Figure G.11 to display in the document screen (along with the Mini toolbar).

To select an option from a shortcut menu with the mouse, click the option. If you are using the keyboard, press the Up or Down Arrow key until the option is selected and then press the Enter key. To close a shortcut menu without choosing an option, click outside the shortcut menu or press the Esc key.

Figure G.11 Word Shortcut Menu

Working with Multiple Programs

As you learn the various applications in the Microsoft Office suite, you will notice many similarities between them. For example, the steps to save, close, and print are virtually the same whether you are working in Word, Excel, or PowerPoint. This consistency between applications greatly enhances your ability to transfer knowledge learned in one application to another within the suite. Another benefit to using Microsoft Office is the ability to have more than one application open at the same time and to integrate content from one program with another. For example, you can open Word and create a document, open Excel and create a spreadsheet, and then copy the Excel spreadsheet into Word.

When you open an application, a button containing an icon representing the application displays on the taskbar. If you open another application, a button containing an icon representing that application displays to the right of the first application button on the taskbar. Figure G.12 shows the taskbar with Word, Excel, Access, and PowerPoint open. To move from one program to another, click the taskbar button representing the desired application.

Customizing Settings

Before beginning computer projects in this textbook, you may need to customize your monitor's settings, change the DPI display setting, and turn on the display of file extensions. Projects in the chapters in this textbook assume that the monitor display is set at 1600 × 900 pixels, the DPI set at 125%, and that the display of file extensions is turned on. If you are unable to make changes to the monitor's resolution or the DPI settings, the projects can still be completed successfully. Some references in the text might not perfectly match what you see on your

Figure G.12 Taskbar with Word, Excel, Access, and PowerPoint Open

screen, so some mental adjustments may need to be made for certain steps. For example, an item in a drop-down gallery might appear in a different column or row than what is indicated in the step instructions.

Before you begin learning the applications in the Microsoft Office 2016 suite, take a moment to check the display settings on the computer you are using. Your monitor's display settings are important because the ribbon in the Microsoft Office suite adjusts to the screen resolution setting of your computer monitor. A computer monitor set at a high resolution will have the ability to show more buttons in the ribbon than will a monitor set to a low resolution. The illustrations in this textbook were created with a screen resolution display set at 1600 × 900 pixels. In Figure G.13, the Word ribbon is shown three ways: at a lower screen resolution (1366 × 768 pixels), at the screen resolution featured throughout this textbook, and at a higher screen resolution (1920 × 1080 pixels). Note the variances in the ribbon in all three examples. If possible, set your display to 1600 × 900 pixels to match the illustrations you will see in this textbook.

Figure G.13 The Home Tab Displayed on a Monitor Set at Different Screen Resolutions

1366 × 768 screen resolution

1600 × 900 screen resolution

1920 × 1080 screen resolution

Project 1 Setting Monitor Display to 1600 × 900

Note: The resolution settings may be locked on lab computers. Also, some laptop screens and small monitors may not be able to display in a 1600 × 900 resolution.

1. At the Windows 10 desktop, right-click in a blank area of the screen.
2. At the shortcut menu, click the *Display settings* option.

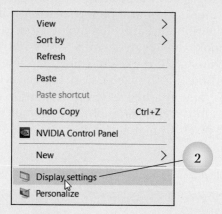

3. At the Settings window with the SYSTEM screen active, scroll down and then click *Advanced display settings*.

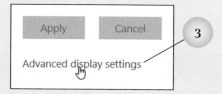

4. Scroll down the Settings window until the *Resolution* option box is visible and take note of the current resolution setting. If the current resolution is already set to 1600 × 900, skip ahead to Step 8.
5. Click in the Resolution option box and then click the 1600 × 900 option at the drop-down list.

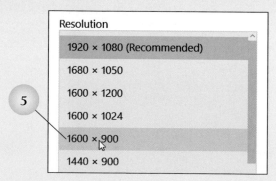

6. Click the Apply button.
7. Click the Keep Changes button.
8. Click the Close button.

Project 2 Changing the DPI Setting

Note: The DPI settings may be locked on lab computers. Also, some laptop screens and small monitors may not allow the DPI settings to be changed.

1. At the Windows 10 desktop, right-click in a blank area of the screen.
2. At the shortcut menu, click the *Display settings* option.
3. At the Settings window, take note of the current DPI percentage next to the text *Change the size of text, apps, and other items*. If the percentage is already set to 125%, skip to Step 5.
4. Click the slider bar below the text *Change the size of text, apps, and other items* and hold down the left mouse button, drag to the right until the DPI percentage is 125%, and then release the mouse button.

5. Close the computer window.

Project 3 Displaying File Extensions

1. At the Windows 10 desktop, click the File Explorer button on the taskbar.

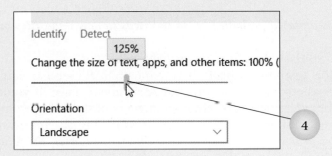

2. At the File Explorer window, click the View tab.
3. Click the *File name extensions* check box in the Show/hide group to insert a check mark.

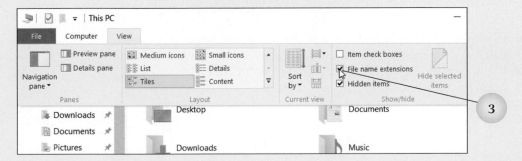

4. Close the computer window.

Data Files

Completing Computer Projects

Some projects in this textbook require that you open an existing file. Project files are saved on OneDrive in a zip file. Before beginning projects and assessments in this book and the accompanying ebook, copy the necessary folder from the zip file to your storage medium (such as a USB flash drive) using File Explorer. Begin downloading the files for this book by going to the ebook and clicking the Ancillary Links button that displays when the ebook displays this page or any chapter opener page with the Data Files tab on it.

Project 4 Downloading Files to a USB Flash Drive

Note: OneDrive is updated periodically, so the steps to download files may vary from the steps below.

1. Insert your USB flash drive into an available USB port.
2. Navigate to this textbook's ebook. If you are a SNAP user, navigate to the ebook by clicking the textbook ebook link on your Assignments page. If you are not a SNAP user, launch your browser and go to http://paradigm.bookshelf.emcp.com, log in, and then click the textbook ebook thumbnail. *Note: The steps in this activity assume you are using the Microsoft Edge browser. If you are using a different browser, the following steps may vary.*
3. Navigate to the ebook page that corresponds to this textbook page.
4. Click the Ancillary Links button in the menu. The menu that appears may be at the top of the window or along the side of the window, depending on the size of the window.

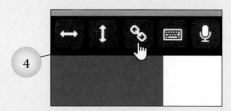

5. At the Ancillary Links dialog box, click the <u>Data Files: All Files</u> hyperlink.

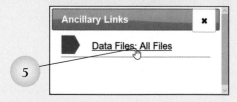

6. Click the Download hyperlink at the top of the window.
7. Click the Open button in the message box when the DataFiles.zip finishes downloading.
8. Right-click the DataFiles folder in the Content pane.
9. Click the *Copy* option in the shortcut menu.

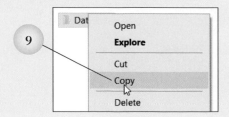

10. Click the USB flash drive that displays in the Navigation pane at the left side of the File Explorer window.
11. Click the Home tab in the File Explorer window.
12. Click the Paste button in the Clipboard group.

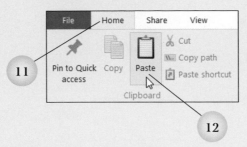

13. Close the File Explorer window by clicking the Close button in the upper right corner of the window.

Project 5 Deleting a File

Note: Check with your instructor before deleting a file.

1. At the Windows 10 desktop, open File Explorer by clicking the File Explorer button on the taskbar.
2. Click the *Downloads* folder in the navigation pane.
3. Right-click *DataFiles.zip*.
4. Click the *Delete* option at the shortcut menu.

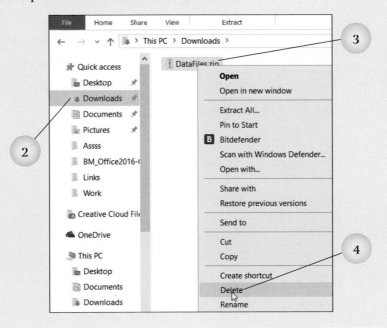

Microsoft Word Level 1

Unit 1

Editing and Formatting Documents

Microsoft® Word

Preparing a Word Document

Performance Objectives

Precheck

Check your current skills to help focus your study.

Upon successful completion of Chapter 1, you will be able to:

1 Open Microsoft Word

2 Create, save, name, print, open, and close a Word document

3 Close Word

4 Open a document from and pin/unpin a document at the *Recent* Option list

5 Edit a document

6 Move the insertion point within a document

7 Scroll within a document

8 Select text

9 Use the Undo and Redo buttons

10 Check spelling and grammar

11 Use the Tell Me and Help features

In this chapter, you will learn to create, save, name, print, open, close, and edit a Word document as well as complete a spelling and grammar check. You will also learn about the Tell Me feature, which provides information and guidance on how to complete a function, and the Help feature, which is an on-screen reference manual that provides information on features and commands for each program in the Microsoft Office suite. Before continuing, make sure you read the *Getting Started* section presented at the beginning of this book. It contains information about computer hardware and software, using the mouse, executing commands, and exploring Help files.

Data Files

Before beginning chapter work, copy the WL1C1 folder to your storage medium and then make WL1C1 the active folder.

SNAP

If you are a SNAP user, launch the Precheck and Tutorials from your Assignments page.

3

Project 1 **Prepare a Word Document**   **2 Parts**

You will create a short document containing information on resumes and then save, print, and close the document.

Preview Finished Project

Tutorial

Opening a Blank Document

Opening Microsoft Word

Microsoft Office 2016 contains a word processing program named Word that can be used to create, save, edit, and print documents. The steps to open Word may vary but generally include clicking the Start button on the Windows 10 desktop and then clicking the Word 2016 tile at the Start menu. At the Word 2016 opening screen, click the *Blank document* template.

Tutorial

Exploring the Word Screen

Creating, Saving, Printing, and Closing a Document

When the Blank document template is clicked, a blank document displays on the screen, as shown in Figure 1.1. The features of the document screen are described in Table 1.1.

At a blank document, type information to create a document. A document is a record containing information such as a letter, report, term paper, table, and so on. Here are some things to consider when typing text:

Quick Steps

Open Word and Open a Blank Document
1. Click Word 2016 tile at Windows Start menu.
2. Click *Blank document* template.

- **Word wrap:** As text is typed in the document, Word wraps text to the next line, so the Enter key does not need to be pressed at the end of each line. A word is wrapped to the next line if it begins before the right margin and continues past the right margin. The only times the Enter key needs to be pressed are to end a paragraph, create a blank line, and end a short line.

- **AutoCorrect:** Word contains a feature that automatically corrects certain words as they are typed. For example, if *adn* is typed instead of *and*, Word automatically corrects it when the spacebar is pressed after typing the word. AutoCorrect will also superscript the letters that follow an ordinal number (a number indicating a position in a series). For example, type *2nd* and then press the spacebar or Enter key, and Word will convert this ordinal number to 2nd.

- **Automatic spelling checker:** By default, Word automatically inserts a red wavy line below any word that is not contained in the Spelling dictionary or automatically corrected by AutoCorrect. This may include misspelled words, proper names, some terminology, and some foreign words. If a typed word is not recognized by the Spelling dictionary, leave it as written if the word is correct. However, if the word is incorrect, delete the word or position the I-beam pointer on the word, click the *right* mouse button, and then click the correct spelling at the shortcut menu.

Hint A book icon displays in the Status bar. A check mark on the book indicates no spelling errors have been detected by the spelling checker, while an X on the book indicates errors. Double-click the book icon to move to the next error. If the book icon is not visible, right-click the Status bar and then click the *Spelling and Grammar Check* option at the shortcut menu.

- **Automatic grammar checker:** Word includes an automatic grammar checker. If the grammar checker detects a sentence containing a grammatical error, a blue wavy line is inserted below the error. The sentence can be left as written or corrected. To correct the sentence, position the I-beam pointer on the error, click the *right* mouse button, and choose from the shortcut menu of possible corrections.

Figure 1.1 Blank Document

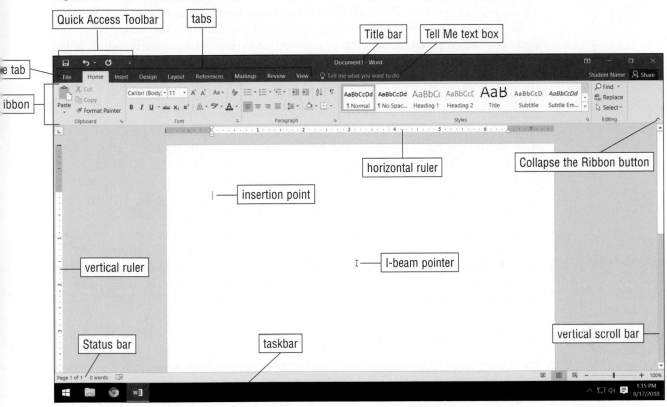

Table 1.1 Microsoft Word Screen Features

Feature	Description
Collapse the Ribbon button	when clicked, removes the ribbon from the screen
File tab	when clicked, displays backstage area, which contains options for working with and managing documents
horizontal ruler	used to set margins, indents, and tabs
I-beam pointer	used to move the insertion point or to select text
insertion point	indicates the location of the next character entered at the keyboard
Quick Access Toolbar	contains buttons for commonly used commands
ribbon	area containing tabs with options and buttons divided into groups
Status bar	displays the numbers of pages and words, plus the view buttons and Zoom slider bar
tabs	contain commands and features organized into groups
taskbar	contains icons for launching programs, buttons for active tasks, and a notification area
Tell Me feature	provides information and guidance on how to complete functions
Title bar	displays the document name followed by the program name
vertical ruler	used to set the top and bottom margins
vertical scroll bar	used to view various parts of the document beyond the screen

- **Spacing punctuation:** Typically, Word uses Calibri as the default typeface, which is a proportional typeface. (You will learn more about typefaces in Chapter 2.) When typing text in a proportional typeface, space once (rather than two times) after end-of-sentence punctuation such as a period, question mark, or exclamation point and after a colon. The characters in a proportional typeface are set closer together, and extra white space at the end of a sentence or after a colon is not needed.

- **Option buttons:** As text is inserted or edited in a document, an option button may display near the text. The name and appearance of this option button varies depending on the action. If a typed word is corrected by AutoCorrect, if an automatic list is created, or if autoformatting is applied to text, the AutoCorrect Options button appears. Click this button to undo the specific automatic action. If text is pasted in a document, the Paste Options button appears near the text. Click this button to display the Paste Options gallery, which has buttons for controlling how the pasted text is formatted.

- **AutoComplete:** Microsoft Word and other Office applications include an AutoComplete feature that inserts an entire item when a few identifying characters are typed. For example, type the letters *Mond* and *Monday* displays in a ScreenTip above the letters. Press the Enter key or press the F3 function key and Word inserts *Monday* in the document.

Tutorial

Entering Text

Using the New Line Command

A Word document is based on a template that applies default formatting. Some basic formatting includes 1.08 line spacing and 8 points of spacing after a paragraph. Each time the Enter key is pressed, a new paragraph begins and 8 points of spacing is inserted after the paragraph. To move the insertion point down to the next line without including the additional 8 points of spacing, use the New Line command, Shift + Enter.

Project 1a Creating a Document

Part 1 of 2

1. Open Word by clicking the Word 2016 tile at the Windows Start menu.
2. At the Word opening screen, click the *Blank document* template. (These steps may vary. Check with your instructor for specific instructions.)
3. At a blank document, type the information shown in Figure 1.2 with the following specifications:
   a. Correct any errors highlighted by the spelling checker or grammar checker as they occur.
   b. Press the spacebar once after end-of-sentence punctuation.
   c. After typing *Created:* press Shift + Enter to move the insertion point to the next line without adding 8 points of additional spacing.
   d. To insert the word *Thursday* at the end of the document, type Thur and then press F3. (This is an example of the AutoComplete feature.)
   e. To insert the word *December*, type Dece and then press the Enter key. (This is another example of the AutoComplete feature.)
   f. Press Shift + Enter after typing *December 6, 2018*.
   g. When typing the last line (the line containing the ordinal numbers), type the ordinal number text and AutoCorrect will automatically convert the letters in the ordinal numbers to a superscript.
4. When you are finished typing the text, press the Enter key. (Keep the document open for the next project.)

Check Your Work

Figure 1.2 Project 1a

The traditional chronological resume lists your work experience in reverse-chronological order (starting with your current or most recent position). The functional style deemphasizes the "where" and "when" of your career and instead groups similar experiences, talents, and qualifications regardless of when they occurred.

Like the chronological resume, the hybrid resume includes specifics about where you worked, when you worked there, and what your job titles were. Like a functional resume, a hybrid resume emphasizes your most relevant qualifications in an expanded summary section, in several "career highlights" bullet points at the top of your resume, or in project summaries.

Created:
Thursday, December 6, 2018
Note: The two paragraphs will become the 2nd and 3rd paragraphs in the 5th section.

Tutorial

Saving with a
New Name

 Save

Quick Steps
Save a Document
1. Click File tab.
2. Click *Save As* option.
3. Click *Browse* option.
4. Type document name in *File name* text box.
5. Press Enter.

Saving a Document with a New Name

Save a document if it is going to be used in the future. Save a new document or save an existing document with a new name at the Save As dialog box.

To save a new document, click the Save button on the Quick Access Toolbar, click the File tab, and then click the *Save* option or the *Save As* option, or press the keyboard shortcut Ctrl + S and the Save As backstage area displays, as shown in Figure 1.3. Click the *Browse* option to display the Save As dialog box, as shown in Figure 1.4.

To save an existing document with a new name, click the File tab, click the *Save As* option to display the Save As backstage area, and then click the *Browse* option to display the Save As dialog box. Press the F12 function key to display the Save As dialog box without having to first display the Save As backstage area. At the Save As dialog box, type the name for the document in the *File name* text box and then press the Enter key or click the Save button.

💡 **Hint** Save a document approximately every 15 minutes or when interrupted.

Figure 1.3 Save As Backstage Area

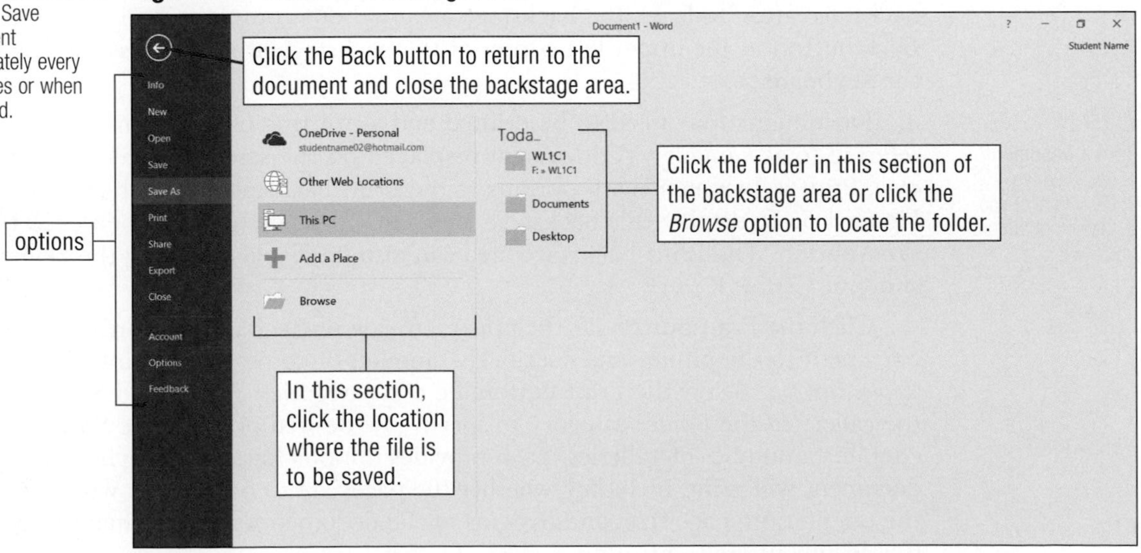

Click the Back button to return to the document and close the backstage area.

options

In this section, click the location where the file is to be saved.

Click the folder in this section of the backstage area or click the *Browse* option to locate the folder.

Figure 1.4 Save As Dialog Box

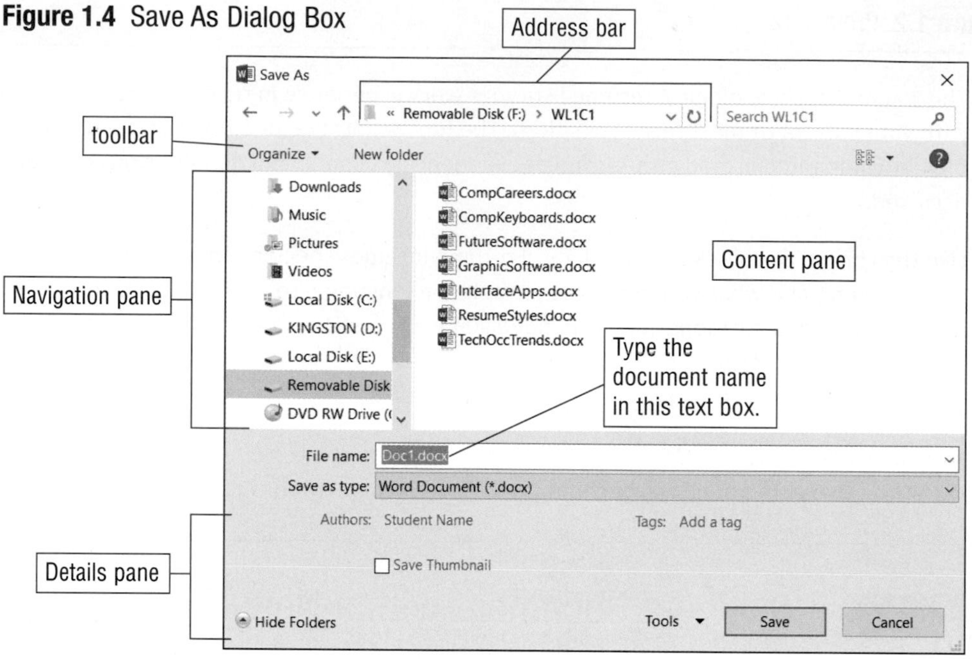

Naming a Document

💡 **Hint** You cannot give a document the same name first in uppercase and then in lowercase letters.

Document names created in Word and other applications in the Microsoft Office suite can be up to 255 characters in length, including the drive letter and any folder names, and they may include spaces. File names cannot include any of the following characters:

forward slash (/)	less-than symbol (<)	quotation marks (" ")
backslash (\)	asterisk (*)	colon (:)
greater-than symbol (>)	question mark (?)	pipe symbol (|)

Printing a Document

Tutorial

Printing a Document

Click the File tab and the backstage area displays. The buttons and options at the backstage area change depending on the option selected at the left side of the backstage area. To leave the backstage area without completing an action, click the Back button in the upper left corner of the backstage area, or press the Esc key on the keyboard.

Quick Steps

Print a Document
1. Click File tab.
2. Click *Print* option.
3. Click Print button.

Documents may need to be printed and a printing of a document on paper is referred to as *hard copy*. A document displayed on the screen is referred to as *soft copy*. Print a document with options at the Print backstage area, shown in Figure 1.5. To display this backstage area, click the File tab and then click the *Print* option. The Print backstage area can also be displayed using the keyboard shortcut Ctrl + P.

Click the Print button, at the upper left side of the backstage area, to send the document to the printer and specify the number of copies to be printed with the *Copies* option. Below the Print button are two categories: *Printer* and *Settings*. Use the gallery in the *Printer* category to specify the desired printer. The *Settings* category contains a number of galleries. Each provides options for specifying how the document will print, including whether the pages are to be collated when printed; the orientation, page size, and margins of the document; and how many pages of the document are to print on a sheet of paper.

Figure 1.5 Print Backstage Area

Back button

Click the Print button to send the document to the specified printer.

Print option

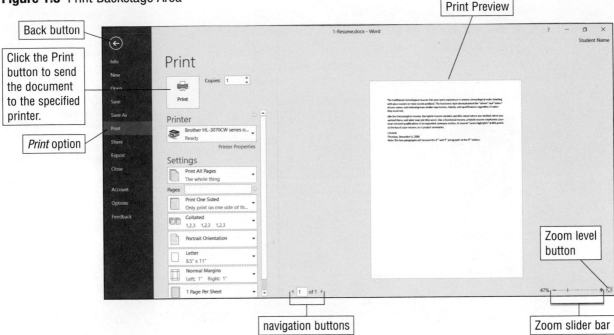

Print Preview

Zoom level button

navigation buttons

Zoom slider bar

 Quick Print

Quick Steps

Close a Document
1. Click File tab.
2. Click *Close* option.

Close Word
Click Close button.

Tutorial

Closing a Document and Closing Word

 Close

Another method for printing a document is to insert the Quick Print button on the Quick Access Toolbar and then click the button. This sends the document directly to the printer without displaying the Print backstage area. To insert the button on the Quick Access Toolbar, click the Customize Quick Access Toolbar button at the right side of the toolbar and then click *Quick Print* at the drop-down list. To remove the Quick Print button from the Quick Access Toolbar, right-click the button and then click the *Remove from Quick Access Toolbar* option at the shortcut menu.

Closing a Document and Closing Word

When a document is saved, it is saved to the specified location and also remains on the screen. To remove the document from the screen, click the File tab and then click the *Close* option or use the keyboard shortcut Ctrl + F4. When a document is closed, it is removed and a blank screen displays. At this screen, open a previously saved document, create a new document, or close Word. To close Word, click the Close button in the upper right corner of the screen. The keyboard shortcut Alt + F4 also closes Word.

Project 1b Saving, Printing, and Closing a Document and Closing Word   Part 2 of 2

1. Save the document you created for Project 1a and name it **1-Resume** (*1-* for Chapter 1 and *Resume* because the document is about resumes) by completing the following steps:
   a. Click the File tab.
   b. Click the *Save As* option.
   c. At the Save As backstage area, click the *Browse* option.
   d. At the Save As dialog box, if necessary, navigate to the WL1C1 folder on your storage medium.

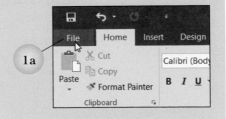

e. Click in the *File name* text box (this selects any text in the box), type 1-Resume, and then press the Enter key.

2. Print the document by clicking the File tab, clicking the *Print* option, and then clicking the Print button at the Print backstage area.

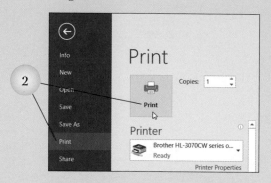

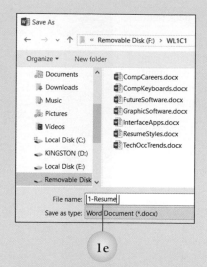

3. Close the document by clicking the File tab and then clicking the *Close* option.
4. Close Word by clicking the Close button in the upper right corner of the screen.

Check Your Work

Project 2 Save a Document with a New Name and the Same Name   2 Parts

You will open a document in the WL1C1 folder on your storage medium, save the document with a new name, add text, and then save the document with the same name. You will also print and then close the document.

Preview Finished Project

Creating a New Document

Quick Steps
Create a New Document
1. Click File tab.
2. Click *New* option.
3. Click *Blank document* template.

When a document is closed, a blank screen displays. To create a new document, display a blank document by clicking the File tab, clicking the *New* option, and then clicking the *Blank document* template. A new document can also be opened with the keyboard shortcut Ctrl + N or by inserting a New button on the Quick Access Toolbar. To insert the button, click the Customize Quick Access Toolbar button at the right side of the toolbar and then click *New* at the drop-down list.

The New backstage area also includes the *Single spaced (blank)* template. Click this template and a new document will open that contains single spacing and no spacing after paragraphs.

Tutorial

Opening a Document from a Removable Disk

Opening a Document

After a document is saved and closed, it can be opened at the Open dialog box, shown in Figure 1.6. To display this dialog box, display the Open backstage area and then click the *Browse* option. Display the Open backstage area by clicking the File tab. If a document is open, click the File tab and then click the *Open* option to display the Open backstage area. Other methods for displaying the Open backstage area include using the keyboard shortcut Ctrl + O, inserting an Open button on the Quick Access Toolbar, or clicking the <u>Open Other Documents</u> hyperlink in the lower left corner of the Word 2016 opening screen.

Figure 1.6 Open Dialog Box

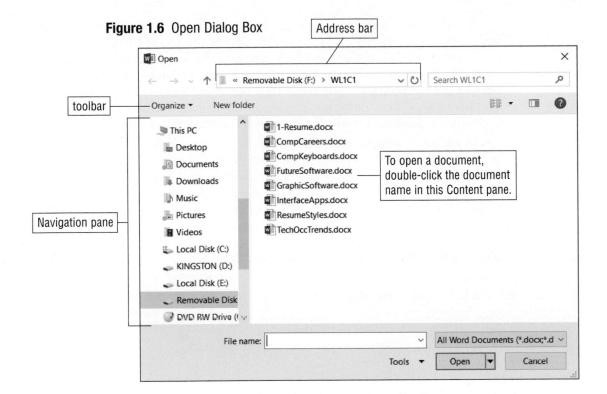

Address bar

toolbar

Navigation pane

To open a document, double-click the document name in this Content pane.

Quick Steps

Open a Document
1. Click File tab.
2. Click *Open* option.
3. Click *Browse* option.
4. Double-click document name.

At the Open backstage area, click the *Browse* option and the Open dialog box displays. Go directly to the Open dialog box without displaying the Open backstage area by pressing Ctrl + F12. At the Open dialog box, navigate to the desired location (such as the drive containing your storage medium), open the folder containing the document, and then double-click the document name in the Content pane.

Opening a Document from the *Recent* Option List

At the Open backstage area with the *Recent* option selected, the names of the most recently opened documents display. By default, Word displays the names of 25 of the most recently opened documents and groups them into categories such as *Today*, *Yesterday*, and perhaps another category such as *Last Week*. To open a document from the *Recent* option list, scroll down the list and then click the document name. The Word 2016 opening screen also displays a list of the names of the most recently opened documents. Click a document name in the Recent list at the opening screen to open the document.

Pinning and Unpinning a Document at the *Recent* Option List

If a document is opened on a regular basis, consider pinning it to the *Recent* option list. To pin a document to the *Recent* option list at the Open backstage area, hover the mouse pointer over the document name and then click the small left-pointing push pin that displays to the right of the document name. The left-pointing push pin changes to a down-pointing push pin and the pinned document is inserted into a new category named *Pinned*. The *Pinned* category displays at the top of the *Recent* option list. The next time the Open backstage area displays, the pinned document displays in the *Pinned* category at the top of the *Recent* option list.

Tutorial

Opening a Document from the *Recent* Option List

Tutorial

Pinning and Unpinning a Document at the *Recent* Option List

A document can also be pinned to the Recent list at the Word 2016 opening screen. When a document is pinned, it displays at the top of the Recent list and the *Recent* option list at the Open backstage area. To "unpin" a document from the Recent or *Recent* option list, click the pin to change it from a down-pointing push pin to a left-pointing push pin. More than one document can be pinned to a list. Another method for pinning and unpinning documents is to use the shortcut menu. Right-click a document name and then click the *Pin to list* or *Unpin from list* option.

In addition to documents, folders can be pinned to a list at the Save As backstage area. The third panel in the Save As backstage area displays a list of the most recently opened folders and groups them into categories such as *Today*, *Yesterday*, and *Last Week*. Pin a folder or folders to the list and a *Pinned* category is created; the folder names display in the category.

Project 2a Opening, Pinning, Unpinning, and Saving a Document

Part 1 of 2

1. Open Word and then open **CompCareers.docx** by completing the following steps:
   a. At the Word opening screen, click the <u>Open Other Documents</u> hyperlink.
   b. At the Open backstage area, click the *Browse* option.
   c. At the Open dialog box, navigate to the external drive containing your storage medium.
   d. Double-click the **WL1C1** folder in the Content pane.
   e. Double-click *CompCareers.docx* in the Content pane.
2. Close **CompCareers.docx**.
3. Press the F12 function key to display the Open dialog box and then double-click *FutureSoftware.docx* in the Content pane to open the document.
4. Close **FutureSoftware.docx**.
5. Pin **CompCareers.docx** to the *Recent* option list by completing the following steps:
   a. Click the File tab.
   b. At the Open backstage area, hover the mouse pointer over **CompCareers.docx** in the *Recent* option list and then click the left-pointing push pin that displays to the right of the document.

   (This creates a new category named *Pinned*, which displays at the top of the list. The **CompCareers.docx** file displays in the *Pinned* category and a down-pointing push pin displays to the right of the document name.)
6. Click *CompCareers.docx* in the *Pinned* category at the top of the *Recent* option list to open the document.
7. Unpin **CompCareers.docx** from the *Recent* option list by completing the following steps:
   a. Click the File tab and then click the *Open* option.
   b. At the Open backstage area, click the down-pointing push pin that displays to the right of **CompCareers.docx** in the *Pinned* category in the *Recent* option list. (This removes the *Pinned* category and changes the pin from a down-pointing push pin to a left-pointing push pin.)
   c. Click the Back button to return to the document.

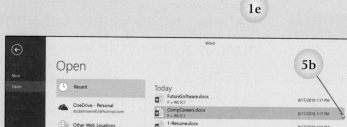

1e

5b

8. With **CompCareers.docx** open, save the document with a new name by completing the following steps:
a. Click the File tab and then click the *Save As* option.
b. At the Save As backstage area, click the *Browse* option.
c. At the Save As dialog box, if necessary, navigate to the WL1C1 folder on your storage medium.
d. Press the Home key on your keyboard to move the insertion point to the beginning of the file name and then type 1-. (Pressing the Home key saves you from having to type the entire document name.)
e. Press the Enter key.

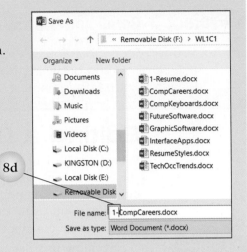

Saving a Document with the Same Name

If changes are made to an existing document, save the changes before closing the document. Consider saving changes to a document on a periodic basis to ensure that no changes are lost if the power is interrupted. Save a document with the same name using the Save button on the Quick Access Toolbar or the *Save* option at the backstage area.

Project 2b **Saving a Document with the Same Name**   Part 2 of 2

1. With **1-CompCareers.docx** open and the insertion point positioned at the beginning of the document, type the text shown in Figure 1.7.
2. Save the changes you just made by clicking the Save button on the Quick Access Toolbar.
3. Print the document by clicking the File tab, clicking the *Print* option, and then clicking the Print button at the Print backstage area. (If your Quick Access Toolbar contains the Quick Print button, you can click the button to send the document directly to the printer.)
4. Close the document by pressing Ctrl + F4.

Check Your Work

Figure 1.7 Project 2b

The majority of new jobs being created in the United States today involve daily work with computers. Computer-related careers include technical support jobs, sales and training, programming and applications development, network and database administration, and computer engineering.

You will open a previously created document, save it with a new name, and then use scrolling and browsing techniques to move the insertion point to specific locations in the document.

Editing a Document

When a document is being edited, text may need to be inserted or deleted. To edit a document, use the mouse, the keyboard, or a combination of the two to move the insertion point to specific locations in the document. To move the insertion point using the mouse, position the I-beam pointer where the insertion point is to be positioned and then click the left mouse button.

Tutorial

Scrolling

Scrolling in a document changes the text display but does not move the insertion point. Use the mouse with the vertical scroll bar, at the right side of the screen, to scroll through text in a document. Click the up scroll arrow at the top of the vertical scroll bar to scroll up through the document and click the down scroll arrow to scroll down through the document.

The scroll bar contains a scroll box that indicates the location of the text in the document screen in relation to the remainder of the document. To scroll up one screen at a time, position the arrow pointer above the scroll box (but below the up scroll arrow) and then click the left mouse button. Position the arrow pointer below the scroll box and click the left button to scroll down a screen. Click and hold down the left mouse button and the action becomes continuous.

Another method for scrolling is to position the arrow pointer on the scroll box, click and hold down the left mouse button, and then drag the scroll box along the scroll bar to reposition text in the document screen. As the scroll box is dragged along the vertical scroll bar in a longer document, page numbers display in a box at the right side of the document screen.

Project 3a Scrolling in a Document

Part 1 of 2

1. Open **InterfaceApps.docx** (from the WL1C1 folder you copied to your storage medium).
2. Save the document with the new name **1-InterfaceApps** to the WL1C1 folder.
3. Position the I-beam pointer at the beginning of the first paragraph and then click the left mouse button.
4. Click the down scroll arrow on the vertical scroll bar several times. (This scrolls down lines of text in the document.) With the mouse pointer on the down scroll arrow, click and hold down the left mouse button and keep it down until the end of the document displays.
5. Position the mouse pointer on the up scroll arrow and click and hold down the left mouse button until the beginning of the document displays.
6. Position the mouse pointer below the scroll box and then click the left mouse button. Continue clicking the mouse button (with the mouse pointer positioned below the scroll box) until the end of the document displays.
7. Position the mouse pointer on the scroll box in the vertical scroll bar. Click and hold down the left mouse button, drag the scroll box to the top of the vertical scroll bar, and then release the mouse button. (Notice that the document page numbers display in a box at the right side of the document screen.)
8. Click in the title at the beginning of the document. (This moves the insertion point to the location of the mouse pointer.)

Moving the Insertion Point to a Specific Line or Page

 Find

Word includes a Go To feature that moves the insertion point to a specific location in a document, such as a line or page. To use the feature, click the Find button arrow in the Editing group on the Home tab, and then click *Go To* at the drop-down list. At the Find and Replace dialog box with the Go To tab selected, move the insertion point to a specific page by typing the page number in the *Enter page number* text box and then pressing the Enter key. Move to a specific line by clicking the *Line* option in the *Go to what* list box, typing the line number in the *Enter line number* text box, and then pressing the Enter key. Click the Close button to close the dialog box.

Moving the Insertion Point with the Keyboard

Tutorial

Moving the Insertion Point and Inserting and Deleting Text

To move the insertion point with the keyboard, use the arrow keys to the right of the regular keyboard or use the arrow keys on the numeric keypad. When using the arrow keys on the numeric keypad, make sure Num Lock is off. Use the arrow keys together with other keys to move the insertion point to various locations in the document, as shown in Table 1.2.

When moving the insertion point, Word considers a word to be any series of characters between spaces. A paragraph is any text that is followed by a single press of the Enter key. A page is text that is separated by a soft or hard page break.

Table 1.2 Insertion Point Movement Commands

To move insertion point	Press
one character left	Left Arrow
one character right	Right Arrow
one line up	Up Arrow
one line down	Down Arrow
one word left	Ctrl + Left Arrow
one word right	Ctrl + Right Arrow
to beginning of line	Home
to end of line	End
to beginning of current paragraph	Ctrl + Up Arrow
to beginning of next paragraph	Ctrl + Down Arrow
up one screen	Page Up
down one screen	Page Down
to top of previous page	Ctrl + Page Up
to top of next page	Ctrl + Page Down
to beginning of document	Ctrl + Home
to end of document	Ctrl + End

Resuming Reading or Editing in a Document

If a previously saved document is opened, pressing Shift + F5 will move the insertion point to the position it was last located when the document was closed.

When opening a multiple-page document, Word remembers the page the insertion point was last positioned. When the document is reopened, Word displays a "Welcome back!" message at the right side of the screen near the vertical scroll bar. The message identifies the page where the insertion point was last located. Click the message and the insertion point is positioned at the top of that page.

Project 3b **Moving the Insertion Point in a Document**

1. With **1-InterfaceApps.docx** open, move the insertion point to line 15 and then to page 3 by completing the following steps:

   a. Click the Find button arrow in the Editing group on the Home tab, and then click *Go To* at the drop-down list.

   b. At the Find and Replace dialog box with the Go To tab selected, click *Line* in the *Go to what* list box.

   c. Click in the *Enter line number* text box, type 15, and then press the Enter key.

   d. Click *Page* in the *Go to what* list box.

   e. Click in the *Enter page number* text box, type 3, and then press the Enter key.

   f. Click the Close button to close the Find and Replace dialog box.

   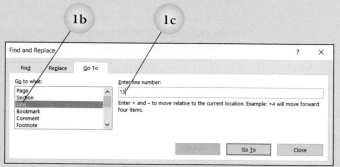

2. Close the document.

3. Open the document by clicking the File tab and then clicking the document name **1-InterfaceApps.docx** in the *Recent* option list in the *Today* category.

4. Move the mouse pointer to the right side of the screen to display the "Welcome back!" message. Hover the mouse pointer over the message and then click the left mouse button. (This positions the insertion point at the top of the third page—the page the insertion point was positioned when you closed the document.)

   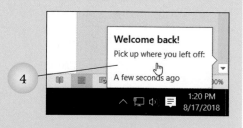

5. Press Ctrl + Home to move the insertion point to the beginning of the document.

6. Practice using the keyboard commands shown in Table 1.2 to move the insertion point within the document.

7. Close **1-InterfaceApps.docx**.

Project 4 Insert and Delete Text
2 Parts

You will open a previously created document, save it with a new name, and then make editing changes to the document. The editing changes will include selecting, inserting, and deleting text and undoing and redoing edits.

Preview Finished Project

Inserting and Deleting Text

Editing a document may include inserting and/or deleting text. To insert text in a document, position the insertion point at the location text is to be typed and then type the text. Existing characters move to the right as text is typed. A number of options are available for deleting text. Some deletion commands are shown in Table 1.3.

Tutorial

Selecting, Replacing, and Deleting Text

Selecting Text

Use the mouse and/or keyboard to select a specific amount of text. Selected text can be deleted or other Word functions can be performed on it. When text is selected, it displays with a gray background, as shown in Figure 1.8, and the Mini toolbar displays. The Mini toolbar contains buttons for common tasks. (You will learn more about the Mini toolbar in Chapter 2.)

Table 1.3 Deletion Commands

To delete	Press
character right of insertion point	Delete key
character left of insertion point	Backspace key
text from insertion point to beginning of word	Ctrl + Backspace
text from insertion point to end of word	Ctrl + Delete

Figure 1.8 Selected Text and Mini Toolbar

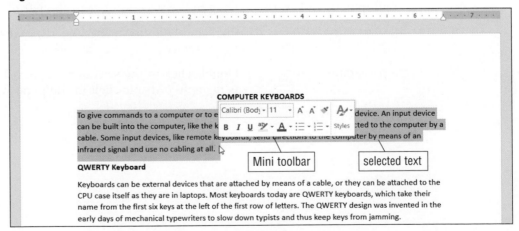

Selecting Text with the Mouse Use the mouse to select a word, line, sentence, paragraph, or entire document. Table 1.4 indicates the steps to follow to select various amounts of text.

To select a specific amount of text, such as a line or paragraph, click in the selection bar. The selection bar is the space at the left side of the document screen between the left edge of the page and the text. When the mouse pointer is positioned in the selection bar, the pointer turns into an arrow pointing up and to the right (instead of to the left).

To select an amount of text other than a word, sentence, or paragraph, position the I-beam pointer on the first character of the text to be selected, click and hold down the left mouse button, drag the I-beam pointer to the last character of the text to be selected, and then release the mouse button. All text between the current insertion point and the I-beam pointer can be selected. To do this, position the insertion point where the selection is to begin, press and hold down the Shift key, click the I-beam pointer at the end of the selection, and then release the Shift key. To cancel a selection using the mouse, click in the document screen.

Select text vertically in a document by holding down the Alt key while dragging with the mouse. This is especially useful when selecting a group of text, such as text set in columns.

Hint If text is selected, any character you type replaces the selected text.

Selecting Text with the Keyboard To select a specific amount of text using the keyboard, turn on the Selection mode by pressing the F8 function key. With the Selection mode activated, use the arrow keys to select the text. To cancel the selection, press the Esc key and then press any arrow key. The Status bar can be customized to indicate that the Selection mode is activated. To do this, right-click on the Status bar and then click *Selection Mode* at the pop-up list. When the F8 function key is pressed to turn on the Selection mode, the words *Extend Selection* display on the Status bar. Text can also be selected with the commands shown in Table 1.5.

Table 1.4 Selecting Text with the Mouse

To select	Complete these steps using the mouse
a word	Double-click the word.
a line of text	Click in the selection bar to the left of the line.
multiple lines of text	Drag in the selection bar to the left of the lines.
a sentence	Press and hold down the Ctrl key and then click in the sentence.
a paragraph	Double-click in the selection bar next to the paragraph, or triple-click in the paragraph.
multiple paragraphs	Drag in the selection bar.
an entire document	Triple-click in the selection bar.

Table 1.5 Selecting Text with the Keyboard

To select	Press
one character to right	Shift + Right Arrow
one character to left	Shift + Left Arrow
to end of word	Ctrl + Shift + Right Arrow
to beginning of word	Ctrl + Shift + Left Arrow
to end of line	Shift + End
to beginning of line	Shift + Home
one line up	Shift + Up Arrow
one line down	Shift + Down Arrow
to beginning of paragraph	Ctrl + Shift + Up Arrow
to end of paragraph	Ctrl + Shift + Down Arrow
one screen up	Shift + Page Up
one screen down	Shift + Page Down
to end of document	Ctrl + Shift + End
to beginning of document	Ctrl + Shift + Home
entire document	Ctrl + A or click Select button in Editing group and then click *Select All*

Project 4a Editing a Document

Part 1 of 2

1. Open **CompKeyboards.docx**. (This document is in the WL1C1 folder you copied to your storage medium.)
2. Save the document with the new name **1-CompKeyboards**.
3. Change the word *give* in the first sentence of the first paragraph to *enter* by double-clicking *give* and then typing enter.
4. Change the second *to* in the first sentence to *into* by double-clicking *to* and then typing into.

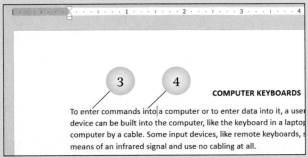

5. Delete the words *means of* (including the space after *of*) in the first sentence in the *QWERTY Keyboard* section.
6. Select the words *and use no cabling at all* and the period that follows at the end of the last sentence in the first paragraph and then press the Delete key.
7. Insert a period immediately following the word *signal*.

8. Delete the heading *QWERTY Keyboard* using the Selection mode by completing the following steps:
   a. Position the insertion point immediately left of the *Q* in *QWERTY*.
   b. Press F8 to turn on the Selection mode.
   c. Press the Down Arrow key.
   d. Press the Delete key.
9. Complete steps similar to those in Step 8 to delete the heading *DVORAK Keyboard*.
10. Begin a new paragraph with the sentence that reads *Keyboards have different physical appearances* by completing the following steps:
    a. Position the insertion point immediately left of the *K* in *Keyboards* (the first word of the fifth sentence in the last paragraph).
    b. Press the Enter key.
11. Save **1-CompKeyboards.docx**.

8a-8c

> To enter commands into a co
> device can be built into the c
> computer by a cable. Some ir
> means of an infrared signal.
>
> **QWERTY Keyboard**
>
> Keyboards can be external de
> itself as they are in laptops. M
> the first six keys at the left of
> of mechanical typewriters to

10a-10b

> To enter commands into a computer or
> device can be built into the computer,
> computer by a cable. Some input devic
> means of an infrared signal.
>
> Keyboards can be external devices that
> itself as they are in laptops. Most keybo
> the first six keys at the left of the first r
> of mechanical typewriters to slow dow
>
> The DVORAK keyboard is an alternative
> commonly used keys are placed close t
> install software on a QWERTY keyboard
> keyboards is convenient especially whe
>
> Keyboards have different physical appe
> that of a calculator, containing number
> "broken" into two pieces to reduce stra
> change the symbol or character entere

Check Your Work

Using the Undo and Redo Buttons

 Undo

 Redo

Hint You cannot undo a save.

Undo typing, formatting, or another action by clicking the Undo button on the Quick Access Toolbar. For example, type text and then click the Undo button and the text is removed. Or, apply formatting to text and then click the Undo button and the formatting is removed.

Click the Redo button on the Quick Access Toolbar to reverse the original action. For example, apply formatting such as underlining to text and then click the Undo button and the underlining is removed. Click the Redo button and the underlining formatting is reapplied to the text. Many Word actions can be undone or redone. Some actions, however, such as printing and saving, cannot be undone or redone.

Word maintains actions in temporary memory. To undo an action performed earlier, click the Undo button arrow. This causes a drop-down list to display. To make a selection from this drop-down list, click the desired action; the action, along with any actions listed above it in the drop-down list, is undone.

1. With **1-CompKeyboards.docx** open, delete the last sentence in the last paragraph using the mouse by completing the following steps:
   a. Hover the I-beam pointer anywhere over the sentence that begins *All keyboards have modifier keys*.
   b. Press and hold down the Ctrl key, and then click the left mouse button, and then release the Ctrl key.

> install software on a QWERTY keyboard that emulates a DVORAK keyboard. The ability to emulate other keyboards is convenient especially when working with foreign languages.
>
> Keyboards have different physical appearances. Many keyboards have a separate numeric keypad, like that of a calculator, containing numbers and mathematical operators. Some keyboards are sloped and "broken" into two pieces to reduce strain. All keyboards have modifier keys that enable the user to change the symbol or character entered when a given key is pressed.

1a-1b

   c. Press the Delete key.
2. Delete the last paragraph by completing the following steps:
   a. Position the I-beam pointer anywhere in the last paragraph (the paragraph that begins *Keyboards have different physical appearances*).
   b. Triple-click the left mouse button.
   c. Press the Delete key.
3. Undo the deletion by clicking the Undo button on the Quick Access Toolbar.
4. Redo the deletion by clicking the Redo button on the Quick Access Toolbar.
5. Select the first sentence in the second paragraph and then delete it.
6. Select the first paragraph in the document and then delete it.
7. Undo the two deletions by completing the following steps:
   a. Click the Undo button arrow.
   b. Click the second *Clear* listed in the drop-down list. (This will redisplay the first paragraph and the first sentence in the second paragraph. The sentence will be selected.)
8. Click outside the sentence to deselect it.
9. Save, print, and then close **1-CompKeyboards.docx**.

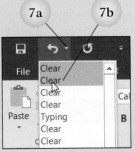

Check Your Work

Project 5 **Complete a Spelling and Grammar Check**   **1 Part**

You will open a previously created document, save it with a new name, and then check the spelling and grammar in the document.

Preview Finished Project

Checking the Spelling and Grammar in a Document

Quick Steps

Check Spelling and Grammar
1. Click Review tab.
2. Click Spelling & Grammar button.
3. Change or ignore errors.
4. Click OK.

 Spelling & Grammar

💡 *Hint* Complete a spelling and grammar check on a portion of a document by selecting the text first and then clicking the Spelling & Grammar button.

Two tools for creating thoughtful and well-written documents are the spelling checker and the grammar checker. The spelling checker finds misspelled words and offers replacement words. It also finds duplicate words and irregular capitalizations. When spell checking a document, the spelling checker compares the words in the document with the words in its dictionary. If the spelling checker finds a match, it passes over the word. If the spelling checker does not find a match, it stops, selects the word, and offers possible corrections.

The grammar checker searches a document for errors in grammar, punctuation, and word usage. If the grammar checker finds an error, it stops and offers possible corrections. The spelling checker and the grammar checker can help create a well-written document but do not eliminate the need for proofreading.

To complete a spelling and grammar check, click the Review tab and then click the Spelling & Grammar button in the Proofing group or press the F7 function key. If Word detects a possible spelling error, the text containing the error is selected and the Spelling task pane displays. The Spelling task pane contains a list box with one or more possible corrections along with buttons to either change or ignore the spelling error, as described in Table 1.6. A definition of the selected word in the list box may display at the bottom of the Spelling task pane if a dictionary is installed.

If Word detects a grammar error, the word(s) or sentence is selected and possible corrections display in the Grammar task pane list box. Depending on the error selected, some or all of the buttons described in Table 1.6 may display in the Grammar task pane and a description of the grammar rule with suggestions may display at the bottom of the task pane. Use the buttons that display to ignore or change the grammar error.

When checking the spelling and grammar in a document, temporarily leave the Spelling task pane or Grammar task pane by clicking in the document. To resume the spelling and grammar check, click the Resume button in the Spelling task pane or Grammar task pane.

Table 1.6 Spelling Task Pane and Grammar Task Pane Buttons

Button	Function
Ignore	during spell checking, skips that occurrence of the word; during grammar checking, leaves currently selected text as written
Ignore All	during spell checking, skips that occurrence of the word and all other occurrences of the word in the document
Add	adds the selected word to the spelling checker dictionary
Delete	deletes the currently selected word(s)
Change	replaces the selected word with the selected word in the task pane list box
Change All	replaces the selected word and all other occurrences of it with the selected word in the task pane list box

1. Open **TechOccTrends.docx**.
2. Save the document with the name **1-TechOccTrends**.
3. Click the Review tab.
4. Click the Spelling & Grammar button in the Proofing group.
5. The spelling checker selects the word *tecnology* and displays the Spelling task pane. The proper spelling is selected in the Spelling task pane list box, so click the Change button (or Change All button).
6. The grammar checker selects the word *too* in the document and displays the Grammar task pane. The correct form of the word is selected in the list box. If definitions of *to* and *too* display at the bottom of the task pane, read the information. Click the Change button.
7. The grammar checker selects the sentence containing the words *downloaded* and *versus*, in which two spaces appear between the words. The Grammar task pane displays in the list box the two words with only one space between them. Read the information about spaces between words that displays at the bottom of the Grammar task pane and then click the Change button.
8. The spelling checker selects the word *sucessful* and offers *successful* in the Spelling task pane list box. Since this word is misspelled in another location in the document, click the Change All button.
9. The spelling checker selects the word *are*, which is used two times in a row. Click the Delete button in the Spelling task pane to delete the second *are*.
10. When the message displays stating that the spelling and grammar check is complete, click OK.
11. Save, print, and then close **1-TechOccTrends.docx**.

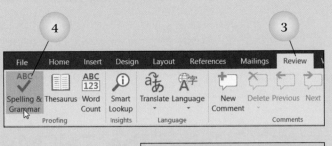

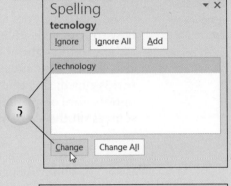

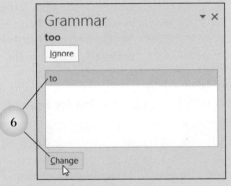

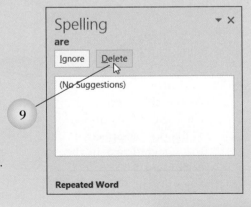

Check Your Work

You will use the Tell Me feature to learn how to double-space text in a document, display the Word Help window with information on autocorrect, and display the Smart Lookup task pane with information on scrolling. You will also use the Help feature to learn more about printing documents.

Preview Finished Project

Tutorial

Using the Tell Me Feature

Using the Tell Me Feature

Word 2016 includes a Tell Me feature that provides information and guidance on how to complete a function. To use Tell Me, click in the *Tell Me* text box on the ribbon to the right of the View tab and then type the function. Type text in the *Tell Me* text box and a drop-down list displays with options that are refined as the text is typed; this is referred to as "word-wheeling." The drop-down list displays options for completing the function, displaying information on the function from sources on the Web, or displaying information on the function in the Word Help window.

The drop-down list also includes a *Smart Lookup* option. Clicking the *Smart Lookup* option will open the Smart Lookup task pane at the right side of the screen. This task pane provides information on the function from a variety of sources on the Internet. The *Smart Lookup* option can also be accessed with the Smart Lookup button on the Review tab or by selecting text, right-clicking the selected text, and then clicking *Smart Lookup* at the shortcut menu.

Project 6a **Using the Tell Me Feature**   **Part 1 of 2**

1. Open **GraphicSoftware.docx** and then save it with the name **1-GraphicSoftware**.
2. Press Ctrl + A to select the entire document.
3. Use the Tell Me feature to learn how to double-space the text in the document by completing the following steps:
   a. Click in the *Tell Me* text box.
   b. Type double space.
   c. Click the *Line and Paragraph Spacing* option.
   d. At the side menu, click the *2.0* option. (This double-spaces the selected text in the document.)
   e. Click in the document to deselect the text.

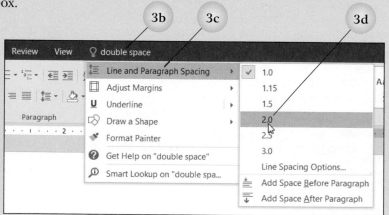

4. Use the Tell Me feature to display the Word Help window with information on AutoCorrect by completing the following steps:
   a. Click in the *Tell Me* text box.
   b. Type autocorrect.
   c. Click the *Get Help on "autocorrect"* option.
   d. At the Word Help window, click a hyperlink to an article that interests you.
   e. After reading the information about autocorrect, close the window by clicking the Close button in the upper right corner of the window.

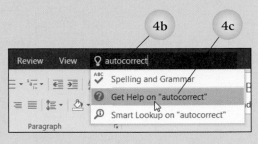

5. Display information on scrolling in the Smart Lookup task pane by completing the following steps:
   a. Click in the *Tell Me* text box.
   b. Type scrolling.
   c. Click the *Smart Lookup on "scrolling"* option. (The first time you use the Smart Lookup feature, the Smart Lookup task pane will display with a message stating that data will be sent to Bing and suggesting that you read the privacy statement for more details. At this message, click the Got it button.)

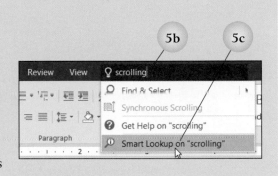

   d. Look at the information that displays in the Smart Lookup task pane on scrolling.
   e. If two options—*Explore* and *Define*—display at the top of the Smart Lookup task pane, click the *Define* option. This will display a definition of the term *scrolling* in the Smart Lookup task pane.
   f. Close the Smart Lookup task pane by clicking the Close button in the upper right corner of the task pane.
6. Save, print, then close **1-GraphicSoftware.docx**.

Check Your Work

Using the Help Feature

Word's Help feature is an on-screen reference manual containing information about Word features and commands. Word's Help feature is similar to the Help features in Excel, PowerPoint, and Access. Get help by using the Tell Me feature or by pressing the F1 function key to display the Word Help window, shown in Figure 1.9.

In this window, type a topic, feature, or question in the search text box and then press the Enter key. Articles related to the search text display in the Word Help window. Click an article to display it in the Word Help window. If the article window contains a <u>Show All</u> hyperlink in the upper right corner, click this hyperlink and the information expands to show all Help information related to the topic. Click the <u>Show All</u> hyperlink and it becomes the <u>Hide All</u> hyperlink.

The Word Help window contains five buttons, which display to the left of the search text box. Use the Back and Forward buttons to navigate within the window. Click the Home button to return to the Word Help window opening screen. To print information on a topic or feature, click the Print button and then click the Print button at the Print dialog box. Click the Use Large Text button in the Word Help window to increase the size of the text in the window.

Figure 1.9 Word Help Window

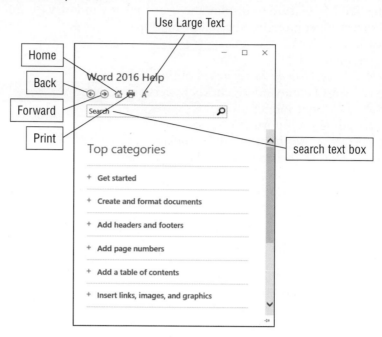

Getting Help from a ScreenTip

Hover the mouse pointer over a certain button such as the Format Painter button or Font Color button and the ScreenTip displays a Help icon and the Tell me more hyperlinked text. Click Tell me more or press the F1 function key and the Word Help window opens with information about the button feature.

Getting Help at the Backstage Area

The backstage area contains a Microsoft Word Help button in the upper right corner of the screen. Display a specific backstage area, click the Microsoft Word Help button, and information on the backstage area displays in the Word Help window.

Getting Help in a Dialog Box

Some dialog boxes contain a Help button. Open a dialog box and then click the Help button and information about the dialog box displays in the Word Help window. After reading and/or printing the information, close the Word Help window and then close the dialog box by clicking the Close button in the upper right corner.

1. Open a new blank document by completing the following steps:
   a. Click the File tab and then click the *New* option.
   b. At the New backstage area, double-click the *Single spaced (blank)* template.

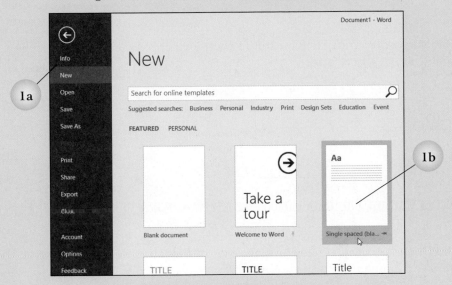

2. Press F1 to display the Microsoft Word Help window.
3. At the Word Help window, click in the search text box, type print preview, and then press the Enter key.
4. When the list of articles displays, click the <u>Print a document in Word</u> hyperlinked article. (You may need to scroll down the Word Help window to display this article.)
5. Scroll down the Word Help window and read the information about printing and previewing documents.
6. Click the Print button in the Word Help window. This displays the Print dialog box. If you want to print information about the topic, click the Print button; otherwise, click the Cancel button to close the dialog box.
7. At the Word Help window, click the Use Large Text button to increase the size of the text in the window.
8. Click the Use Large Text button again to return the text to the normal size.
9. Click the Back button to return to the previous window.
10. Click the Home button to return to the original Word Help window screen.
11. Click the Close button to close the Word Help window.
12. Hover your mouse over the Format Painter button in the Clipboard group on the Home tab.

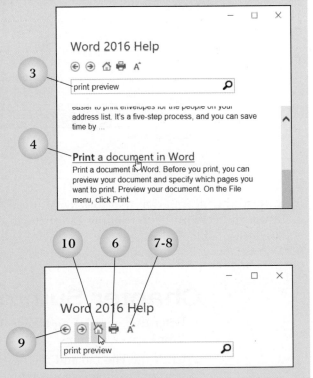

13. Click the <u>Tell me more</u> hyperlinked text at the bottom of the ScreenTip.
14. Read the information in the Word Help window about the Format Painter feature.
15. Click the Close button to close the Word Help window.
16. Click the File tab.
17. Click the Microsoft Word Help button in the upper right corner of the screen.

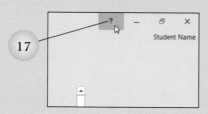
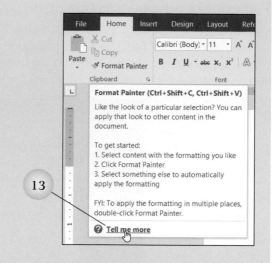

18. Look at the information that displays in the Word Help window and then close the window.
19. Click the Back button to return to the document.
20. Click the Paragraph group dialog box launcher in the lower right corner of the Pararaph group on the Home tab.

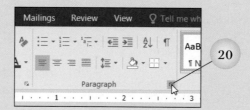

21. Click the Help button in the upper right corner of the Paragraph dialog box.

22. Read the information that displays in the Word Help window.
23. Close the Word Help window and then close the Paragraph dialog box.
24. Close the blank document.

Chapter Summary

- Refer to Figure 1.1 and Table 1.1 for an example and a list, respectively, of key Word screen features.
- Click the File tab and the backstage area displays, containing options for working with and managing documents.
- Document names can contain a maximum of 255 characters, including the drive letter and folder names, and may include spaces.
- The Quick Access Toolbar contains buttons for commonly used commands.

- The ribbon contains tabs with options and buttons divided into groups.
- The insertion point displays as a blinking vertical line and indicates the position of the next character to be entered in the document.
- The insertion point can be moved throughout the document without interfering with text by using the mouse, the keyboard, or the mouse combined with the keyboard.
- The scroll box on the vertical scroll bar indicates the location of the text in the document in relation to the remainder of the document.
- The insertion point can be moved by character, word, screen, or page and from the first to the last character in a document. Refer to Table 1.2 for keyboard insertion point movement commands.
- Delete text by character, word, line, several lines, or partial page using specific keys or by selecting text using the mouse or the keyboard. Refer to Table 1.3 for deletion commands.
- A specific amount of text can be selected using the mouse or the keyboard. Refer to Table 1.4 for information on selecting with the mouse, and refer to Table 1.5 for information on selecting with the keyboard.
- Use the Undo button on the Quick Access Toolbar to undo an action such as typing, deleting, or formatting text. Use the Redo button to redo something that has been undone with the Undo button.
- The spelling checker matches the words in a document with the words in its dictionary. If a match is not found, the word is selected and possible corrections are suggested in the Spelling task pane. The grammar checker searches a document for errors in grammar, punctuation, and word usage. When a grammar error is detected, possible corrections display in the Grammar task pane along with information about the grammar rule or error. Refer to Table 1.6 for Spelling task pane and Grammar task pane buttons.
- The Tell Me feature provides information and guidance on how to complete a function. The *Tell Me* text box is on the ribbon to the right of the View tab.
- Word's Help feature is an on-screen reference manual containing information about Word features and commands. Press the F1 function key to display the Word Help window.
- The Word Help window (Figure 1.9) contains five buttons, which are to the left of the search text box: the Back, Forward, Home, Print, and Use Large Text buttons.
- Hover the mouse pointer over a certain button and the ScreenTip displays a Help icon and the <u>Tell me more</u> hyperlinked text. Click this hyperlinked text to display the Word Help window, which contains information about the button feature.
- Some dialog boxes and the backstage area contain a help button that when clicked displays information about the dialog box or backstage area.

Commands Review

FEATURE	RIBBON TAB, GROUP	BUTTON, OPTION	KEYBOARD SHORTCUT
AutoComplete entry			F3
close document	File, *Close*		Ctrl + F4
close Word		✕	Alt + F4
Find and Replace dialog box with Go To tab selected	Home, Editing	🔍, *Go To*	Ctrl + G
Leave backstage area		←	Esc
Move insertion point to previous location when document was closed			Shift + F5
new blank document	File, *New*	*Blank document*	Ctrl + N
New Line command			Shift + Enter
Open backstage area	File, *Open*		Ctrl + O
Open dialog box	File, *Open*		Ctrl + F12
Print backstage area	File, *Print*		Ctrl + P
redo an action		↷	Ctrl + Y
save	File, *Save*	💾	Ctrl + S
Save As backstage area	File, *Save As*		
Save As dialog box	File, *Save As*		F12
Selection mode			F8
spelling and grammar checker	Review, Proofing	ABC ✓	F7
Tell Me feature		💡 Tell me what you want to do	Alt + Q
undo an action		↶ ▾	Ctrl + Z
Word Help			F1

Workbook

Chapter study tools and assessment activities are available in the *Workbook* ebook. These resources are designed to help you further develop and demonstrate mastery of the skills learned in this chapter.

Microsoft®
Word

Formatting Characters and Paragraphs

Performance Objectives

Upon successful completion of Chapter 2, you will be able to:

1 Change the font, font size, and choose font effects

2 Format selected text with buttons on the Mini toolbar

3 Apply styles from style sets

4 Apply themes

5 Customize style sets and themes.

6 Change the alignment of text in paragraphs

7 Indent text in paragraphs

8 Increase and decrease spacing before and after paragraphs

9 Repeat the last action

10 Automate formatting with Format Painter

11 Change line spacing

12 Reveal and compare formatting

The appearance of a document in the document screen and when printed is called the *format*. A Word document is based on a template that applies default formatting. Some of the default formats include 11-point Calibri font, line spacing of 1.08, 8 points of spacing after each paragraph, and left-aligned text. In this chapter, you will learn about changing the typeface, type size, and typestyle as well as applying font effects such as bold and italic. The Paragraph group on the Home tab includes buttons for applying formatting to paragraphs of text. In Word, a paragraph is any amount of text followed by a press of the Enter key. In this chapter, you will learn to format paragraphs by changing text alignment, indenting text, applying formatting with Format Painter, and changing line spacing.

SNAP

Data Files

Before beginning chapter work, copy the WL1C2 folder to your storage medium and then make WL1C2 the active folder.

Preview Finished Project

Project 1 Apply Character Formatting

4 Parts

You will open a document containing a glossary of terms, add additional text, and then format the document by applying character formatting.

Tutorial

Applying Font
Formatting Using
the Font Group

Applying Font Formatting

The Font group, shown in Figure 2.1, contains a number of options and buttons for applying character formatting to text in a document. The top row contains options for changing the font and font size as well as buttons for increasing and decreasing the size of the font, changing the text case, and clearing formatting. Remove character formatting (as well as paragraph formatting) applied to text by clicking the Clear All Formatting button in the Font group. Remove only character formatting from selected text by pressing the keyboard shortcut Ctrl + spacebar. The bottom row contains buttons for applying typestyles such as bold, italic, and underline and for applying text effects, highlighting, and color.

Hint Change
the default font by
selecting the font at
the Font dialog box and
then clicking the Set As
Default button.

A Word document is based on a template that formats text in 11-point Calibri. This default may need to be changed to another font for such reasons as altering the mood of the document, enhancing its visual appeal, and increasing its readability. A font consists of three elements: typeface, type size, and typestyle.

Hint Use a serif
typeface for text-
intensive documents.

A typeface is a set of characters with a common design and shape and can be decorative or plain and either monospaced or proportional. Word refers to a typeface as a *font*. A monospaced typeface allots the same amount of horizontal space for each character, while a proportional typeface allots varying amounts of space for different characters. Typefaces are divided into two main categories: serif and sans serif. A serif is a small line at the end of a character stroke. Consider using a serif typeface for text-intensive documents because the serifs help move the reader's eyes across the page. Use a sans serif typeface for headings, headlines, and advertisements. Some popular typefaces are shown in Table 2.1.

Figure 2.1 Font Group Option Boxes and Buttons

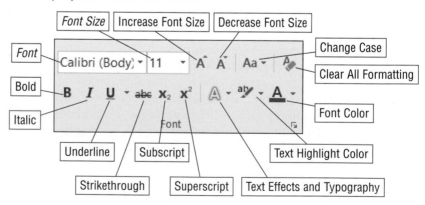

Table 2.1 Categories of Typefaces

Serif Typefaces	Sans Serif Typefaces	Monospaced Typefaces
Cambria	Calibri	Consolas
Constantia	Candara	Courier New
Times New Roman	Corbel	Lucida Console
Bookman Old Style	Arial	MS Gothic

Type is generally set in proportional size. The size of proportional type is measured vertically in units called *points*. A point is approximately ¹/₇₂ of an inch—the higher the point size, the larger the characters. Within a typeface, characters may have varying styles. Type styles are divided into four main categories: regular, bold, italic, and bold italic.

💡 *Hint* Press Ctrl +] to increase font size by 1 point and press Ctrl + [to decrease font size by 1 point.

Use the *Font* option box arrow in the Font group to change the font. Select the text and then click the *Font* option box arrow and a drop-down gallery of font options displays. Hover the mouse pointer over a font option and the selected text in the document displays with the font applied. Continue hovering the mouse pointer over different font options to see how the selected text displays in each font.

The *Font* option drop-down gallery is an example of the live preview feature, which displays how the font formatting affects text without having to return to the document. The live preview feature is also available with the drop-down gallery of font sizes that displays when the *Font Size* option box arrow is clicked.

Project 1a   Changing the Font and Font Size   Part 1 of 4

1. Open **CompTerms.docx** and then save it with the name **2-CompTerms**.
2. Change the typeface to Cambria by completing the following steps:
   a. Select the entire document by pressing Ctrl + A. (You can also select all text in the document by clicking the Select button in the Editing group and then clicking *Select All* at the drop-down list.)
   b. Click the *Font* option box arrow, scroll down the drop-down gallery until *Cambria* displays, and then hover the mouse pointer over *Cambria*. This displays a live preview of the text set in Cambria.
   c. Click the *Cambria* option.

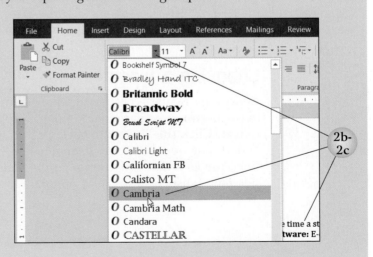

3. Change the type size to 14 points by completing the following steps:
   a. With the text in the document still selected, click the *Font Size* option box arrow.
   b. At the drop-down gallery, hover the mouse pointer over *14* and look at the live preview of the text with 14 points applied.
   c. Click the *14* option.

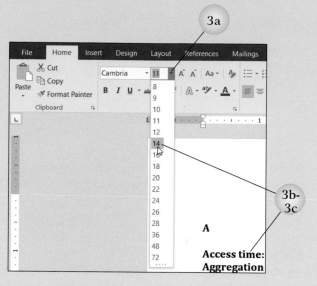

4. Change the type size and typeface by completing the following steps:
   a. Click the Decrease Font Size button in the Font group three times. (This decreases the size to 10 points.)
   b. Click the Increase Font Size button two times. (This increases the size to 12 points.)
   c. Click the *Font* option box arrow, scroll down the drop-down gallery, and then click *Constantia*. (The most recently used fonts display at the beginning of the gallery, followed by a listing of all fonts.)

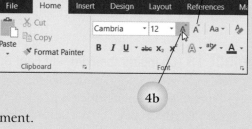

5. Deselect the text by clicking anywhere in the document.
6. Save **2-CompTerms.docx**.

Check Your Work

Choosing a Typestyle

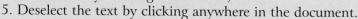

B Bold

I Italic

U ▾ Underline

Apply a particular typestyle to text with the Bold, Italic, or Underline buttons in the bottom row in the Font group. More than one typestyle can be applied to text. Click the Underline button arrow and a drop-down gallery displays with underlining options such as a double line, dashed line, and thicker underline. Click the *Underline Color* option at the Underline button drop-down gallery and a side menu displays with color options.

1. With **2-CompTerms.docx** open, press Ctrl + Home to move the insertion point to the beginning of the document.
2. Type a heading for the document by completing the following steps:
   a. Click the Bold button in the Font group. (This turns on bold formatting.)
   b. Click the Underline button in the Font group. (This turns on underline formatting.)
   c. Type Glossary of Terms.
3. Press Ctrl + End to move the insertion point to the end of the document.
4. Type the text shown in Figure 2.2 with the following specifications:
   a. While typing, make the appropriate text bold, as shown in the figure, by completing the following steps:
      1) Click the Bold button in the Font group. (This turns on bold formatting.)
      2) Type the text.
      3) Click the Bold button in the Font group. (This turns off bold formatting.)
   b. Press the Enter key two times after typing the *C* heading.
   c. While typing, italicize the appropriate text, as shown in the figure, by completing the following steps:
      1) Click the Italic button in the Font group.
      2) Type the text.
      3) Click the Italic button in the Font group.
5. After typing the text, press the Enter key two times and then press Ctrl + Home to move the insertion point to the beginning of the document.
6. Change the underlining below the title by completing the following steps:
   a. Select the title *Glossary of Terms*.
   b. Click the Underline button arrow and then click the third underline option from the top of the drop-down gallery (*Thick underline*).
   c. Click the Underline button arrow, point to the *Underline Color* option, and then click the *Red* color (second color option in the *Standard Colors* section).

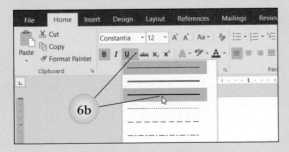

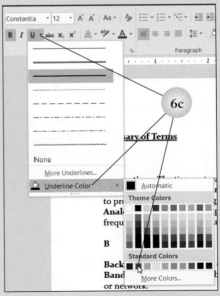

7. With the title still selected, change the font size to 14 points.
8. Save **2-CompTerms.docx**.

Check Your Work

Figure 2.2 Project 1b

C

Chip: A thin wafer of *silicon* containing electronic circuitry that performs various functions, such as mathematical calculations, storage, or controlling computer devices.
Cluster: A group of two or more *sectors* on a disk, which is the smallest unit of storage space used to store data.
Coding: A term used by programmers to refer to the act of writing source code.
Crackers: A term coined by computer hackers for those who intentionally enter (or hack) computer systems to damage them.

 Tutorial

Highlighting Text

 Clear All Formatting

 Change Case

 Strikethrough

 Subscript

 Superscript

 Text Effects and Typography

 Text Highlight Color

 Font Color

Choosing a Font Effect

Apply font effects with some of the buttons in the top and bottom rows in the Font group, or clear all formatting from selected text with the Clear All Formatting button. Change the case of text with the Change Case button drop-down list. Click the Change Case button in the top row in the Font group and a drop-down list displays with the options *Sentence case*, *lowercase*, *UPPERCASE*, *Capitalize Each Word*, and *tOGGLE cASE*. The case of selected text can also be changed with the keyboard shortcut Shift + F3. Each time Shift + F3 is pressed, the selected text displays in the next case option in the list.

The bottom row in the Font group contains buttons for applying font effects. Use the Strikethrough button to draw a line through selected text. This has a practical application in some legal documents in which deleted text must be retained in the document. Use the Subscript button to create text that is lowered slightly below the line, as in the chemical formula H_2O. Use the Superscript button to create text that is raised slightly above the text line, as in the mathematical equation four to the third power (written as 4^3). Click the Text Effects and Typography button in the bottom row and a drop-down gallery displays with effect options. Use the Text Highlight Color button to highlight specific text in a document and use the Font Color button to change the color of text.

Applying Formatting Using Keyboard Shortcuts

Several of the options and buttons in the Font group have keyboard shortcuts. For example, press Ctrl + B to turn bold formatting on or off and press Ctrl + I to turn italic formatting on or off. Position the mouse pointer on an option or button and an enhanced ScreenTip displays with the name of the option or button; the keyboard shortcut, if any; a description of the action performed by the option or button; and sometimes, access to the Word Help window. Table 2.2 identifies the keyboard shortcuts available for options and buttons in the Font group.

Table 2.2 Font Group Option and Button Keyboard Shortcuts

Font Group Option/Button	Keyboard Shortcut
Font	Ctrl + Shift + F
Font Size	Ctrl + Shift + P
Increase Font Size	Ctrl + Shift + > OR Ctrl +]
Decrease Font Size	Ctrl + Shift + < OR Ctrl + [
Bold	Ctrl + B
Italic	Ctrl + I
Underline	Ctrl + U
Subscript	Ctrl + =
Superscript	Ctrl + Shift + +
Change Case	Shift + F3

Tutorial

Applying Font
Formatting Using
the Mini Toolbar

Formatting with the Mini Toolbar

When text is selected, the Mini toolbar displays above the selected text, as shown in Figure 2.3. Click a button on the Mini toolbar to apply formatting to the selected text. When the mouse pointer is moved away from the Mini toolbar, the toolbar disappears.

Figure 2.3 Mini Toolbar

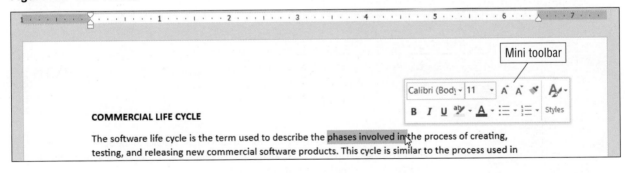

1. With **2-CompTerms.docx** open, move the insertion point to the beginning of the term *Chip*, press the Enter key, and then press the Up Arrow key.
2. Type the text shown in Figure 2.4. Create each superscript number by clicking the Superscript button, typing the number, and then clicking the Superscript button.
3. Remove underlining and change the case of the text in the title by completing the following steps:
   a. Select the title *Glossary of Terms*.
   b. Remove all formatting from the title by clicking the Clear All Formatting button in the Font group.
   c. Click the Change Case button in the Font group and then click *UPPERCASE* at the drop-down list.
   d. Click the Text Effects and Typography button in the Font group and then click the *Gradient Fill - Blue, Accent 1, Reflection* option (second column, second row) at the drop-down gallery.
   e. Change the font size to 14 points.
4. Strike through text by completing the following steps:
   a. Select the words and parentheses *(or hack)* in the *Crackers* definition.
   b. Click the Strikethrough button in the Font group.

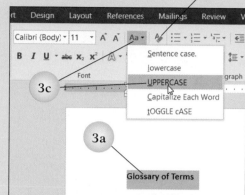

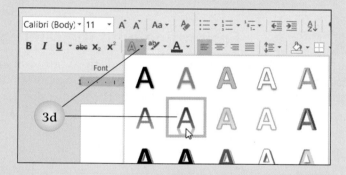

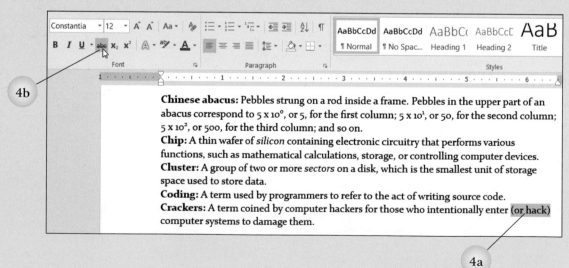

5. Change the font color by completing the following steps:
   a. Press Ctrl + A to select the entire document.
   b. Click the Font Color button arrow.
   c. Click the *Dark Red* color (first color option in the *Standard Colors* section) at the drop-down gallery.
   d. Click in the document to deselect text.
6. Highlight text in the document by completing the following steps:
   a. Click the Text Highlight Color button arrow in the Font group and then click the *Yellow* color (first column, first row) at the drop-down palette. (This causes the mouse pointer to display as an I-beam pointer with a highlighter pen attached.)
   b. Select the term *Beta-testing* and the definition that follows.
   c. Click the Text Highlight Color button arrow and then click the *Turquoise* color (third column, first row).
   d. Select the term *Cluster* and the definition that follows.
   e. Click the Text Highlight Color button arrow and then click the *Yellow* color at the drop-down gallery.
   f. Click the Text Highlight Color button to turn off highlighting.
7. Apply italic formatting using the Mini toolbar by completing the following steps:
   a. Select the text *one-stop shopping* in the definition for the term *Aggregation software*. (When you select the text, the Mini toolbar displays.)
   b. Click the Italic button on the Mini toolbar.
   c. Select the word *bits* in the definition for the term *Bandwidth* and then click the Italic button on the Mini toolbar.
8. Save **2-CompTerms.docx**.

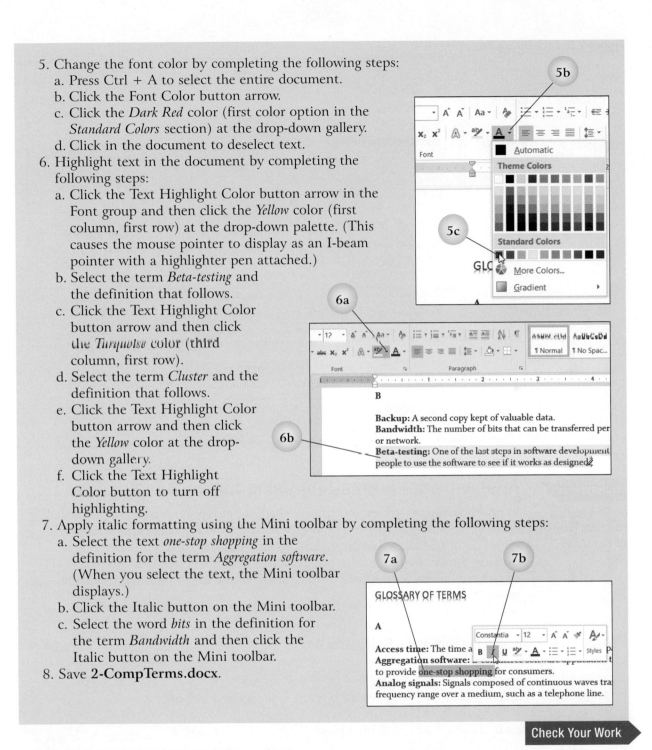

Check Your Work

Figure 2.4 Project 1c

Chinese abacus: Pebbles strung on a rod inside a frame. Pebbles in the upper part of an abacus correspond to 5×10^0, or 5, for the first column; 5×10^1, or 50, for the second column; 5×10^2, or 500, for the third column; and so on.

Figure 2.5 Font Dialog Box

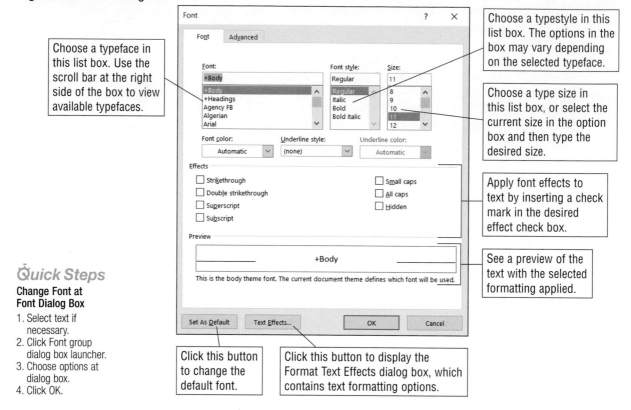

Choose a typeface in this list box. Use the scroll bar at the right side of the box to view available typefaces.

Choose a typestyle in this list box. The options in the box may vary depending on the selected typeface.

Choose a type size in this list box, or select the current size in the option box and then type the desired size.

Apply font effects to text by inserting a check mark in the desired effect check box.

See a preview of the text with the selected formatting applied.

Click this button to change the default font.

Click this button to display the Format Text Effects dialog box, which contains text formatting options.

Tutorial

Applying Font Formatting Using the Font Dialog Box

Applying Font Formatting Using the Font Dialog Box

In addition to options and buttons in the Font group, options at the Font dialog box, shown in Figure 2.5, can be used to change the typeface, type size, and typestyle of text as well as apply font effects. Display the Font dialog box by clicking the Font group dialog box launcher. The dialog box launcher is a small square containing a diagonal-pointing arrow in the lower right corner of the Font group.

Project 1d Changing the Font at the Font Dialog Box

Part 4 of 4

1. With **2-CompTerms.docx** open, press Ctrl + End to move the insertion point to the end of the document. (Make sure the insertion point is positioned a double space below the last line of text.)
2. Type Created by Susan Ashby and then press the Enter key.
3. Type Wednesday, February 21, 2018.
4. Change the font to 13-point Candara and the color to standard dark blue for the entire document by completing the following steps:
   a. Press Ctrl + A to select the entire document.
   b. Click the Font group dialog box launcher.

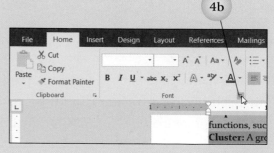

4b

c. At the Font dialog box, type can in the *Font* option box (this displays fonts that begin with *can*) and then click *Candara* in the *Font* list box.

d. Click in the *Size* option box and then type 13.

e. Click the *Font color* option box arrow and then click the *Dark Blue* color option (ninth option in the *Standard Colors* section).

f. Click OK to close the dialog box.

5. Double-underline text by completing the following steps:

a. Select *Wednesday, February 21, 2018*.

b. Click the Font group dialog box launcher.

c. At the Font dialog box, click the *Underline style* option box arrow and then click the double-line option at the drop-down list.

d. Click OK to close the dialog box.

6. Change text to small caps by completing the following steps:

a. Select the text *Created by Susan Ashby* and *Wednesday, February 21, 2018*.

b. Display the Font dialog box.

c. Click the *Small caps* check box in the *Effects* section. (This inserts a check mark in the check box.)

d. Click OK to close the dialog box.

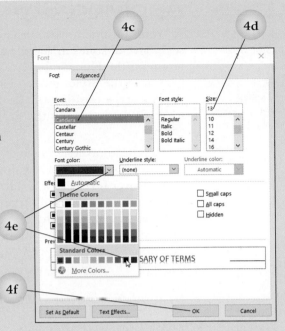

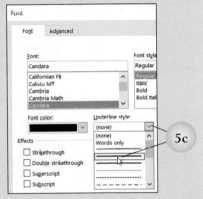

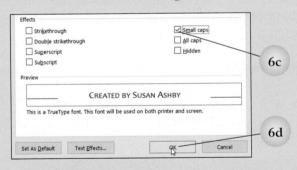

7. Save, print, and then close **2-CompTerms.docx**.

Check Your Work

Project 2 Apply Styles and Themes

3 Parts

You will open a document containing information on the life cycle of software, apply styles to text, and then change the style set. You will also apply a theme and then change the theme colors and fonts.

Preview Finished Project

Applying Styles from a Style Set

Tutorial

Applying Styles and Style Sets

Q̄uick Steps

Apply a Style
1. Position insertion point in text or paragraph of text.
2. Click More Styles button in Styles group.
3. Click style.

A Word document contains a number of predesigned formats grouped into style sets. Several styles in the default style set display in the styles gallery in the Styles group on the Home tab. Display additional styles by clicking the More Styles button in the Styles group. This displays a drop-down gallery of style options. To apply a style, position the insertion point in the text or paragraph of text, click the More Styles button in the Styles group, and then click the style at the drop-down gallery.

If a heading style (such as Heading 1, Heading 2, and so on) is applied to text, the text below the heading can be collapsed and expanded. Hover the mouse pointer over text with a heading style applied and a collapse triangle (solid, right- and down-pointing triangle) displays to the left of the heading. Click this collapse triangle and any text below the heading is collapsed (hidden). Redisplay the text below a heading by hovering the mouse over the heading text until an expand triangle displays (hollow, right-pointing triangle) and then click the expand triangle. This expands (redisplays) the text below the heading.

Removing Default Formatting

A Word document contains some default formatting, including 8 points of spacing after paragraphs and line spacing of 1.08. (You will learn more about these formatting options later in this chapter.) This default formatting, as well as any character formatting applied to text in the document, can be removed by applying the No Spacing style to the text. This style is in the styles gallery in the Styles group.

Changing the Style Set

Q̄uick Steps

Change Style Set
1. Click Design tab.
2. Click style set.

Word provides a number of style sets containing styles that apply formatting to text in a document. To change the style set, click the Design tab and then click the style set in the style sets gallery in the Document Formatting group.

Project 2a   Applying Styles and Changing the Style Set   Part 1 of 3

1. Open **SoftwareCycle.docx** and then save it with the name **2-SoftwareCycle**.
2. Position the insertion point anywhere in the title *COMMERCIAL LIFE CYCLE* and then click the *Heading 1* style in the Styles group.

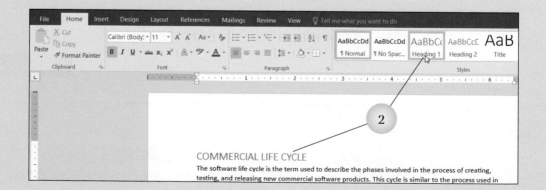

3. Position the insertion point anywhere in the heading *Proposal and Planning* and then click the *Heading 2* style in the styles gallery in the Styles group.

4. Position the insertion point anywhere in the heading *Design* and then click the *Heading 2* style in the styles gallery.

5. Apply the Heading 2 style to the remaining headings (*Implementation*, *Testing*, and *Public Release and Support*).

6. Collapse and expand text below the heading with the Heading 1 style applied by completing the following steps:

   a. Hover the mouse pointer over the heading *COMMERCIAL LIFE CYCLE* until a collapse triangle displays at the left side of the heading and then click the triangle. (This collapses all the text below the heading.)

   b. Click the expand triangle at the left side of the heading *COMMERCIAL LIFE CYCLE*. (This redisplays the text in the document.)

7. Click the Design tab.

8. Click the *Casual* style set in the style sets gallery in the Document Formatting group (the ninth option in the style set). (Notice how the Heading 1 and Heading 2 formatting changes.)

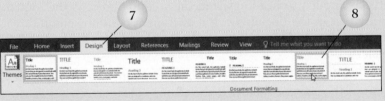

9. Save and then print **2-SoftwareCycle.docx**.

Check Your Work

Tutorial

Applying and Modifying a Theme

 Themes

Quick Steps
Apply a Theme
1. Click Design tab.
2. Click Themes button.
3. Click theme.

Applying a Theme

Word provides a number of themes for formatting text in a document. A theme is a set of formatting choices that includes a color theme (a set of colors), a font theme (a set of heading and body text fonts), and an effects theme (a set of lines and fill effects). To apply a theme, click the Design tab and then click the Themes button in the Document Formatting group. At the drop-down gallery, click the theme. Hover the mouse pointer over a theme and the live preview feature will display the document with the theme formatting applied. Applying a theme is an easy way to give a document a professional look.

1. With **2-SoftwareCycle.docx** open, click the
   Design tab and then click the Themes button in
   the Document Formatting group.
2. At the drop-down gallery, hover your mouse
   pointer over several different themes and
   notice how the text formatting changes in your
   document.
3. Click the *Organic* theme.
4. Save and then print **2-SoftwareCycle.docx**.

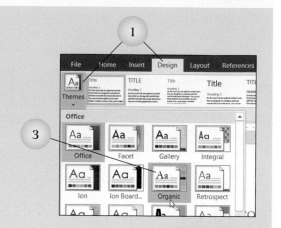

Check Your Work

Modifying a Theme

Modify the color applied by a style or theme with the Colors button in the
Document Formatting group. Click the Colors button and a drop-down gallery
displays with named color schemes. Modify the fonts applied to text in a
document with the Fonts button in the Document Formatting group. Click this
button and a drop-down gallery displays with font choices. Each font group in the
drop-down gallery contains two choices. The first choice in the group is the font
that is applied to headings, and the second choice is the font that is applied to
body text in the document. If a document contains graphics with lines and fills, a
specific theme effect can be applied with options at the Effects button drop-down
gallery.

The buttons in the Document Formatting group display a visual representation of the current theme. If the theme colors are changed, the small color squares
in the Themes button and the Colors button reflect the change. Change the theme
fonts and the *As* on the Themes button and the uppercase *A* on the Fonts button
reflect the change. If the theme effects are changed, the circle in the Effects button
reflects the change.

The Paragraph Spacing button in the Document Formatting group on the
Design tab contains predesigned paragraph spacing options. To change paragraph
spacing, click the Paragraph Spacing button and then click the option at the drop-
down gallery. Hover the mouse pointer over an option at the drop-down gallery and
after a moment a ScreenTip displays with information about the formatting applied
by the option. For example, hover the mouse pointer over the *Compact* option at the
side menu and a ScreenTip displays indicating that selecting the *Compact* option will
change the spacing before paragraphs to 0 points, the spacing after paragraphs to 4
points, and the line spacing to single line spacing.

1. With **2-SoftwareCycle.docx** open, click the Colors button in the Document Formatting group on the Design tab and then click *Red Orange* at the drop-down gallery. (Notice how the colors in the title and headings change.)
2. Click the Fonts button and then click the *Corbel* option. (Notice how the document text font changes.)
3. Click the Paragraph Spacing button and then, one at a time, hover the mouse pointer over each paragraph spacing option, beginning with *Compact*. For each option, read the ScreenTip that explains the paragraph spacing applied by the option.
4. Click the *Double* option.
5. Scroll through the document and notice the paragraph spacing.
6. Change the paragraph spacing by clicking the Paragraph Spacing button and then clicking *Compact*.
7. Save, print, and then close **2-SoftwareCycle.docx**.

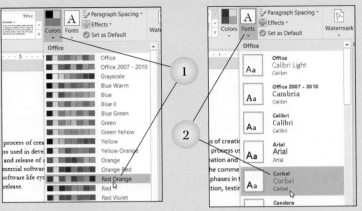

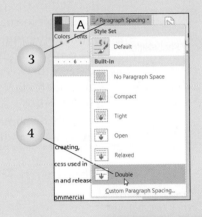

Check Your Work

Project 3 **Apply Paragraph Formatting and Use Format Painter** **6 Parts**

You will open a report on intellectual property and fair use issues and then format the report by changing the alignment of text in paragraphs, applying spacing before and after paragraphs of text, and repeating the last formatting command.

Preview Finished Project

Tutorial

Changing
Paragraph
Alignment

Changing Paragraph Alignment

By default, paragraphs in a Word document are aligned at the left margin and are ragged at the right margin. Change this default alignment with buttons in the Paragraph group on the Home tab or with keyboard shortcuts, as shown in Table 2.3. The alignment of text in paragraphs can be changed before text is typed or the alignment of existing text can be changed.

Table 2.3 Paragraph Alignment Buttons and Keyboard Shortcuts

To align text	Paragraph Group Button	Keyboard Shortcut
At the left margin		Ctrl + L
Between margins		Ctrl + E
At the right margin		Ctrl + R
At the left and right margins		Ctrl + J

Changing Paragraph Alignment as Text Is Typed

≡ Center

¶ Show/Hide ¶

≡ Align Right

≡ Align Left

If the alignment is changed before text is typed, the alignment formatting is inserted in the paragraph mark. Type text and press the Enter key and the paragraph formatting is continued. For example, click the Center button in the Paragraph group, type text for the first paragraph, and then press the Enter key; the center alignment formatting is still active and the insertion point displays centered between the left and right margins. To display the paragraph symbols in a document, click the Show/Hide ¶ button in the Paragraph group. With the Show/Hide ¶ button active (displays with a gray background), nonprinting formatting symbols display, such as the paragraph symbol ¶ indicating a press of the Enter key or a dot indicating a press of the spacebar.

Changing Paragraph Alignment of Existing Text

💡 **Hint** Align text to help the reader follow the message of a document and to make the layout look appealing.

To change the alignment of existing text in a paragraph, position the insertion point anywhere within the paragraph. The entire paragraph does not need to be selected. To change the alignment of several adjacent paragraphs in a document, select a portion of the first paragraph through a portion of the last paragraph. All the text in the paragraphs does not need to be selected.

To return paragraph alignment to the default (left-aligned), click the Align Left button in the Paragraph group. All paragraph formatting can also be returned to the default with the keyboard shortcut Ctrl + Q. This keyboard shortcut removes paragraph formatting from selected text. To remove all formatting from selected text, including character and paragraph formatting, click the Clear All Formatting button in the Font group.

Project 3a Changing Paragraph Alignment

Part 1 of 6

1. Open **IntelProp.docx**. (Some of the default formatting in this document has been changed.)
2. Save the document with the name **2-IntelProp**.
3. Click the Show/Hide ¶ button in the Paragraph group on the Home tab to turn on the display of nonprinting characters.

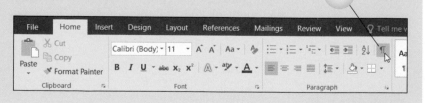

4. Press Ctrl + A to select the entire document and then change the paragraph alignment to justified alignment by clicking the Justify button in the Paragraph group.
5. Press Ctrl + End to move the insertion point to the end of the document.
6. Press the Enter key.
7. Press Ctrl + E to move the insertion point to the middle of the page.
8. Type Prepared by Clarissa Markham.
9. Press Shift + Enter and then type Edited by Joshua Streeter.

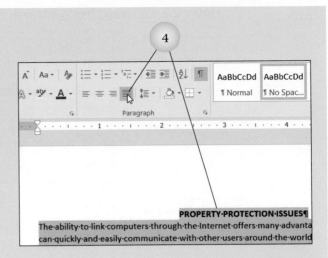

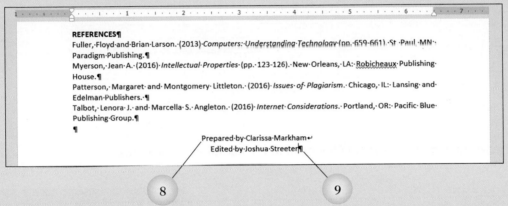

10. Click the Show/Hide ¶ button in the Paragraph group to turn off the display of nonprinting characters.
11. Save **2-IntelProp.docx**.

Check Your Work

Quick Steps

Change Paragraph Alignment
Click alignment button in Paragraph group on Home tab.
OR
1. Click Paragraph group dialog box launcher.
2. Click *Alignment* option box arrow.
3. Click alignment option.
4. Click OK.

Changing Alignment at the Paragraph Dialog Box

Along with buttons in the Paragraph group and keyboard shortcuts, paragraph alignment can be changed with the *Alignment* option box at the Paragraph dialog box, shown in Figure 2.6. Display this dialog box by clicking the Paragraph group dialog box launcher. At the Paragraph dialog box, click the *Alignment* option box arrow. At the drop-down list, click the alignment option and then click OK to close the dialog box.

Figure 2.6 Paragraph Dialog Box with Indents and Spacing Tab Selected

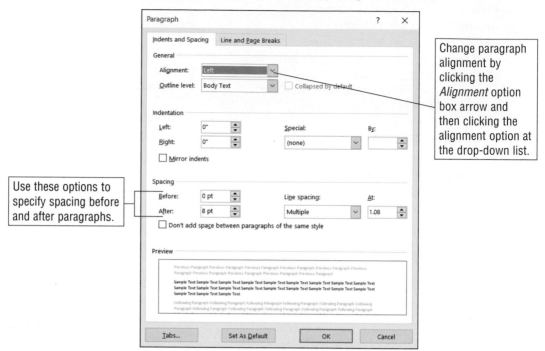

Change paragraph alignment by clicking the *Alignment* option box arrow and then clicking the alignment option at the drop-down list.

Use these options to specify spacing before and after paragraphs.

Project 3b Changing Paragraph Alignment at the Paragraph Dialog Box

1. With **2-IntelProp.docx** open, change the paragraph alignment by completing the following steps:
   a. Select the entire document.
   b. Click the Paragraph group dialog box launcher.
   c. At the Paragraph dialog box with the Indents and Spacing tab selected, click the *Alignment* option box arrow and then click the *Left* option.
   d. Click OK to close the dialog box.
   e. Deselect the text.
2. Change the paragraph alignment by completing the following steps:
   a. Press Ctrl + End to move the insertion point to the end of the document.
   b. Position the insertion point anywhere in the text *Prepared by Clarissa Markham*.
   c. Click the Paragraph group dialog box launcher.
   d. At the Paragraph dialog box with the Indents and Spacing tab selected, click the *Alignment* option box arrow and then click the *Right* option.
   e. Click OK to close the dialog box. (The line of text containing the name *Clarissa Markham* and the line of text containing the name *Joshua Streeter* are both aligned at the right since you used the New Line command, Shift + Enter, to separate the lines of text without creating a new paragraph.)
3. Save and then print **2-IntelProp.docx**.

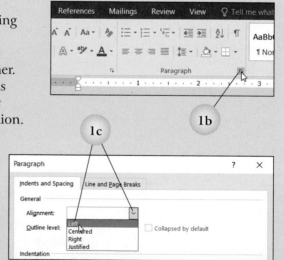

Check Your Work

Indenting Text in Paragraphs

Quick Steps

Indent Text in Paragraph

Drag indent marker(s)
on horizontal ruler.
OR
Press keyboard
shortcut keys.
OR
1. Click Paragraph
   group dialog box
   launcher.
2. Insert measurement
   in *Left, Right,* and/or
   By text box.
3. Click OK.

To indent text from the left margin, the right margin, or both margins, use the indent buttons in the Paragraph group on the Layout tab, keyboard shortcuts, options from the Paragraph dialog box, markers on the horizontal ruler, or the Alignment button above the vertical ruler. Figure 2.7 identifies indent markers on the horizontal ruler and the Alignment button. Refer to Table 2.4 for methods for indenting text in a document. If the horizontal ruler is not visible, display the ruler by clicking the View tab and then clicking the *Ruler* check box in the Show group to insert a check mark.

Figure 2.7 Horizontal Ruler and Indent Markers

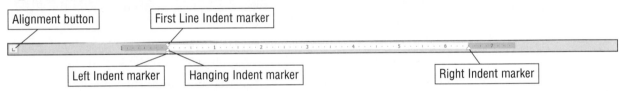

Table 2.4 Methods for Indenting Text

Indent	Methods for Indenting
First line of paragraph	• Press the Tab key. • Display the Paragraph dialog box, click the *Special* option box arrow, click *First line*, and then click OK. • Drag the First Line Indent marker on the horizontal ruler. • Click the Alignment button, until the First Line Indent symbol displays and then click the horizontal ruler at the desired location.
Text from left margin	• Click the Increase Indent button in the Paragraph group on the Home tab to increase the indent or click the Decrease Indent button to decrease the indent. • Insert a measurement in the *Indent Left* measurement box in the Paragraph group on the Layout tab. • Press Ctrl + M to increase the indent or press Ctrl + Shift + M to decrease the indent. • Display the Paragraph dialog box, type the indent measurement in the *Left* measurement box, and then click OK. • Drag the Left Indent marker on the horizontal ruler.

continues

Table 2.4 Methods for Indenting Text—*Continued*

Indent	Methods for Indenting
Text from right margin	• Insert a measurement in the *Indent Right* measurement box in the Paragraph group on the Layout tab. • Display the Paragraph dialog box, type the indent measurement in the *Right* measurement box, and then click OK. • Drag the Right Indent marker on the horizontal ruler.
All lines of text except the first (called a *hanging indent*)	• Press Ctrl + T. (Press Ctrl + Shift + T to remove a hanging indent.) • Display the Paragraph dialog box, click the *Special* option box arrow, click *Hanging*, and then click OK. • Click the Alignment button, left of the horizontal ruler and above the vertical ruler until the Hanging Indent symbol displays and then click the horizontal ruler at the desired location. • Drag the Hanging Indent marker on the horizontal ruler.
Text from both left and right margins	• Display the Paragraph dialog box, type the indent measurement in the *Left* measurement box, type the indent measurement in the *Right* measurement box, and then click OK. • Insert a measurements in the *Indent Right* and *Indent Left* measurement boxes in the Paragraph group on the Layout tab. • Drag the Left Indent marker on the horizontal ruler and then drag the Right Indent marker on the horizontal ruler.

Project 3c Indenting Text

Part 3 of 6

1. With **2-IntelProp.docx** open, indent the first line of text in each paragraph by completing the following steps:
   a. Select the first two paragraphs of text in the document (the text after the title *PROPERTY PROTECTION ISSUES* and before the heading *Intellectual Property*).
   b. Make sure the horizontal ruler displays. (If it does not display, click the View tab and then click the *Ruler* check box in the Show group to insert a check mark.)
   c. Position the mouse pointer on the First Line Indent marker on the horizontal ruler, click and hold down the left mouse button, drag the marker to the 0.5-inch mark, and then release the mouse button.
   d. Select the paragraphs of text in the *Intellectual Property* section and then drag the First Line Indent marker on the horizontal ruler to the 0.5-inch mark.

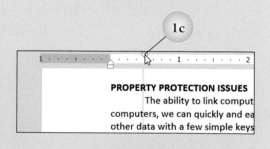

e. Select the paragraphs of text in the *Fair Use* section, click the Alignment button until the First Line Indent symbol displays, and then click the horizontal ruler at the 0.5-inch mark.

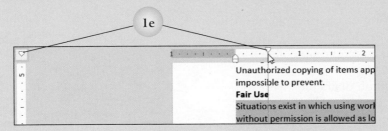

f. Position the insertion point anywhere in the paragraph of text below the heading *Intellectual Property Protection*, make sure the First Line Indent symbol displays on the Alignment button, and then click the 0.5-inch mark on the horizontal ruler.

2. Since the text in the second paragraph in the *Fair Use* section is a quote, indent the text from the left and right margins by completing the following steps:

   a. Position the insertion point anywhere in the second paragraph in the *Fair Use* section (the paragraph that begins *[A] copyrighted work, including such*).

   b. Click the Paragraph group dialog box launcher.

   c. At the Paragraph dialog box with the Indents and Spacing tab selected, select the current measurement in the *Left* measurement box and then type 0.5.

   d. Select the current measurement in the *Right* measurement box and then type 0.5.

   e. Click the *Special* option box arrow and then click *(none)* at the drop-down list.

   f. Click OK or press the Enter key.

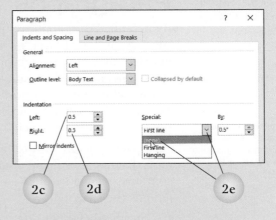

3. Create a hanging indent for the first paragraph in the *REFERENCES* section by positioning the insertion point anywhere in the first paragraph below the heading *REFERENCES* and then pressing Ctrl + T.

4. Create a hanging indent for the second paragraph in the *REFERENCES* section by completing the following steps:

   a. Position the insertion point anywhere in the second paragraph in the *REFERENCES* section.

   b. Click the Alignment button until the Hanging Indent symbol displays.

   c. Click the 0.5-inch mark on the horizontal ruler.

5. Create a hanging indent for the third and fourth paragraphs by completing the following steps:
   a. Select a portion of the third and fourth paragraphs.
   b. Click the Paragraph group dialog box launcher.
   c. At the Paragraph dialog box with the Indents and Spacing tab selected, click the *Special* option box arrow and then click *Hanging* at the drop-down list.
   d. Click OK or press the Enter key.
6. Save **2-IntelProp.docx**.

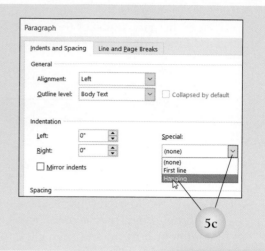

5c

Check Your Work

Tutorial

Changing Spacing Before and After Paragraphs

💡 **Hint** Line spacing determines the amount of vertical space between lines, while paragraph spacing determines the amount of space above or below paragraphs of text.

Spacing Before and After Paragraphs

By default, Word applies 8 points of additional spacing after a paragraph. This spacing can be removed or it can be increased or decreased, and spacing can be inserted above the paragraph. To change spacing before or after a paragraph, use the *Before* and *After* measurement boxes in the Paragraph group on the Layout tab, or the *Before* and *After* options at the Paragraph dialog box with the Indents and Spacing tab selected. Spacing can also be added before and after paragraphs at the Line and Paragraph Spacing button drop-down list.

Spacing before or after a paragraph is part of the paragraph and will be moved, copied, or deleted with the paragraph. If a paragraph, such as a heading, contains spacing before it and the paragraph falls at the top of a page, Word ignores the spacing.

Spacing before or after paragraphs is added in points and 1 vertical inch contains approximately 72 points. To add spacing before or after a paragraph, click the Layout tab, select the current measurement in the *Before* or *After* measurement box, and then type the number of points. The up or down arrows at the *Before* and *After* measurement boxes can also be clicked to increase or decrease the amount of spacing.

Automating Formatting

Applying consistent formatting in a document, especially a multiple-page document, can be time consuming. Word provides options for applying formatting automatically. Use the Repeat command to repeat the last action, such as applying formatting, or the Format Painter to apply formatting to multiple locations in a document.

Repeating the Last Command

Formatting applied to text can be applied to other text in the document using the Repeat command. To use this command, apply the formatting, move the insertion point to the next location the formatting is to be applied, and then press the F4 function key or the keyboard shortcut Ctrl + Y. The Repeat command will repeat only the last command executed.

Project 3d Spacing Before and After Paragraphs and Repeating the Last Command   Part 4 of 6

1. With **2-IntelProp.docx** open, add 6 points of spacing before and after each paragraph in the document by completing the following steps:
   a. Select the entire document.
   b. Click the Layout tab.
   c. Click the *Before* measurement box up arrow. (This inserts *6 pt* in the box.)
   d. Click the *After* measurement box up arrow two times. (This inserts *6 pt* in the box.)
2. Add an additional 6 points of spacing above the headings by completing the following steps:
   a. Position the insertion point anywhere in the heading *Intellectual Property* and then click the *Before* measurement box up arrow. (This changes the measurement to *12 pt*.)
   b. Position the insertion point anywhere in the heading *Fair Use* and then press F4. (F4 is the Repeat command.)
   c. Position the insertion point anywhere in the heading *Intellectual Property Protection* and then press F4.
   d. Position the insertion point anywhere in the heading *REFERENCES* and then press Ctrl + Y. (Ctrl + Y is also the Repeat command.)
3. Save **2-IntelProp.docx**.

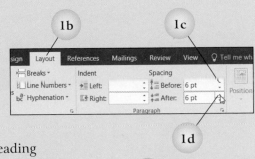
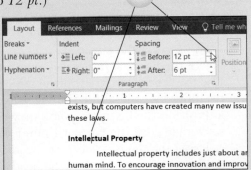

Check Your Work

Formatting with Format Painter

The Clipboard group on the Home tab contains a button for copying formatting and displays in the Clipboard group with a paintbrush. To use this button, called Format Painter, position the insertion point anywhere in text containing the desired formatting, click the Format Painter button, and then select the text to which the formatting is to be applied. When the Format Painter button is clicked, the I-beam pointer displays with a paintbrush attached. To apply the formatting a single time, click the Format Painter button. To apply the formatting in more than one location in the document, double-click the Format Painter button and then select the text to which the formatting is to be applied. When finished, click the Format Painter button to turn it off. The Format Painter button can also be turned off by pressing the Esc key.

Quick Steps

Format with Format Painter
1. Format text then position insertion point within formatted text.
2. Double-click Format Painter button.
3. Select text to apply formatting.
4. Click Format Painter button.

1. With **2-IntelProp.docx** open, click the Home tab.
2. Select the entire document and then change the font to 12-point Cambria.
3. Select the title *PROPERTY PROTECTION ISSUES*, click the Center button in the Paragraph group, and then change the font to 16-point Candara.
4. Apply 16-point Candara formatting to the heading *REFERENCES* by completing the following steps:
   a. Click anywhere in the title *PROPERTY PROTECTION ISSUES*.
   b. Click the Format Painter button in the Clipboard group.

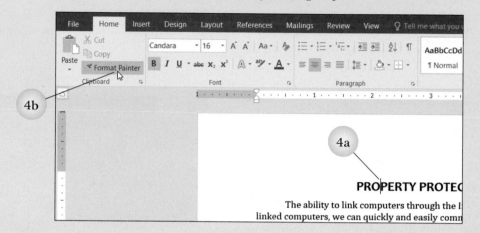

4b

4a

PROPERTY PROTEC

The ability to link computers through the I
linked computers, we can quickly and easily comr

   c. Press Ctrl + End to move the insertion point to the end of the document and then click anywhere in the heading *REFERENCES*. (This applies the 16-point Candara formatting and centers the text.)
5. Select the heading *Intellectual Property* and then change the font to 14-point Candara.
6. Use the Format Painter button and apply 14-point Candara formatting to the other headings by completing the following steps:
   a. Position the insertion point anywhere in the heading *Intellectual Property*.
   b. Double-click the Format Painter button in the Clipboard group.
   c. Using the mouse, select the heading *Fair Use*.
   d. Using the mouse, select the heading *Intellectual Property Protection*.
   e. Click the Format Painter button in the Clipboard group. (This turns off the feature and deactivates the button.)
   f. Deselect the heading.
7. Save **2-IntelProp.docx**.

Check Your Work

Tutorial

Changing Line Spacing

Line and
Paragraph
Spacing

Changing Line Spacing

The default line spacing for a document is 1.08. (The line spacing for the IntelProp.docx file, which you opened at the beginning of Project 3, had been changed to single line spacing.) In certain situations, Word automatically adjusts the line spacing. For example, if a large character or object, such as a graphic, is inserted into a line, Word increases the line spacing of that line. The line spacing for a section or an entire document can also be changed.

Quick Steps

Change Line Spacing
1. Click Line and Paragraph Spacing button.
2. Click option.
OR
Press keyboard shortcut command.
OR
1. Click Paragraph group dialog box launcher.
2. Click *Line Spacing* option box arrow.
3. Click line spacing option.
4. Click OK.
OR
1. Click Paragraph group dialog box launcher.
2. Type line measurement in *At* measurement box
3. Click OK.

Change line spacing using the Line and Paragraph Spacing button in the Paragraph group on the Home tab, keyboard shortcuts, or options from the Paragraph dialog box. Table 2.5 displays the keyboard shortcuts to change line spacing.

Line spacing can also be changed at the Paragraph dialog box with the *Line spacing* option or the *At* measurement box. Click the *Line spacing* option box arrow and a drop-down list displays with a variety of spacing options, such as *Single*, *1.5 lines*, and *Double*. A specific line spacing measurement can be entered in the *At* measurement box. For example, to change the line spacing to 1.75 lines, type *1.75* in the *At* measurement box.

Table 2.5 Line Spacing Keyboard Shortcuts

Press	To change line spacing to
Ctrl + 1	single line spacing
Ctrl + 2	double line spacing
Ctrl + 5	1.5 line spacing

Project 3f Changing Line Spacing

Part 6 of 6

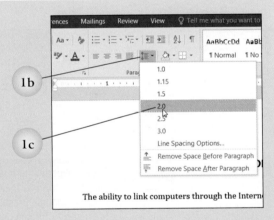

1. With **2-IntelProp.docx** open, change the line spacing for all paragraphs to double spacing by completing the following steps:
   a. Select the entire document.
   b. Click the Line and Paragraph Spacing button in the Paragraph group on the Home tab.
   c. Click *2.0* at the drop-down list.
2. With the entire document still selected, press Ctrl + 5. (This changes the line spacing to 1.5 lines.)
3. Change the line spacing to 1.2 lines using the Paragraph dialog box by completing the following steps:
   a. With the entire document still selected, click the Paragraph group dialog box launcher.
   b. At the Paragraph dialog box, make sure the Indents and Spacing tab is selected, click in the *At* measurement box, and then type 1.2. (This measurement box is to the right of the *Line spacing* option box.)
   c. Click OK or press the Enter key.
   d. Deselect the text.
4. Save, print, and then close **2-IntelProp.docx**.

Check Your Work

You will open a document containing two computer-related problems to solve, reveal the formatting, compare the formatting, and make formatting changes.

Preview Finished Project

Revealing and Comparing Formatting

Display formatting applied to specific text in a document at the Reveal Formatting task pane, shown in Figure 2.8. The Reveal Formatting task pane displays font, paragraph, and section formatting applied to text where the insertion point is positioned or to selected text. Display the Reveal Formatting task pane with the keyboard shortcut Shift + F1. Generally, a collapse triangle (a solid right-and-down-pointing triangle) precedes *Font* and *Paragraph* and an expand triangle (a hollow right-pointing triangle) precedes *Section* in the *Formatting of selected text* list box in the Reveal Formatting task pane. Click the collapse triangle to hide any items below a heading and click the expand triangle to reveal items. Some of the items below headings in the *Formatting of selected text* list box are hyperlinks. Click a hyperlink and a dialog box displays with the specific option.

Figure 2.8 Reveal Formatting Task Pane

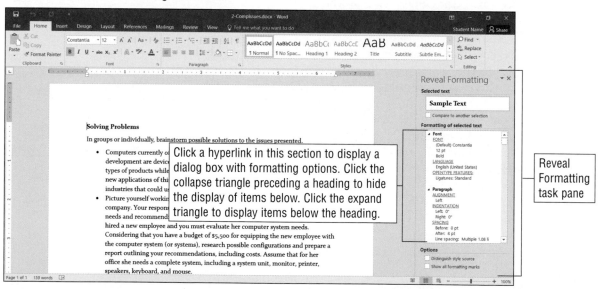

Project 4a **Revealing Formatting**

Part 1 of 2

1. Open **CompIssues.docx** and then save it with the name **2-CompIssues**.
2. Press Shift + F1 to display the Reveal Formatting task pane.
3. Click anywhere in the heading *Solving Problems* and then notice the formatting information in the Reveal Formatting task pane.
4. Click in the bulleted paragraph and notice the formatting information in the Reveal Formatting task pane.

Compare Formatting
1. Press Shift + F1 to display Reveal Formatting task pane.
2. Click or select text.
3. Click *Compare to another selection* check box.
4. Click or select text.

Along with displaying formatting applied to text, the Reveal Formatting task pane can be used to compare formatting of two text selections to determine what is different. To compare formatting, select the first instance of formatting to be compared, click the *Compare to another selection* check box, and then select the second instance of formatting to be compared. Any differences between the two selections display in the *Formatting differences* list box.

Project 4b Comparing Formatting   Part 2 of 2

1. With **2-CompIssues.docx** open, make sure the Reveal Formatting task pane displays. If it does not, turn it on by pressing Shift + F1.
2. Select the first bulleted paragraph (the paragraph that begins *Computers currently offer both*).
3. Click the *Compare to another selection* check box to insert a check mark.
4. Select the second bulleted paragraph (the paragraph that begins *Picture yourself working in the*).
5. Determine the formatting differences by reading the information in the *Formatting differences* list box. (The list box displays *12 pt -> 11 pt* below the <u>FONT</u> hyperlink, indicating that the difference is point size.)
6. Format the second bulleted paragraph so it is set in 12-point size.
7. Click the *Compare to another selection* check box to remove the check mark.
8. Select the word *visual*, which displays in the first sentence in the first bulleted paragraph.
9. Click the *Compare to another selection* check box to insert a check mark.
10. Select the word *audio*, which displays in the first sentence of the first bulleted paragraph.
11. Determine the formatting differences by reading the information in the *Formatting differences* list box.
12. Format the word *audio* so it matches the formatting of the word *visual*.
13. Click the *Compare to another selection* check box to remove the check mark.
14. Close the Reveal Formatting task pane by clicking the Close button in the upper right corner of the task pane.
15. Save, print, and then close **2-CompIssues.docx**.

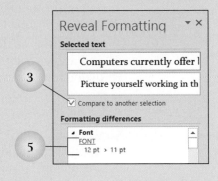

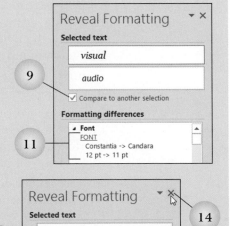

Check Your Work

Chapter Summary

- A font consists of three elements: typeface, type size, and typestyle.

- A typeface (font) is a set of characters with a common design and shape. Typefaces are either monospaced, allotting the same amount of horizontal space for each character, or proportional, allotting varying amounts of space for different characters. Proportional typefaces are divided into two main categories: serif and sans serif.

- Type size is measured in point size; the higher the point size, the larger the characters.

- A typestyle is a variation of style within a certain typeface, such as bold, italic, or underline. Apply typestyle formatting with some of the buttons in the Font group on the Home tab.

- Apply font effects with some of the buttons in the Font group on the Home tab, such as superscript, subscript, and strikethrough.

- The Mini toolbar automatically displays above selected text. Use options and buttons on this toolbar to apply formatting to selected text.

- Use options at the Font dialog box to change the font, font size, and font style and apply specific effects. Display this dialog box by clicking the Font group dialog box launcher.

- A Word document contains a number of predesigned formats grouped into style sets. Change to a different style set by clicking the Design tab and then clicking the style set in the styles set gallery in the Document Formatting group.

- Apply a theme and change theme colors, fonts, and effects with buttons in the Document Formatting group on the Design tab.

- Click the Paragraph Spacing button in the Document Formatting group on the Design tab to apply a predesigned paragraph spacing option to text in a document.

- By default, paragraphs in a Word document are aligned at the left margin and ragged at the right margin. Change this default alignment with buttons in the Paragraph group, at the Paragraph dialog box, or with keyboard shortcuts.

- To turn on or off the display of nonprinting characters, such as paragraph marks, click the Show/Hide ¶ button in the Paragraph group on the Home tab.

- Indent text in paragraphs with indent buttons in the Paragraph group on the Home tab, buttons in the Paragraph group on the Layout tab, keyboard shortcuts, options from the Paragraph dialog box, markers on the horizontal ruler, or the Alignment button above the vertical ruler.

- Increase and/or decrease spacing before and after paragraphs using the *Before* and *After* measurement boxes in the Paragraph group on the Layout tab or using the *Before* and/or *After* options at the Paragraph dialog box.

- Repeat the last command by pressing the F4 function key or the keyboard shortcut Ctrl + Y.

- Use the Format Painter button in the Clipboard group on the Home tab to copy formatting already applied to text to different locations in the document.

- Change line spacing with the Line and Paragraph Spacing button in the Paragraph group on the Home tab, keyboard shortcuts, or options from the Paragraph dialog box.

- Display the Reveal Formatting task pane to display formatting applied to text. Use the *Compare to another selection* option in the task pane to compare formatting of two text selections to determine what is different.

Commands Review

FEATURE	RIBBON TAB, GROUP	BUTTON	KEYBOARD SHORTCUT
bold text	Home, Font	B	Ctrl + B
center-align text	Home, Paragraph	≡	Ctrl + E
change case of text	Home, Font	Aa ⁻	Shift + F3
clear all formatting	Home, Font	🅐	
clear character formatting			Ctrl + spacebar
clear paragraph formatting			Ctrl + Q
decrease font size	Home, Font	A˅	Ctrl + Shift + < OR Ctrl + [
display or hide nonprinting characters	Home, Paragraph	¶	Ctrl + Shift + *
font	Home, Font		
font color	Home, Font	A ⁻	
Font dialog box	Home, Font	⌜	Ctrl + Shift + F
font size	Home, Font		
Format Painter	Home, Clipboard	�**✸**	Ctrl + Shift + C
Help			F1
highlight text	Home, Font	ab⁄ ⁻	
increase font size	Home, Font	A˄	Ctrl + Shift + > OR Ctrl +]
italicize text	Home, Font	I	Ctrl + I
justify text	Home, Paragraph	≡	Ctrl + J
left-align text	Home, Paragraph	≡	Ctrl + L
line spacing	Home, Paragraph	‡≡ ⁻	Ctrl + 1 (single) Ctrl + 2 (double) Ctrl + 5 (1.5)
Paragraph dialog box	Home, Paragraph	⌜	
paragraph spacing	Design, Document Formatting	🖹	
repeat last action			F4 or Ctrl + Y
Reveal Formatting task pane			Shift + F1

FEATURE	RIBBON TAB, GROUP	BUTTON	KEYBOARD SHORTCUT
right-align text	Home, Paragraph		Ctrl + R
spacing after paragraph	Layout, Paragraph		
spacing before paragraph	Layout, Paragraph		
strikethrough text	Home, Font		
subscript text	Home, Font		Ctrl + =
superscript text	Home, Font		Ctrl + Shift + +
text effects and typography	Home, Font		
theme colors	Design, Document Formatting		
theme effects	Design, Document Formatting		
theme fonts	Design, Document Formatting		
themes	Design, Document Formatting		
underline text	Home, Font		Ctrl + U

Workbook

Chapter study tools and assessment activities are available in the
Workbook ebook. These resources are designed to help you further
develop and demonstrate mastery of the skills learned in this chapter.

Microsoft®
Word

Customizing Paragraphs

Performance Objectives

Upon successful completion of Chapter 3, you will be able to:

1 Apply numbering and bulleting formatting to text

2 Apply paragraph borders and shading

3 Sort paragraph text

4 Set, clear, and move tabs on the horizontal ruler and at the Tabs dialog box

5 Cut, copy, and paste text in a document

6 Use the Paste Options button to specify how text is pasted in a document

7 Use the Clipboard task pane to copy and paste text within and between documents

Precheck

Check your current skills to help focus your study.

As you learned in Chapter 2, Word contains a variety of options for formatting text in paragraphs. In this chapter you will learn how to apply numbering and bulleted formatting to text, how to apply borders and shading to paragraphs of text, how to sort paragraphs of text, and how to manipulate tabs on the horizontal ruler and at the Tabs dialog box. Editing some documents might include selecting and then deleting, moving, or copying text. You can perform this type of editing with buttons in the Clipboard group on the Home tab or with keyboard shortcuts.

Data Files

Before beginning chapter work, copy the WL1C3 folder to your storage medium and then make WL1C3 the active folder.

SNAP

If you are a SNAP user, launch the Precheck and Tutorials from your Assignments page.

Project 1 **Format a Document on Computer Technology** **3 Parts**

You will open a document containing information on computer technology, type numbered text in the document, and apply numbering and bulleted formatting to paragraphs in the document.

Preview Finished Project

Applying Numbering and Bullets

 Numbering

Bullets

Automatically number paragraphs or insert bullets before paragraphs using buttons in the Paragraph group on the Home tab. Use the Numbering button to insert numbers before specific paragraphs and use the Bullets button to insert bullets.

Tutorial

Creating
Numbered Lists

Quick Steps
Type Numbered
Paragraphs
1. Type 1.
2. Press spacebar.
3. Type text.
4. Press Enter.

Hint Define a new numbering format by clicking the Numbering button arrow and then clicking *Define New Number Format*.

Creating Numbered Lists

Type *1.* and then press the spacebar and Word indents the number 0.25 inch from the left margin and hang-indents the text in the paragraph 0.5 inch from the left margin. Additionally, when the Enter key is pressed to end the first item, *2.* is inserted 0.25 inch from the left margin at the beginning of the next paragraph. Continue typing items and Word inserts the next number in the list. To turn off numbering, press the Enter key two times or click the Numbering button in the Paragraph group on the Home tab. (Paragraph formatting can be removed from a paragraph, including automatic numbering, with the keyboard shortcut Ctrl + Q. Remove all formatting, including character and paragraph formatting from selected text, by clicking the Clear All Formatting button in the Font group on the Home tab.)

Press the Enter key two times between numbered paragraphs and the automatic numbering is removed. To turn it back on, type the next number in the list (and the period) followed by a space. Word will automatically indent the number and hang-indent the text. To insert a line break without inserting a bullet or number, press Shift + Enter.

When the AutoFormat feature inserts numbering and indents text, the AutoCorrect Options button displays. Click this button and a drop-down list displays with options for undoing and/or stopping the automatic numbering. An AutoCorrect Options button also displays when AutoFormat inserts automatic bulleting in a document.

Project 1a Creating a Numbered List

Part 1 of 3

1. Open **TechInfo.docx** and then save it with the name **3-TechInfo**.
2. Press Ctrl + End to move the insertion point to the end of the document and then type the text shown in Figure 3.1. Apply bold formatting and center the title *Technology Career Questions*. When typing the numbered paragraphs, complete the following steps:
   a. Type 1. and then press the spacebar. (The *1.* is indented 0.25 inch from the left margin and the first paragraph of text is indented 0.5 inch from the left margin. Also, the AutoCorrect Options button displays. Use this button if you want to undo or stop automatic numbering.)
   b. Type the paragraph of text and then press the Enter key. (This moves the insertion point down to the next paragraph and inserts an indented number *2* followed by a period.)

c. Continue typing the remaining text. (Remember, you do not need to type the paragraph number and period—they are automatically inserted. The last numbered item will wrap differently on your screen than shown in Figure 3.1.)

d. After typing the last question, press the Enter key two times. (This turns off paragraph numbering.)

3. Save **3-TechInfo.docx**.

Check Your Work

Figure 3.1 Project 1a

Technology Career Questions

1. What is your ideal technical job?
2. Which job suits your personality?
3. Which is your first-choice certificate?
4. How does the technical job market look in your state right now? Is the job market wide open or are the information technology career positions limited?

Automatic numbering is turned on by default. Turn off automatic numbering at the AutoCorrect dialog box with the AutoFormat As You Type tab selected, as shown in Figure 3.2. To display this dialog box, click the File tab and then click *Options*. At the Word Options dialog box, click the *Proofing* option in the left panel and then click the AutoCorrect Options button in the *AutoCorrect options* section of the dialog box. At the AutoCorrect dialog box, click the AutoFormat As You Type tab and then click the *Automatic numbered lists* check box to remove the check mark. Click OK to close the AutoCorrect dialog box and then click OK to close the Word Options dialog box.

Figure 3.2 AutoCorrect Dialog Box with AutoFormat As You Type Tab Selected

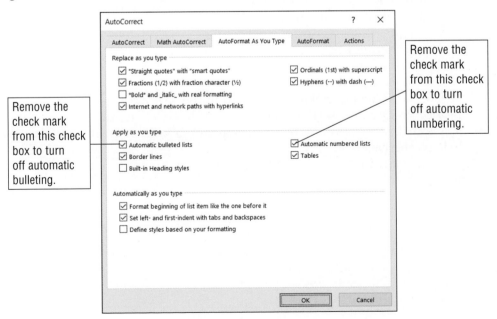

Quick Steps
Create a Numbered List
1. Select text.
2. Click Numbering button.

Numbering formatting can be turned on or applied to existing text with the Numbering button in the Paragraph group on the Home tab. Click the Numbering button to turn on numbering, type text, and then click the button again to turn off numbering, or select existing text and then click the Numbering button to apply numbering formatting.

Project 1b   Applying Numbering Formatting

Part 2 of 3

1. With **3-TechInfo.docx** open, apply numbers to paragraphs by completing the following steps:
   a. Select the five paragraphs of text in the *Technology Information Questions* section.
   b. Click the Numbering button in the Paragraph group on the Home tab.

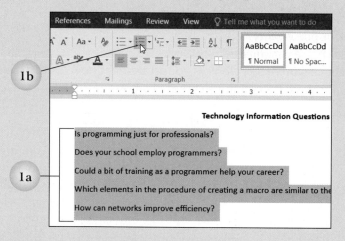

2. Add text between paragraphs 4 and 5 in the *Technology Information Questions* section by completing the following steps:
   a. Position the insertion point immediately right of the question mark at the end of the fourth paragraph.
   b. Press the Enter key.
   c. Type What kinds of networks are used in your local area?

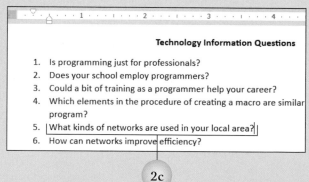

3. Delete the second question (paragraph) in the *Technology Information Questions* section by completing the following steps:
   a. Select the text of the second paragraph. (You will not be able to select the number.)
   b. Press the Delete key.
4. Save **3-TechInfo.docx**.

Check Your Work

Creating Bulleted Lists

In addition to automatically numbering paragraphs, Word's AutoFormat feature creates bulleted lists. A bulleted list with a hanging indent is automatically created when a paragraph begins with the symbol *, >, or -. Type one of the symbols and then press the spacebar and the AutoFormat feature inserts a bullet 0.25 inch from the left margin and indents the text following the bullet another 0.25 inch. Change the indent of bulleted text by pressing the Tab key to demote text or pressing Shift + Tab to promote text. Word uses different bullets for demoted text.

Bulleted formatting can be turned on or applied to existing text with the Bullets button in the Paragraph group on the Home tab. Click the Bullets button to turn on bulleting, type text, and then click the button again to turn off bulleting. Or, select existing text and then click the Bullets button to apply bulleted formatting. The automatic bulleting feature can be turned off at the AutoCorrect dialog box with the AutoFormat As You Type tab selected.

Quick Steps

Type Bulleted List
1. Type *, >, or -
   symbol.
2. Press spacebar.
3. Type text.
4. Press Enter.

Create Bulleted List
1. Select text.
2. Click Bullets button.

Project 1c Creating a Bulleted List and Applying Bulleted Formatting   Part 3 of 3

1. With **3-TechInfo.docx** open, press Ctrl + End to move the insertion point to the end of the document and then press the Enter key.
2. Type Technology Timeline: Computer Design bolded and centered, as shown in Figure 3.3, and then press the Enter key.
3. Turn off bold formatting and change to left alignment.
4. Type a greater-than symbol (>), press the spacebar, type the text of the first bulleted paragraph in Figure 3.3, and then press the Enter key.
5. Press the Tab key (which demotes the bullet to a hollow circle) and then type the bulleted text.
6. Press the Enter key (which displays another hollow circle bullet), type the bulleted text, and then press the Enter key.
7. Press Shift + Tab (which promotes the bullet to an arrow), type the bulleted text, and then press the Enter key two times (which turns off bullets).
8. Promote bulleted text by positioning the insertion point at the beginning of the text *1958: Jack Kilby, an engineer* and then pressing Shift + Tab. Promote the other hollow circle bullet to an arrow. (The four paragraphs of text should be preceded by arrow bullets.)
9. Format the paragraphs of text in the *Technology Timeline: Computers in the Workplace* section as a bulleted list by completing the following steps:
   a. Select the paragraphs of text in the *Technology Timeline: Computers in the Workplace* section.
   b. Click the Bullets button in the Paragraph group. (Word will insert the same arrow bullets that you inserted in Step 2. Word keeps the same bullet formatting until you choose a different bullet style.)
10. Save, print, and then close **3-TechInfo.docx**.

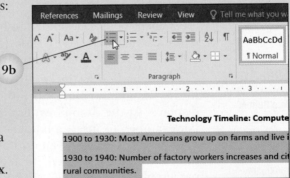

Check Your Work

Figure 3.3 Project 1c

Technology Timeline: Computer Design

➤ 1937: Dr. John Atanasoff and Clifford Berry design and build the first electronic digital computer.
  o 1958: Jack Kilby, an engineer at Texas Instruments, invents the integrated circuit, thereby laying the foundation for fast computers and large-capacity memory.
  o 1981: IBM enters the personal computer field by introducing the IBM-PC.
➤ 2004: Wireless computer devices, including keyboards, mice, and wireless home networks, become widely accepted among users.

Project 2 **Customize a Document on Chapter Questions**   **3 Parts**

You will open a document containing chapter questions and then apply border and shading formatting to text.

Preview Finished Project

Adding Emphasis to Paragraphs

To call attention to or to highlight specific text in a paragraph, consider adding emphasis to the text by applying paragraph borders and/or shading. Apply borders with the Borders button on the Home tab and shading with the Shading button. Additional borders and shading options are available at the Borders and Shading dialog box.

 Borders

Tutorial

Applying Borders

Applying Paragraph Borders

Every paragraph in a Word document contains an invisible frame and a border can be applied to the frame around the paragraph. Apply a border to specific sides of the paragraph frame or to all sides. Add borders to paragraphs using the Borders button in the Paragraph group on the Home tab or using options at the Borders and Shading dialog box.

When a border is added to a paragraph of text, the border expands and contracts as text is inserted or deleted from the paragraph. Insert a border around the active paragraph or around selected paragraphs.

One method for inserting a border is to use options from the Borders button in the Paragraph group. Click the Borders button arrow and a drop-down list displays. At the drop-down list, click the option that will insert the desired border. For example, to insert a border at the bottom of the paragraph, click the *Bottom Border* option. Clicking an option will add the border to the paragraph where the insertion point is located. To add a border to more than one paragraph, select the paragraphs first and then click the option.

Quick Steps
Apply Borders with Borders Button
1. Select text.
2. Click Borders button arrow.
3. Click border option at drop-down list.

1. Open **Questions.docx** and then save it with the name **3-Questions**.
2. Insert an outside border to specific text by completing the following steps:
   a. Select text from the heading *Chapter 1 Questions* through the four bulleted paragraphs.
   b. In the Paragraph group, click the Borders button arrow.
   c. Click the *Outside Borders* option at the drop-down list.
3. Select text from the heading *Chapter 2 Questions* through the five bulleted paragraphs and then click the Borders button in the Paragraph group. (The button will apply the border option that was previously selected.)
4. Save **3-Questions.docx**.

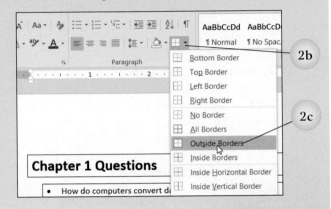

Check Your Work

Quick Steps

Apply Borders at the Borders and Shading Dialog Box
1. Select text.
2. Click Borders button arrow.
3. Click *Borders and Shading* option.
4. Choose options in dialog box.
5. Click OK.

To further customize paragraph borders, use options at the Borders and Shading dialog box shown in Figure 3.4. Display this dialog box by clicking the Borders button arrow and then clicking *Borders and Shading* at the drop-down list. At the Borders and Shading dialog box, specify the border setting, style, color, and width.

Figure 3.4 Borders and Shading Dialog Box with the Borders Tab Selected

Click the *Style* list box arrow to display additional line styles.

Click the *Color* option box arrow to display a drop-down list of color options.

Click the *Width* option box arrow to display a drop-down list of width options.

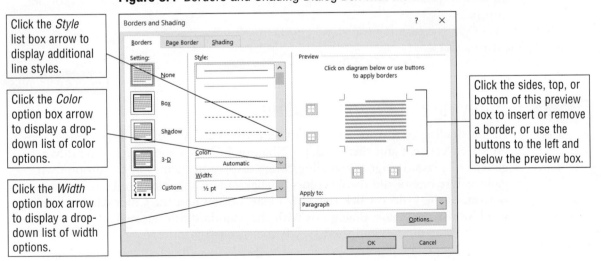

Click the sides, top, or bottom of this preview box to insert or remove a border, or use the buttons to the left and below the preview box.

1. With **3-Questions.docx** open, remove the paragraph borders around the heading *Chapter 1 Questions* by completing the following steps:
   a. Position the insertion point anywhere in the heading *Chapter 1 Questions*.
   b. Click the Borders button arrow and then click *No Border* at the drop-down list.
2. Apply a bottom border to the heading *Chapter 1 Questions* by completing the following steps:
   a. Click the Borders button arrow.
   b. Click the *Borders and Shading* option.
   c. At the Borders and Shading dialog box, click the *Style* list box down arrow two times. (This displays a double-line option.)
   d. Click the double-line option.
   e. Click the *Color* option box arrow.
   f. Click the *Blue* color option (eighth option in the *Standard Colors* section).
   g. Click the *Width* option box arrow.
   h. Click the *3/4 pt* option at the drop-down list.
   i. Click the *None* option in the *Setting* section.
   j. Click the bottom border of the box in the *Preview* section.
   k. Click the OK button to close the dialog box and apply the border.
3. Apply the same border to the other heading by completing the following steps:
   a. With the insertion point positioned in the heading *Chapter 1 Questions*, click the Format Painter button.
   b. Click anywhere in the heading *Chapter 2 Questions*.
4. Save **3-Questions.docx**.

Check Your Work

Applying Paragraph Shading

Applying Shading

 Shading

Quick Steps

Apply Shading
1. Select text.
2. Click Shading button.
OR
1. Click Borders button arrow.
2. Click *Borders and Shading* option.
3. Click Shading tab.
4. Choose options in dialog box.
5. Click OK.

Apply shading to text in a document with the Shading button in the Paragraph group. Select text and then click the Shading button arrow, and a drop-down gallery displays. Paragraph shading colors display in themes in the drop-down gallery. Use one of the theme colors or click one of the standard colors at the bottom of the gallery. Click the *More Colors* option and the Colors dialog box displays. At the Colors dialog box with the Standard tab selected, click a color or click the Custom tab and then specify a custom color.

Paragraph shading can also be applied to paragraphs in a document using options at the Borders and Shading dialog box with the Shading tab selected. Display this dialog box by clicking the Borders button arrow and then clicking the *Borders and Shading* option. At the Borders and Shading dialog box, click the Shading tab. Use options in the dialog box to specify a fill color, choose a pattern style, and specify a color for the dots that make up the pattern.

1. With **3-Questions.docx** open, apply paragraph shading to the heading *Chapter 1 Questions* by completing the following steps:
   a. Click anywhere in the heading *Chapter 1 Questions*.
   b. Click the Shading button arrow.
   c. Click the *Blue, Accent 5, Lighter 80%* color option (ninth column, second row in the *Theme Colors* section).

2. Apply the same blue shading to the other heading by completing the following steps:
   a. With the insertion point positioned in the heading *Chapter 1 Questions*, click the Format Painter button.
   b. Click anywhere in the heading *Chapter 2 Questions*.

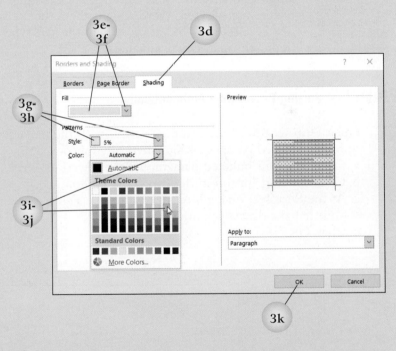

3. Apply shading to text with options at the Borders and Shading dialog box by completing the following steps:
   a. Select the four bulleted paragraphs below the heading *Chapter 1 Questions*.
   b. Click the Borders button arrow.
   c. Click the *Borders and Shading* option.
   d. At the Borders and Shading dialog box, click the Shading tab.
   e. Click the *Fill* option box arrow.
   f. Click the *Gold, Accent 4, Lighter 80%* color option (eighth column, second row).
   g. Click the *Style* option box arrow.
   h. Click the *5%* option.
   i. Click the *Color* option box arrow.
   j. Click the *Blue, Accent 5, Lighter 60%* color option (ninth column, third row in the *Theme Colors* section).
   k. Click OK to close the dialog box.

4. Apply the same shading to the bulleted paragraphs below the heading *Chapter 2 Questions* by completing the following steps:
   a. Click anywhere in the bulleted paragraphs below the heading *Chapter 1 Questions*.
   b. Click the Format Painter button.
   c. Select the five bulleted paragraphs below the heading *Chapter 2 Questions*.

5. Save, print, and then close **3-Questions.docx**.

Check Your Work

Project 3 **Sort Text in a Document on Online Shopping** **1 Part**

You will open a document on online shopping and then sort several different paragraphs of text.

Preview Finished Project

Tutorial

Sorting Text in Paragraphs

Sorting Text in Paragraphs

Text arranged in paragraphs can be sorted alphabetically by the first character of each paragraph. The first character can be a number, symbol (such as $ or #), or letter. Type paragraphs to be sorted at the left margin or indented at a tab. Unless specific paragraphs are selected for sorting, Word sorts the entire document.

 Sort

To sort text in paragraphs, open the document. If the document contains text that should not be included in the sort, select the specific paragraphs to be sorted. Click the Sort button in the Paragraph group and the Sort Text dialog box displays. At this dialog box, click OK.

Quick Steps

Sort Paragraphs of Text
1. Click Sort button.
2. Make changes as needed at Sort Text dialog box.
3. Click OK.

The *Type* option at the Sort Text dialog box will display *Text*, *Number*, or *Date* depending on the text selected. Word attempts to determine the data type and chooses one of the three options. For example, if numbers with mathematical values are selected, Word assigns them the *Number* type. However, if a numbered list is selected, Word assigns them the *Text* type since the numbers do not represent mathematical values.

Project 3 **Sorting Paragraphs Alphabetically** **Part 1 of 1**

1. Open **OnlineShop.docx** and then save it with the name **3-OnlineShop**.
2. Sort the bulleted paragraphs alphabetically by completing the following steps:
   a. Select the four bulleted paragraphs in the section *Advantages of Online Shopping*.
   b. Click the Sort button in the Paragraph group.
   c. At the Sort Text dialog box, make sure that *Paragraphs* displays in the *Sort by* option box and that the *Ascending* option is selected.
   d. Click OK.

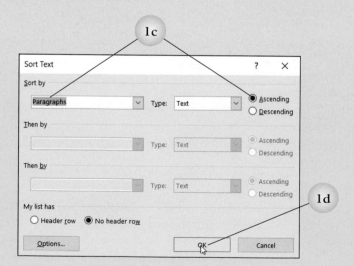

3. Sort the numbered paragraphs by completing the following steps:
   a. Select the six numbered paragraphs in the section *Online Shopping Safety Tips*.
   b. Click the Sort button in the Paragraph group.
   c. Click OK at the Sort Text dialog box.
4. Sort alphabetically the three paragraphs below the title *REFERENCES* by completing the following steps:
   a. Select the paragraphs below the title *REFERENCES*.
   b. Click the Sort button in the Paragraph group.
   c. Click the *Type* option box arrow and then click *Text* at the drop-down list.
   d. Click OK.
5. Save, print, and then close **3-OnlineShop.docx**.

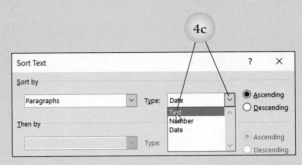

Check Your Work

Project 4   Prepare a Document on Workshops and Training Dates   4 Parts

You will set and move tabs on the horizontal ruler and at the Tabs dialog box and type tabbed text about workshops, training dates, and a table of contents.

Preview Finished Project

Setting and Modifying Tabs

A Word document includes a variety of default settings, such as margins and line spacing. One of these defaults is a left tab set every 0.5 inch. In some situations, these default tabs are appropriate; in others, custom tabs may be needed. Two methods are available for setting tabs: set tabs on the horizontal ruler or at the Tabs dialog box.

Setting and Modifying Tabs on the Horizontal Ruler

Use the horizontal ruler to set, move, and delete tabs. If the ruler is not visible, click the View tab and then click the *Ruler* check box in the Show group to insert a check mark. By default, tabs are set every 0.5 inch on the horizontal ruler. With a left tab, text aligns at the left edge of the tab. The other types of tabs that can be set on the horizontal ruler are center, right, decimal, and bar. Use the Alignment button above the vertical ruler to specify types of tabs. Each time the Alignment button is clicked, a different tab or paragraph symbol displays. Table 3.1 shows the tab symbols and what type of tab each symbol will set.

To set a left tab on the horizontal ruler, make sure the left tab symbol (see Table 3.1) displays on the Alignment button. Position the arrow pointer on the tick mark (the vertical line on the ruler) where the tab is to be set and then click the left mouse button. When a tab is set on the horizontal ruler, any default tabs to the left are automatically deleted by Word. Set a center, right, decimal, or bar tab on the horizontal ruler in a similar manner.

Table 3.1 Alignment Button Tab Symbols

Alignment Button Symbol	Type of Tab
L	left
⊥	center
⌐	right
⊥·	decimal
I	bar

Hint Position the insertion point in any paragraph of text, and tabs for the paragraph appear on the horizontal ruler.

If the tab symbol on the Alignment button is changed, the symbol remains in place until it is changed again or Word is closed. If Word is closed and then reopened, the Alignment button displays with the left tab symbol.

To set a tab at a specific measurement on the horizontal ruler, press and hold down the Alt key, position the arrow pointer at the desired position, and then click and hold down the left mouse button. This displays two measurements in the white portion of the horizontal ruler. The first measurement is the location of the arrow pointer on the ruler in relation to the left margin. The second measurement is the distance from the arrow pointer to the right margin. With the left mouse button held down, position the tab symbol at the desired location and then release the mouse button followed by the Alt key.

Project 4a Setting Left, Center, and Right Tabs on the Horizontal Ruler

Part 1 of 4

1. Press Ctrl + N to open a new blank document.
2. Type WORKSHOPS centered and bolded, as shown in Figure 3.5.
3. Press the Enter key. In the new paragraph, change the paragraph alignment back to left and then turn off bold formatting.
4. Set a left tab at the 0.5-inch mark, a center tab at the 3.25-inch mark, and a right tab at the 6-inch mark by completing the following steps:
   a. Click the Show/Hide ¶ button in the Paragraph group on the Home tab to turn on the display of nonprinting characters.
   b. Make sure the horizontal ruler is displayed. (If it is not displayed, click the View tab and then click the *Ruler* check box in the Show group to insert a check mark.)
   c. Make sure the left tab symbol displays in the Alignment button.
   d. Position the arrow pointer on the 0.5-inch mark on the horizontal ruler and then click the left mouse button.

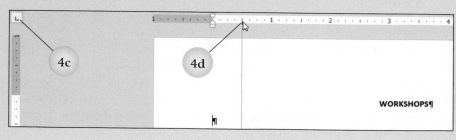

e. Position the arrow pointer on the Alignment button and then click the left mouse button until the center tab symbol displays (see Table 3.1).

f. Position the arrow pointer on the 3.25-inch mark on the horizontal ruler. Press and hold down the Alt key and then click and hold down the left mouse button. Make sure the first measurement on the horizontal ruler displays as *3.25"* and then release both the mouse button and the Alt key.

g. Position the arrow pointer on the Alignment button and then click the left mouse button until the right tab symbol displays (see Table 3.1).

h. Position the arrow pointer below the 6-inch mark on the horizontal ruler. Press and hold down the Alt key and then click and hold down the left mouse button. Make sure the first measurement on the horizontal ruler displays as *6"* and then release both the mouse button and the Alt key.

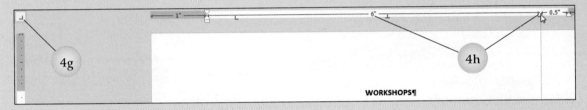

5. Type the text in columns, as shown in Figure 3.5. Press the Tab key before typing each column entry and press Shift + Enter after typing each entry in the third column. Bold the title and column headings as shown in the figure.

6. After typing the final entry in the last column entry, press the Enter key two times.

7. Press Ctrl + Q to remove paragraph formatting (tab settings) below the columns from the current paragraph.

8. Click the Show/Hide ¶ button to turn off the display of nonprinting characters.

9. Save the document and name it **3-Tabs**.

Check Your Work

Figure 3.5 Project 4a

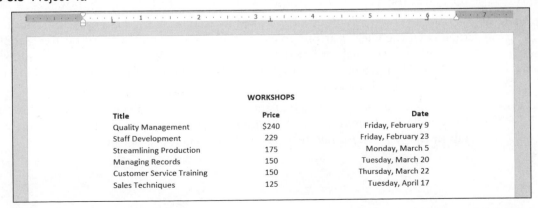

After a tab has been set on the horizontal ruler, it can be moved to a new location. To move a tab, position the arrow pointer on the tab symbol on the ruler, click and hold down the left mouse button, drag the symbol to the new location on the ruler, and then release the mouse button. To delete a tab from the ruler, position the arrow pointer on the tab symbol to be deleted, click and hold down the left mouse button, drag down into the document, and then release the mouse button.

When typing text in columns, press the Enter key or press Shift + Enter to end each line. If the Enter key is used to end each line, all lines of text in columns will need to be selected to make changes. To make changes to columns of text with line breaks inserted using Shift + Enter, the insertion point needs to be positioned only in one location in the columns of text.

Project 4b Moving Tabs

1. With **3-Tabs.docx** open, position the insertion point anywhere in the first entry in the tabbed text.
2. Position the arrow pointer on the left tab symbol at the 0.5-inch mark on the horizontal ruler, click and hold down the left mouse button, drag the left tab symbol to the 1-inch mark on the ruler, and then release the mouse button. *Hint: Use the Alt key to help you position the tab symbol precisely.*

3. Position the arrow pointer on the right tab symbol at the 6-inch mark on the horizontal ruler, click and hold down the left mouse button, drag the right tab symbol to the 5.5-inch mark on the ruler, and then release the mouse button. *Hint: Use the Alt key to help you position the tab symbol precisely.*
4. Save **3-Tabs.docx**.

Check Your Work

Setting and Modifying Tabs at the Tabs Dialog Box

Use the Tabs dialog box, shown in Figure 3.6, to set tabs at specific measurements, set tabs with preceding leaders, and clear one tab or all tabs. To display the Tabs dialog box, click the Paragraph group dialog box launcher. At the Paragraph dialog box, click the Tabs button in the lower left corner of the dialog box.

To clear an individual tab at the Tabs dialog box, specify the tab position and then click the Clear button. To clear all tabs, click the Clear All button. A left, right, center, decimal, or bar tab can be set at the Tabs dialog box. (For an example of a bar tab, refer to Figure 3.7.) A left, right, center, or decimal tab can be set with preceding leaders.

To change the type of tab at the Tabs dialog box, display the dialog box and then click the desired tab in the *Alignment* section. Type the measurement for the tab in the *Tab stop position* text box and then click the Set button.

Figure 3.6 Tabs Dialog Box

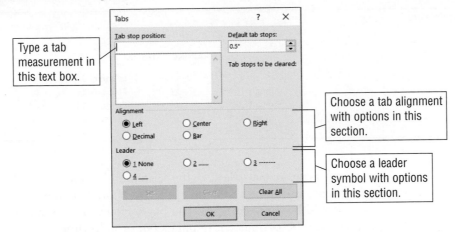

Type a tab measurement in this text box.

Choose a tab alignment with options in this section.

Choose a leader symbol with options in this section.

Project 4c Setting Left Tabs and a Bar Tab at the Tabs Dialog Box

Part 3 of 4

1. With **3-Tabs.docx** open, press Ctrl + End to move the insertion point to the end of the document.
2. Type the title TRAINING DATES bolded and centered (as shown in Figure 3.7), press the Enter key, return the paragraph alignment to left, and then turn off bold formatting.
3. Display the Tabs dialog box and then set left tabs and a bar tab by completing the following steps:
   a. Click the Paragraph group dialog box launcher.
   b. At the Paragraph dialog box, click the Tabs button in the lower left corner of the dialog box.
   c. Make sure *Left* is selected in the *Alignment* section of the dialog box.
   d. Type 1.75 in the *Tab stop position* text box.
   e. Click the Set button.
   f. Type 4 in the *Tab stop position* text box and then click the Set button.
   g. Type 3.25 in the *Tab stop position* text box, click *Bar* in the *Alignment* section, and then click the Set button.
   h. Click OK to close the Tabs dialog box.

   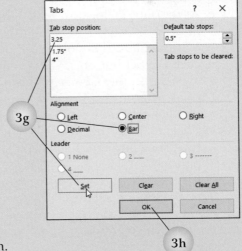

4. Type the text in columns, as shown in Figure 3.7. Press the Tab key before typing each column entry and press Shift + Enter to end each line. After typing *February 26*, press the Enter key.
5. Clear tabs below the columns from the current paragraph by completing the following steps:
   a. Click the Paragraph group dialog box launcher.
   b. At the Paragraph dialog box, click the Tabs button.
   c. At the Tabs dialog box, click the Clear All button.
   d. Click OK.
6. Press the Enter key.
7. Remove the 8 points of spacing after the last entry in the text by completing the following steps:
   a. Position the insertion point anywhere in the *January 24* entry.
   b. Click the Line and Paragraph Spacing button in the Paragraph group on the Home tab.
   c. Click the *Remove Space After Paragraph* option.
8. Save **3-Tabs.docx**.

Check Your Work

Figure 3.7 Project 4c

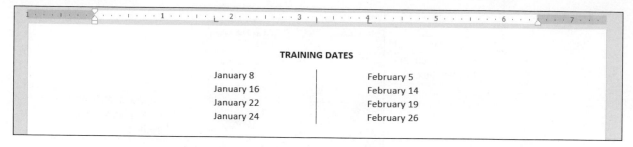

TRAINING DATES

January 8	February 5
January 16	February 14
January 22	February 19
January 24	February 26

Four types of tabs (left, right, center, and decimal) can be set with leaders. Leaders are useful in a table of contents or other material where the reader's eyes should be directed across the page. Figure 3.8 shows an example of leaders. Leaders can be periods (.), hyphens (-), or underlines (_). To add leaders to a tab, click the type of leader in the *Leader* section of the Tabs dialog box.

Project 4d Setting a Left Tab and a Right Tab with Period Leaders

1. With **3-Tabs.docx** open, press Ctrl + End to move the insertion point to the end of the document.
2. Type the title TABLE OF CONTENTS bolded and centered, as shown in Figure 3.8.
3. Press the Enter key and then return the paragraph alignment to left and turn off bold formatting.
4. Set a left tab and then a right tab with period leaders by completing the following steps:
   a. Click the Paragraph group dialog box launcher.
   b. Click the Tabs button in the lower left corner of the Paragraph dialog box.
   c. At the Tabs dialog box, make sure *Left* is selected in the *Alignment* section of the dialog box.
   d. With the insertion point positioned in the *Tab stop position* text box, type 1 and then click the Set button.
   e. Type 5.5 in the *Tab stop position* text box.
   f. Click *Right* in the *Alignment* section of the dialog box.
   g. Click *2 ......* in the *Leader* section of the dialog box and then click the Set button.
   h. Click OK to close the dialog box.
5. Type the text in columns, as shown in Figure 3.8. Press the Tab key before typing each column entry and press Shift + Enter to end each line.
6. Save, print, and then close **3-Tabs.docx**.

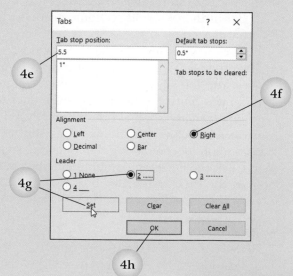

Check Your Work

Figure 3.8 Project 4d

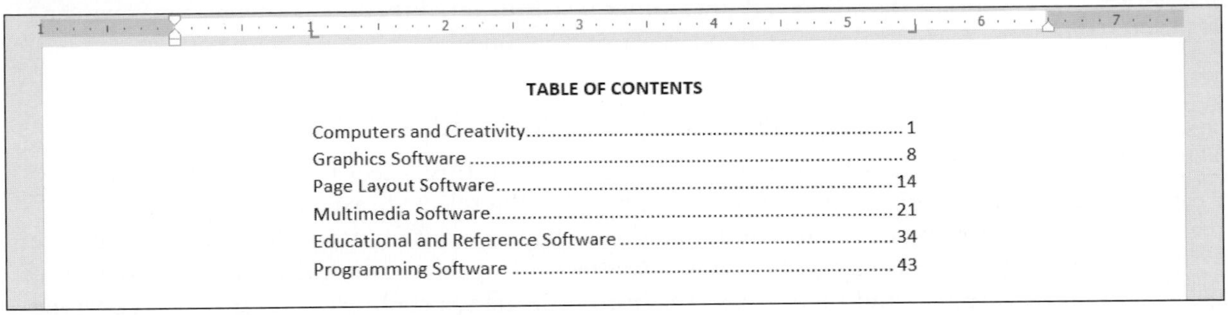

TABLE OF CONTENTS

Project 5 **Move and Copy Text in a Document on Online Shopping Tips**   **2 Parts**

You will open a document containing information on online shopping safety tips and then cut, copy, and paste text in the document.

Preview Finished Project

Tutorial

Cutting, Copying, and Pasting Text

Cutting, Copying, and Pasting Text

When editing a document, specific text may need to be deleted, moved to a different location in the document, or copied to various locations in the document. These activites can be completed using buttons in the Clipboard group on the Home tab.

Deleting Selected Text

Hint The Clipboard content is deleted when the computer is turned off. Text you want to save permanently should be saved as a separate document.

Word offers several different methods for deleting text from a document. To delete a single character, use either the Delete key or the Backspace key. To delete more than a single character, select the text and then press the Delete key on the keyboard or click the Cut button in the Clipboard group. If the Delete key is used to delete selected text, the text is deleted permanently. (Deleted text can be restored with the Undo button on the Quick Access Toolbar.)

Using the Cut button in the Clipboard group will remove the selected text from the document and insert it in the Clipboard, which is a temporary area of memory. The Clipboard holds text while it is being moved or copied to a new location in the document or to a different document.

Cutting and Pasting Text

Cut

Paste

Quick Steps

Move Selected Text
1. Select text.
2. Click Cut button.
3. Position insertion point.
4. Click Paste button.

To move text to a different location in the document, select the text, click the Cut button in the Clipboard group, position the insertion point at the location the text is to be inserted, and then click the Paste button in the Clipboard group.

Selected text can also be moved using the shortcut menu. To do this, select the text and then position the insertion point inside the selected text until it turns into an arrow pointer. Click the right mouse button and then click *Cut* at the shortcut menu. Position the insertion point where the text is to be inserted, click the right mouse button, and then click *Paste* at the shortcut menu. Keyboard shortcuts are also available for cutting and pasting text. Use Ctrl + X to cut text and Ctrl + V to paste text.

Quick Steps

Move Text with the Mouse
1. Select text.
2. Position mouse pointer in selected text.
3. Click and hold down left mouse button and drag to new location.
4. Release left mouse button.

OR

1. Select text.
2. Press Ctrl + X.
3. Move to new location.
4. Click Ctrl + V.

When selected text is cut from a document and inserted in the Clipboard, it stays in the Clipboard until other text is inserted there. For this reason, text can be pasted from the Clipboard more than once.

Moving Text by Dragging with the Mouse

The mouse can be used to move text. To do this, select text to be moved and then position the I-beam pointer inside the selected text until it turns into an arrow pointer. Click and hold down the left mouse button, drag the arrow pointer (which displays with a gray box attached) to the location the selected text is to be inserted, and then release the button. If the selected text is inserted in the wrong location, click the Undo button immediately.

Project 5a Moving and Dragging Selected Text

Part 1 of 2

1. Open **ShoppingTips.docx** and then save it with the name **3-ShoppingTips**.
2. Move a paragraph by completing the following steps:
   a. Select the paragraph that begins with *Only buy at secure sites,* including the blank line below the paragraph.
   b. Click the Cut button in the Clipboard group on the Home tab.
   c. Position the insertion point at the beginning of the paragraph that begins with *Look for sites that follow.*
   d. Click the Paste button in the Clipboard group. (If the first and second paragraphs are not separated by a blank line, press the Enter key.)
3. Following steps similar to those in Step 2, move the paragraph that begins with *Never provide your social* before the paragraph that begins *Look for sites that follow privacy* and after the paragraph that begins *Only buy at secure.*

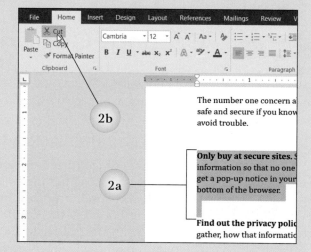

4. Use the mouse to select the paragraph that begins with *Keep current with the latest Internet,* including one blank line below the paragraph.
5. Move the I-beam pointer inside the selected text until it displays as an arrow pointer.
6. Click and hold down the left mouse button, drag the arrow pointer (which displays with a small gray box attached) so that the insertion point (which displays as a black vertical bar) is positioned at the beginning of the paragraph that begins with *Never provide your social,* and then release the mouse button.
7. Deselect the text.
8. Save **3-ShoppingTips.docx**.

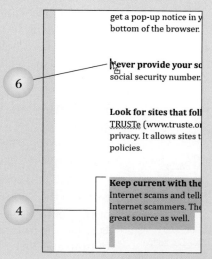

Check Your Work

Using the Paste Options Button

When selected text is pasted, the Paste Options button displays in the lower right corner of the text. Click this button (or press the Ctrl key on the keyboard) and the *Paste Options* gallery displays, as shown in Figure 3.9. Use buttons in this gallery to specify how the text is pasted in the document. Hover the mouse pointer over a button in the gallery and the live preview displays the text in the document as it will appear when pasted.

By default, pasted text retains the formatting of the selected text. This can be changed to match the formatting of the pasted text with the formatting of where the text is pasted or to paste only the text without retaining formatting. To determine the function of any button in the *Paste Options* gallery, hover the mouse pointer over the button and a ScreenTip displays with an explanation of the function as well as the keyboard shortcut. For example, hover the mouse pointer over the first button from the left in the *Paste Options* gallery and the ScreenTip displays with *Keep Source Formatting (K)*. Click this button or press K on the keyboard and the pasted text keeps its original formatting.

Figure 3.9 Paste Options Button Drop-Down List

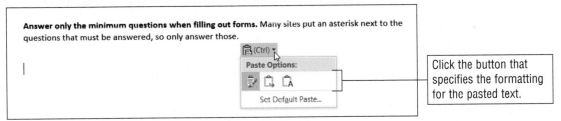

Click the button that specifies the formatting for the pasted text.

Project 5b Using the Paste Options Button

Part 2 of 2

1. With **3-ShoppingTips.docx** open, open **Tip.docx**.
2. Select the paragraph of text in the document, including the blank line below the paragraph, and then click the Copy button in the Clipboard group.
3. Close **Tip.docx**.
4. Press Ctrl + End to move the insertion point to the end of **3-ShoppingTips.docx**.
5. Click the Paste button in the Clipboard group.
6. Click the Paste Options button that displays at the end of the paragraph and then click the second button in the *Paste Options* gallery (Merge Formatting button). (This changes the font so it matches the font of the other paragraphs in the document.)
7. Save, print, and then close **3-ShoppingTips.docx**.

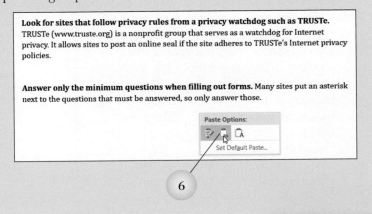

Check Your Work

You will copy and paste text in a document announcing a staff meeting for the Technical Support Team.

Preview Finished Project

Copying and Pasting Text

 Copy

Ṻuick Steps

Copy Selected Text
1. Select text.
2. Click Copy button.
3. Position insertion point.
4. Click Paste button.

Copying selected text can be useful in documents that contain repeated information. Use copy and paste to insert duplicate portions of text in a document instead of retyping them. Copy selected text to a different location using the Copy and Paste buttons in the Clipboard group on the Home tab, the mouse, or the keyboard shortcuts, Ctrl + C and Ctrl + V.

To use the mouse to copy text, select the text and then position the I-beam pointer inside the selected text until it becomes an arrow pointer. Click and hold down the left mouse button and also press and hold down the Ctrl key. Drag the arrow pointer (which displays with a small gray box and a box containing a plus [+] symbol) and a black vertical bar moves with the pointer. Position the black bar in the desired location, release the mouse button, and then release the Ctrl key.

Project 6 Copying Text   Part 1 of 1

1. Open **StaffMtg.docx** and then save it with the name **3-StaffMtg**.
2. Copy the text in the document to the end of the document by completing the following steps:
   a. Select all of the text in the document and include one blank line below the text. *Hint:* **Click the Show/Hide ¶ button to turn on the display of nonprinting characters. When you select the text, select one of the paragraph markers below the text.**
   b. Click the Copy button in the Clipboard group.
   c. Move the insertion point to the end of the document.
   d. Click the Paste button in the Clipboard group.
3. Paste the text again at the end of the document. To do this, position the insertion point at the end of the document and then click the Paste button in the Clipboard group. (This inserts a copy of the text from the Clipboard.)
4. Select all the text in the document using the mouse and include one blank line below the text. (Consider turning on the display of nonprinting characters.)
5. Move the I-beam pointer inside the selected text until it becomes an arrow pointer.
6. Click and hold down the Ctrl key and then the left mouse button. Drag the arrow pointer (which displays with a box with a plus symbol inside) so the vertical black bar is positioned at the end of the document, release the mouse button, and then release the Ctrl key.
7. Deselect the text.
8. Make sure all the text fits on one page. If not, consider deleting any extra blank lines.
9. Save, print, and then close **3-StaffMtg.docx**.

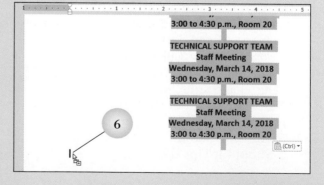

Check Your Work

Project 7 Create a Contract Negotiations Document   1 Part

You will use the Clipboard task pane to copy and paste paragraphs to and from separate documents to create a contract negotiations document.

Preview Finished Project

Tutorial

Using the Clipboard Task Pane

Using the Clipboard Task Pane

Use the Clipboard task pane to collect and paste multiple items. Up to 24 different items can be collected and then pasted in various locations. To display the Clipboard task pane, click the Clipboard group task pane launcher in the lower right corner of the Clipboard group. The Clipboard task pane displays at the left side of the screen in a manner similar to what is shown in Figure 3.10.

Select the text or object to be copied and then click the Copy button in the Clipboard group. Continue selecting text or items and clicking the Copy button. To insert an item from the Clipboard task pane into the document, position the insertion point in the desired location and then click the option in the Clipboard task pane representing the item. Click the Paste All button to paste all of the items in the Clipboard task pane into the document. If the copied item is text, the first 50 characters display in the list box on the Clipboard task pane. When all the items are inserted, click the Clear All button to remove any remaining items.

Quick Steps

Use the Clipboard
1. Click Clipboard group task pane launcher.
2. Select and copy text.
3. Position insertion point.
4. Click option in Clipboard task pane.

Hint You can copy items to the Clipboard from various Microsoft Office applications and then paste them into any Office file.

Figure 3.10 Clipboard Task Pane

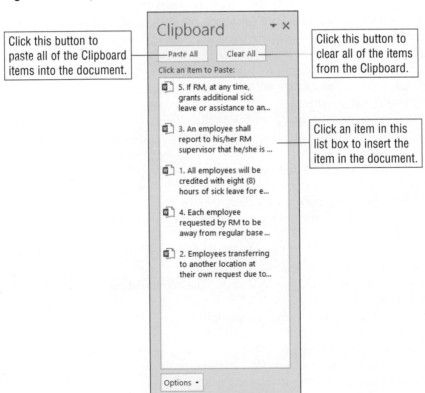

Click this button to paste all of the Clipboard items into the document.

Click this button to clear all of the items from the Clipboard.

Click an item in this list box to insert the item in the document.

1. Open **ContractItems.docx**.
2. Display the Clipboard task pane by clicking the Clipboard group task pane launcher in the bottom right corner of the Clipboard group. (If the Clipboard task pane list box contains any text, click the Clear All button in the upper right corner of the Clipboard task pane.)
3. Select paragraph 1 in the document (the *1.* is not selected) and then click the Copy button in the Clipboard group.
4. Select paragraph 3 in the document (the *3.* is not selected) and then click the Copy button in the Clipboard group.
5. Close **ContractItems.docx**.
6. Paste the paragraphs by completing the following steps:
   a. Press Ctrl + N to display a new blank document. (If the Clipboard task pane does not display, click the Clipboard group task pane launcher.)
   b. Type CONTRACT NEGOTIATION ITEMS centered and bolded.
   c. Press the Enter key, turn off bold formatting, and return the paragraph alignment to left alignment.
   d. Click the Paste All button in the Clipboard task pane to paste both paragraphs in the document.
   e. Click the Clear All button in the Clipboard task pane.
7. Open **UnionContract.docx**.
8. Select and then copy each of the following paragraphs:
   a. Paragraph 2 in the *Transfers and Moving Expenses* section.
   b. Paragraph 4 in the *Transfers and Moving Expenses* section.
   c. Paragraph 1 in the *Sick Leave* section.
   d. Paragraph 3 in the *Sick Leave* section.
   e. Paragraph 5 in the *Sick Leave* section.
9. Close **UnionContract.docx**.
10. Make sure the insertion point is positioned at the end of the document, on a new line, and then paste the paragraphs by completing the following steps:
    a. Click the button in the Clipboard task pane representing paragraph 2. (When the paragraph is inserted in the document, the paragraph number changes to *3.*)
    b. Click the button in the Clipboard task pane representing paragraph 4.
    c. Click the button in the Clipboard task pane representing paragraph 3.
    d. Click the button in the Clipboard task pane representing paragraph 5.
11. Click the Clear All button in the upper right corner of the Clipboard task pane.
12. Close the Clipboard task pane.
13. Save the document and name it **3-NegotiateItems**.
14. Print and then close **3-NegotiateItems.docx**.

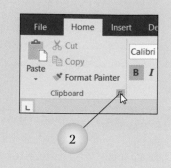

2

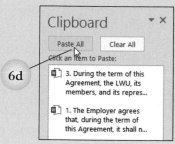

6d

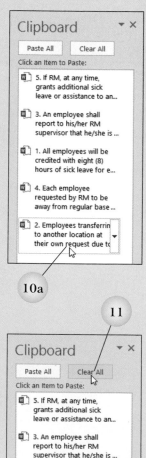

10a

11

Check Your Work

Chapter Summary

- Number paragraphs using the Numbering button in the Paragraph group on the Home tab and insert bullets before paragraphs using the Bullets button.

- Remove all paragraph formatting from a paragraph by pressing the keyboard shortcut Ctrl + Q. Remove all character and paragraph formatting by clicking the Clear All Formatting button in the Font group.

- The AutoCorrect Options button displays when the AutoFormat feature inserts numbers. Click this button to display options for undoing and/or stopping automatic numbering.

- A bulleted list with a hanging indent is automatically created when a paragraph begins with *, >, or -. The type of bullet inserted depends on the type of character entered.

- Automatic numbering and bulleting can be turned off at the AutoCorrect dialog box with the AutoFormat As You Type tab selected.

- A paragraph created in Word contains an invisible frame and a border can be added to this frame. Click the Borders button arrow to display a drop-down list of border options.

- Use options at the Borders and Shading dialog box with the Borders tab selected to add a customized border to a paragraph or selected paragraphs.

- Apply shading to text by clicking the Shading button arrow and then clicking a color at the drop-down gallery. Use options at the Borders and Shading dialog box with the Shading tab selected to add shading or a pattern to a paragraph or selected paragraphs.

- Use the Sort button in the Paragraph group on the Home tab to sort text in paragraphs alphabetically by the first character of each paragraph, which can be a number, symbol, or letter.

- By default, tabs are set every 0.5 inch. Tab settings can be changed on the horizontal ruler or at the Tabs dialog box.

- Use the Alignment button above the vertical ruler to select a left, right, center, decimal, or bar tab. When a tab is set on the horizontal ruler, any default tabs to the left are automatically deleted.

- After a tab has been set on the horizontal ruler, it can be moved or deleted using the mouse pointer.

- At the Tabs dialog box, any of the five types of tabs can be set at a specific measurement. Tabs also can be set with preceding leaders, which can be periods, hyphens, or underlines. Individual tabs or all tabs can be cleared at the Tabs dialog box.

- Cut, copy, and paste text using buttons in the Clipboard group on the Home tab, with options at the shortcut menu, or with keyboard shortcuts.

- When selected text is pasted, the Paste Options button displays in the lower right corner of the text. Click the button and the *Paste Options* gallery displays with buttons for specifying how text is pasted in the document.

- With the Clipboard task pane, up to 24 items can be copied and then pasted in various locations in a document or other document.

- Display the Clipboard task pane by clicking the Clipboard group task pane launcher in the Clipboard group on the Home tab.

Commands Review

FEATURE	RIBBON TAB, GROUP	BUTTON, OPTION	KEYBOARD SHORTCUT
borders	Home, Paragraph		
Borders and Shading dialog box	Home, Paragraph	, Borders and Shading	
bullets	Home, Paragraph		
clear all formatting	Home, Font		
clear paragraph formatting			Ctrl + Q
Clipboard task pane	Home, Clipboard		
copy text	Home, Clipboard		Ctrl + C
cut text	Home, Clipboard		Ctrl + X
New Line command			Shift + Enter
numbering	Home, Paragraph		
Paragraph dialog box	Home, Paragraph		
paste text	Home, Clipboard		Ctrl + V
shading	Home, Paragraph		
Sort Text dialog box	Home, Paragraph		
Tabs dialog box	Home, Paragraph	, Tabs	

Workbook

Chapter study tools and assessment activities are available in the *Workbook* ebook. These resources are designed to help you further develop and demonstrate mastery of the skills learned in this chapter.

Microsoft®

Word

Formatting Pages

Performance Objectives

Precheck

Check your current skills to help focus your study.

Upon successful completion of Chapter 4, you will be able to:

1 Change document views

2 Navigate in a document with the Navigation pane

3 Change margins, page orientation, and paper size

4 Format pages at the Page Setup dialog box

5 Insert a page break, blank page, and cover page

6 Insert page numbering

7 Insert and edit predesigned headers and footers

8 Insert a watermark, page background color, and page border

9 Find and replace text and formatting

A document generally displays in Print Layout view. This default view can be changed with buttons in the view area on the Status bar or with options on the View tab. The Navigation pane provides one method for navigating in a document. A Word document, by default, contains 1-inch top, bottom, left, and right margins. Change these default margins with the Margins button in the Page Setup group on the Layout tab or with options at the Page Setup dialog box. A variety of features can be inserted in a Word document, including a page break, blank page, and cover page, as well as page numbers, headers, footers, a watermark, page color, and page border. Use options at the Find and Replace dialog box to search for specific text or formatting and replace it with other text or formatting.

SNAP

If you are a SNAP user, launch the Precheck and Tutorials from your Assignments page.

You will open a document containing information on navigating and searching the web, change document views, hide and show white space at the tops and bottoms of pages, and navigate in the document using the Navigation pane.

Tutorial

Changing
Document Views

Changing Document Views

By default, a Word document displays in Print Layout view. This view displays the document on the screen as it will appear when printed. Other views are available, such as Draft and Read Mode. Change views with buttons in the view area on the Status bar (see Figure 4.1) or with options on the View tab.

Displaying a Document in Draft View

Change to Draft view and the document displays in a format for efficient editing and formatting. At this view, margins and other features, such as headers and footers, do not display on the screen. Change to Draft view by clicking the View tab and then clicking the Draft button in the Views group.

 Draft

Displaying a Document in Read Mode View

Read Mode view displays a document in a format for easy viewing and reading. Change to Read Mode view by clicking the Read Mode button in the view area on the Status bar or by clicking the View tab and then clicking the Read Mode button in the Views group. Navigate in Read Mode view using the keys on the keyboard, as shown in Table 4.1. Other methods for navigating in Read Mode view include clicking at the right side of the screen or clicking the Next button (right-pointing arrow in a circle) to display the next pages and by clicking at the left side of the screen or clicking the Previous button (left-pointing arrow in a circle) to display the previous pages.

Read Mode

Read Mode

The File, Tools, and View tabs display in the upper left corner of the screen in Read Mode view. Click the File tab to display the backstage area. Click the Tools tab and a drop-down list displays options for finding specific text in the document and searching for information on the Internet using the Smart Lookup feature. Click the View tab and options display for customizing what appears in Read Mode view. Use View tab options to display the Navigation pane to navigate to specific locations in the document, show comments inserted in the document, change column widths or page layout, and change the page colors in Read Mode view.

Figure 4.1 View Buttons and Zoom Slider Bar

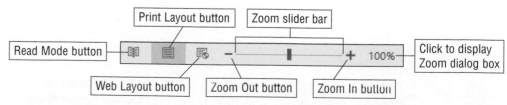

Table 4.1 Keyboard Commands in Read Mode View

Press this key	To complete this action
Page Down key, Right Arrow key, or spacebar	display next two pages
Page Up key, Left Arrow key, or Backspace key	display previous two pages
Home	display first page in document
End	display last page in document
Esc	return to previous view

If a document contains an object such as a table, SmartArt graphic, image, or shape, zoom in on the object in Read Mode view by double-clicking it. The display size of the object increases and a button containing a magnifying glass with a plus symbol inside (🔍) displays just outside the upper right corner of the object. Click this button to zoom in even more on the object. Click the button again and the object returns to the original zoom size. Click outside the object to return it to its original display size. To close Read Mode view and return to the previous view, press the Esc key or click the View tab and then click *Edit Document* at the drop-down list.

Changing the Display Percentage

Tutorial

Changing
the Display
Percentage

 Zoom

 Zoom Out

 Zoom In

 100%

💡 *Hint* Click the 100% at the right side of the Zoom slider bar to display the Zoom dialog box.

📶 Ribbon Display Options

By default, a document displays at 100%. This display percentage can be changed with the Zoom slider bar at the right side of the Status bar (see Figure 4.1) and with options in the Zoom group on the View tab. To change the display percentage with the Zoom slider bar, drag the button on the bar to increase or decrease the percentage. Click the Zoom Out button at the left side of the slider bar to decrease the display percentage or click the Zoom In button to increase the display percentage.

Click the Zoom button in the Zoom group on the View tab to display the Zoom dialog box that contains options for changing the display percentage. If the display percentage has been changed, return to the default by clicking the 100% button in the Zoom group on the View tab. Click the One Page button to display the entire page on the screen and click the Multiple Pages button to display multiple pages on the screen. Click the Page Width button and the document expands across the screen.

Changing Ribbon Display Options

Use the Ribbon Display Options button in the upper right corner of the screen to view more of a document. Click the Ribbon Display Options button and a drop-down list displays with three options: *Auto-hide Ribbon*, *Show Tabs*, and *Show Tabs and Commands*. The default is Show Tabs and Commands, which displays the Quick Access Toolbar, ribbon, and Status bar on the screen. Click the first option, *Auto-hide Ribbon*, and the Quick Access Toolbar, ribbon, and Status bar are hidden, allowing more of the document to be visible on the screen. To temporarily redisplay these features, click at the top of the screen. Turn these features back on by clicking the Ribbon Display Options button and then clicking the *Show Tabs and Commands* option. Click the *Show Tabs* option at the drop-down list and the tabs display on the ribbon while the buttons and commands remain hidden.

Tutorial

Hiding and
Showing White
Space

Hide White
Space

Show White
Space

Hiding and Showing White Space

In Print Layout view, a page displays as it will appear when printed, including the white spaces at the top and the bottom of the page representing the document's margins. To save space on the screen in Print Layout view, the white space can be removed by positioning the mouse pointer at the top edge or bottom edge of a page or between pages until the pointer displays as the Hide White Space icon and then double-clicking the left mouse button. To redisplay the white space, position the mouse pointer on the thin gray line separating pages until the pointer turns into the Show White Space icon and then double-click the left mouse button.

Project 1a Changing Views and Hiding/Showing White Space

Part 1 of 2

1. Open **WebReport.docx** and then save it with the name **4-WebReport**.
2. Click the View tab and then click the Draft button in the Views group.
3. Click the Zoom Out button (to the left of the Zoom slider bar) three times. (This changes the display percentage and *70%* displays at the right side of the Zoom In button.)

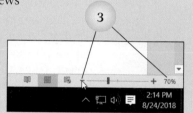

4. Using the mouse, drag the Zoom slider bar button to the middle until *100%* displays at the right side of the Zoom In button.
5. Click the Print Layout button in the view area on the Status bar.
6. Click the Zoom button in the Zoom group on the View tab.
7. At the Zoom dialog box, click the *75%* option and then click OK.

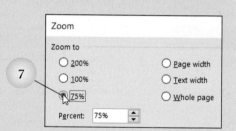

8. Return the display percentage to the default by clicking the 100% button in the Zoom group.
9. Click the Read Mode button in the view area on the Status bar.
10. Increase the display size of the table at the right side of the screen by double-clicking the table. (If the table is not visible, click the Next button at the right side of the screen to view the next page.)
11. Click the button containing a magnifying glass with a plus symbol that displays outside the upper right corner of the table. (This increases the zoom.)

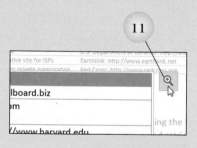

12. Click outside the table to return it to the original display size.
13. Practice navigating in Read Mode view using the actions shown in Table 4.1 (except the last action).
14. Press the Esc key to return to the Print Layout view.
15. Click the Ribbon Display Options button in the upper right corner of the screen and then click *Auto-hide Ribbon* at the drop-down list.

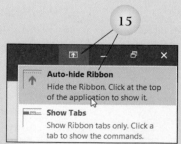

16. Press Ctrl + End to display the last page in the document and then press the Page Up key until the beginning of the document displays.
17. Click at the top of the screen to temporarily redisplay the Quick Access Toolbar, ribbon, and Status bar.
18. Click the Ribbon Display Options button and then click *Show Tabs* at the drop-down list.

19. Click the Ribbon Display Options button and then click *Show Tabs and Commands* at the drop-down list.
20. Press Ctrl + Home to move the insertion point to the beginning of the document.
21. Hide the white spaces at the tops and bottoms of pages by positioning the mouse pointer at the top edge of the page until the pointer turns into the Hide White Space icon and then double-clicking the left mouse button.
22. Scroll through the document and notice the display of pages.
23. Redisplay the white spaces at the tops and bottoms of pages by positioning the mouse pointer on any thin gray line separating pages until the pointer turns into the Show White Space icon and then double-clicking the left mouse button.
24. Save **4-WebReport.docx**.

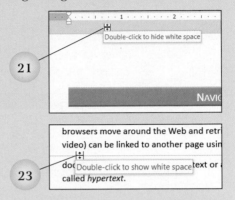

Navigating Using the Navigation Pane

Among the features that Word provides for navigating in a document is the Navigation pane, shown in Figure 4.2. Click the *Navigation Pane* check box in the Show group on the View tab to insert a check mark and the Navigation pane displays at the left side of the screen and includes a search text box and a pane with three tabs. Click the Headings tab to display titles and headings with styles applied. Click a title or heading in the pane to move the insertion point to that title or heading. Click the Pages tab to display a thumbnail of each page. Click a thumbnail to move the insertion point to the specific page. Click the Results tab to browse the current search results in the document. Close the Navigation pane by clicking the *Navigation Pane* check box in the Show group on the View tab to remove the check mark or by clicking the Close button in the upper right corner of the pane.

Quick Steps

Display Navigation Pane
1. Click View tab.
2. Click *Navigation Pane* check box.

Figure 4.2 Navigation Pane

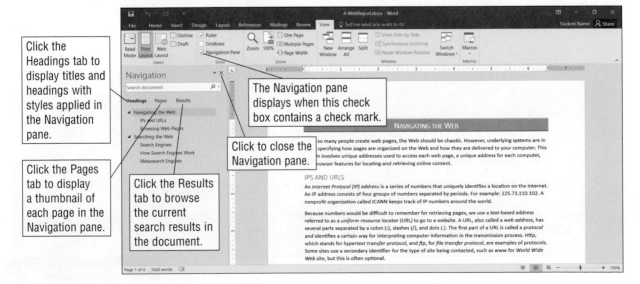

Click the Headings tab to display titles and headings with styles applied in the Navigation pane.

The Navigation pane displays when this check box contains a check mark.

Click to close the Navigation pane.

Click the Pages tab to display a thumbnail of each page in the Navigation pane.

Click the Results tab to browse the current search results in the document.

1. With **4-WebReport.docx** open, make sure the document displays in Print Layout view.
2. Display the Navigation pane by clicking the View tab and then clicking the *Navigation Pane* check box in the Show group to insert a check mark.
3. Click the *Navigating the Web* heading in the Navigation pane.

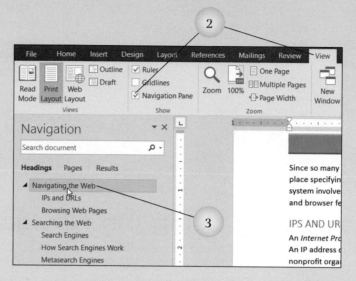

4. Click the *Searching the Web* heading in the Navigation pane.
5. Click the Pages tab in the Navigation pane to display the page thumbnails in the pane.
6. Click the page 4 thumbnail in the Navigation pane.
7. Scroll up the pane and then click the page 1 thumbnail.
8. Close the Navigation pane by clicking the Close button in the upper right corner of the pane.
9. Save and then close **4-WebReport.docx**.

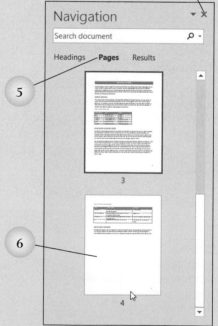

Project 2 Format a Document on Online Etiquette Guidelines

2 Parts

You will open a document containing information on guidelines for online etiquette and then change the margins, page orientation, and page size.

Preview Finished Project

Changing Page Setup

The Page Setup group on the Layout tab contains a number of options for changing pages in a document. Use options in the Page Setup group to perform such actions as changing margins, orientation, and page size and inserting page breaks. The Pages group on the Insert tab contains three buttons for inserting a cover page, blank page, and page break.

Changing Margins

 Margins

Changing Margins

Change page margins with options at the Margins button drop-down list, as shown in Figure 4.3. To display this list, click the Layout tab and then click the Margins button in the Page Setup group. To change the margins, click one of the preset margins in the drop-down list. Be aware that most printers require a minimum margin (between ¼ and ⅜ inch) because they cannot print to the edge of the page.

Tutorial

Changing Page Orientation

Orientation

Changing Page Orientation

Click the Orientation button in the Page Setup group on the Layout tab and two options display: *Portrait* and *Landscape*. At the portrait orientation, which is the default, the page is 11 inches tall and 8.5 inches wide. At the landscape orientation, the page is 8.5 inches tall and 11 inches wide. Change the page orientation and the page margins automatically shift—the left and right margin measurements become the top and bottom margin measurements.

Tutorial

Changing Paper Size

 Size

Changing Paper Size

By default, Word uses a paper size of 8.5 inches wide and 11 inches tall. Change this default setting with options at the Size button drop-down list. Display this drop-down list by clicking the Size button in the Page Setup group on the Layout tab.

Quick Steps

Change Margins
1. Click Layout tab.
2. Click Margins button.
3. Click margin option.

Change Page Orientation
1. Click Layout tab.
2. Click Orientation button.
3. Click orientation option.

Change Paper Size
1. Click Layout tab.
2. Click Size button.
3. Click size option.

Figure 4.3 Margins Button Drop-Down List

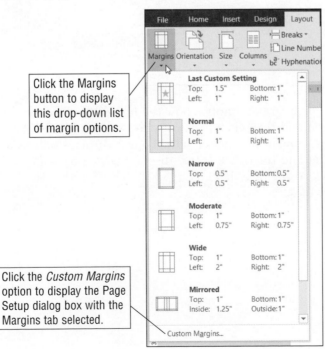

1. Open **Netiquette.docx** and then save it with the name **4-Netiquette**.
2. Click the Layout tab.
3. Click the Margins button in the Page Setup group and then click the *Narrow* option.
4. Click the Orientation button in the Page Setup group and then click *Landscape* at the drop-down list.

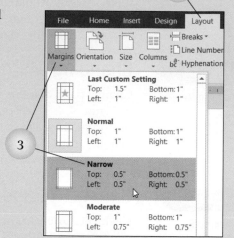

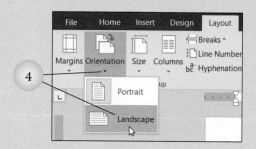

5. Scroll through the document and notice how the text displays on the page in landscape orientation.
6. Click the Orientation button in the Page Setup group and then click *Portrait* at the drop-down list. (This changes the orientation back to the default.)
7. Click the Size button in the Page Setup group and then click the *Executive* option (displays with *7.25" × 10.5"* below *Executive*). If this option is not available, choose an option with a similar paper size.

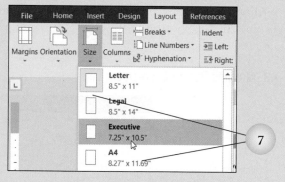

8. Scroll through the document and notice how the text displays on the page.
9. Click the Size button and then click *Legal* (displays with *8.5" × 14"* below *Legal*).
10. Scroll through the document and notice how the text displays on the page.
11. Click the Size button and then click *Letter* (displays with *8.5" × 11"* below *Letter*). (This returns the size back to the default.)
12. Save **4-Netiquette.docx**.

Check Your Work

Quick Steps
Change Margins at the Page Setup Dialog Box
1. Click Layout tab.
2. Click Page Setup group dialog box launcher.
3. Specify margins.
4. Click OK.

Change Paper Size at the Page Setup Dialog Box
1. Click Layout tab.
2. Click Size button.
3. Click *More Paper Sizes* at drop-down list.
4. Specify size.
5. Click OK.

Changing Margins at the Page Setup Dialog Box

The Margins button in the Page Setup group provides a number of preset margins. If these margins do not provide the desired margins, set specific margins at the Page Setup dialog box with the Margins tab selected, as shown in Figure 4.4. Display this dialog box by clicking the Page Setup group dialog box launcher or by clicking the Margins button and then clicking *Custom Margins* at the bottom of the drop-down list.

To change one of the margins, select the current measurement in the *Top*, *Bottom*, *Left*, or *Right* measurement box and then type the new measurement, or click the measurement box up arrow to increase the measurement or the measurement box down arrow to decrease the measurement. As the margin measurements change at the Page Setup dialog box, the sample page in the *Preview* section shows the effects of the changes.

Changing Paper Size at the Page Setup Dialog Box

The Size button drop-down list contains a number of preset paper sizes. If these sizes do not provide the desired paper size, specify a paper size at the Page Setup dialog box with the Paper tab selected. Display this dialog box by clicking the Size button in the Page Setup group and then clicking *More Paper Sizes* at the bottom of the drop-down list.

Figure 4.4 Page Setup Dialog Box with Margins Tab Selected

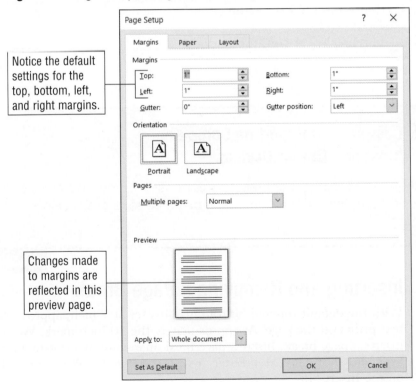

Notice the default settings for the top, bottom, left, and right margins.

Changes made to margins are reflected in this preview page.

1. With **4-Netiquette.docx** open, make sure the Layout tab is selected.
2. Click the Page Setup group dialog box launcher.
3. At the Page Setup dialog box with the Margins tab selected, click the *Top* measurement box up arrow until *0.7"* displays.
4. Click the *Bottom* measurement box up arrow until *0.7"* displays.
5. Select the current measurement in the *Left* measurement box and then type 0.75.
6. Select the current measurement in the *Right* measurement box and then type 0.75.
7. Click OK to close the dialog box.
8. Click the Size button in the Page Setup group and then click *More Paper Sizes* at the drop-down list.
9. At the Page Setup dialog box with the Paper tab selected, click the *Paper size* option box arrow and then click *Legal* at the drop-down list.
10. Click OK to close the dialog box.
11. Scroll through the document and notice how the text displays on the page.
12. Click the Size button in the Page Setup group and then click *Letter* at the drop-down list.
13. Save, print, and then close **4-Netiquette.docx**.

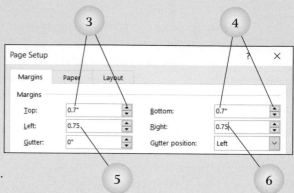

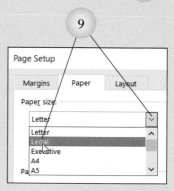

Check Your Work

Project 3 Customize a Report on Computer Input and Output Devices

3 Parts

You will open a document containing information on computer input and output devices and then insert page breaks, a blank page, a cover page, and page numbering.

Preview Finished Project

Inserting and Removing a Page Break

With the default top and bottom margins set at 1 inch, approximately 9 inches of text prints on the page. At approximately the 10-inch mark, Word automatically inserts a page break. Insert a page break manually in a document with the keyboard shortcut Ctrl + Enter or with the Page Break button in the Pages group on the Insert tab.

A page break inserted by Word is considered a soft page break and a page break inserted manually is considered a hard page break. Soft page breaks automatically adjust if text is added to or deleted from a document. Hard page breaks do not adjust and are therefore less flexible than soft page breaks.

Insert a Page Break
1. Click Insert tab.
2. Click Page Break button.
OR
Press Ctrl + Enter.

If text is added to or deleted from a document containing a hard page break, check the break to determine whether it is still in a desirable location. Display a hard page break, along with other nonprinting characters, by clicking the Show/Hide ¶ button in the Paragraph group on the Home tab. A hard page break displays as a row of dots with the words *Page Break* in the center. To delete a hard page break, position the insertion point at the beginning of the page break and then press the Delete key. If the display of nonprinting characters is turned off, delete a hard page break by positioning the insertion point immediately below the page break and then pressing the Backspace key.

Project 3a Inserting Page Breaks

Parts 1 of 3

1. Open **CompDevices.docx** and then save it with the name **4-CompDevices**.
2. Change the top margin by completing the following steps:
   a. Click the Layout tab.
   b. Click the Page Setup group dialog box launcher.
   c. At the Page Setup dialog box, click the Margins tab and then type 1.5 in the *Top* measurement box.
   d. Click OK to close the dialog box.
3. Insert a page break at the beginning of the heading *Mouse* by completing the following steps:
   a. Position the insertion point at the beginning of the heading *Mouse* (at the bottom of page 1).
   b. Click the Insert tab and then click the Page Break button in the Pages group.
4. Move the insertion point to the beginning of the title *COMPUTER OUTPUT DEVICES* (on the second page) and then insert a page break by pressing Ctrl + Enter.
5. Move the insertion point to the beginning of the heading *Printer* and then press Ctrl + Enter to insert a page break.
6. Delete a page break by completing the following steps:
   a. Click the Home tab.
   b. Click the Show/Hide ¶ button in the Paragraph group.
   c. Scroll up to display the bottom of the third page, position the insertion point at the beginning of the page break (displays with the words *Page Break*), and then press the Delete key.
   d. Press the Delete key again to remove the blank line.
   e. Turn off the display of nonprinting characters by clicking the Show/Hide ¶ button in the Paragraph group on the Home tab.
7. Save **4-CompDevices.docx**.

Check Your Work

Inserting and Removing a Blank Page

Click the Blank Page button in the Pages group on the Insert tab to insert a blank page at the position of the insertion point. This might be useful in a document where a blank page is needed for an illustration, graphic, or figure. When a blank page is inserted, Word inserts a page break and then inserts another page break to create the blank page. To remove a blank page, turn on the display of nonprinting characters and then delete the page breaks.

Inserting and Removing a Cover Page

Consider inserting a cover page to improve the visual appeal of a document or to prepare it for distribution to others. Use the Cover Page button in the Pages group on the Insert tab to insert a predesigned cover page and then type personalized text in the placeholders on the page. Click the Cover Page button and a drop-down list displays with visual representations of the cover pages. Scroll through the list and then click a predesigned cover page option.

A predesigned cover page contains location placeholders, in which specific text is entered. For example, a cover page might contain the *[Document title]* placeholder. Click the placeholder to select it and then type personalized text. Delete a placeholder by clicking the placeholder to select it, clicking the placeholder tab, and then pressing the Delete key. Remove a cover page by clicking the Cover Page button and then clicking *Remove Current Cover Page* at the drop-down list.

Quick Steps

Insert Blank Page
1. Click Insert tab.
2. Click Blank Page button.

Insert Cover Page
1. Click Insert tab.
2. Click Cover Page button.
3. Click cover page at drop-down list.

Hint Adding a cover page gives a document a polished and professional look.

Project 3b Inserting a Blank Page and a Cover Page

1. With **4-CompDevices.docx** open, create a blank page by completing the following steps:
   a. Move the insertion point to the beginning of the heading *Touchpad and Touchscreen* on the second page.
   b. Click the Insert tab.
   c. Click the Blank Page button in the Pages group.
2. Insert a cover page by completing the following steps:
   a. Press Ctrl + Home to move the insertion point to the beginning of the document.
   b. Click the Cover Page button in the Pages group.
   c. Scroll down the drop-down list and then click the *Motion* cover page.

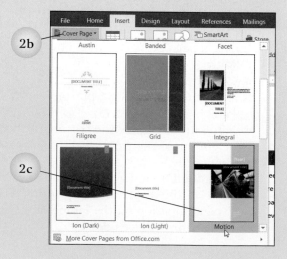

d. Click the *[Document title]* placeholder and then type Computer Devices.

2d

e. Click the *[Year]* placeholder. Click the placeholder down arrow and then click the Today button at the bottom of the drop-down calendar.

f. Click the *[Company name]* placeholder and then type Drake Computing. (If a name displays in the placeholder, select the name and then type Drake Computing.)

g. Select the name above the company name and then type your first and last names. If, instead of a name, the *[Author name]* placeholder displays above the company name, click the placeholder and then type your first and last names.

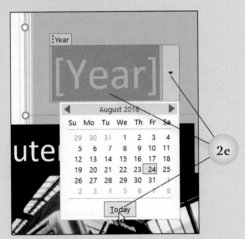

2e

3. Remove the blank page you inserted in Step 1 by completing the following steps:

a. Move the insertion point immediately right of the period that ends the last sentence in the paragraph of text in the *Trackball* section the bottom of page 3).

b. Press the Delete key on the keyboard approximately six times until the heading *Touchpad and Touchscreen* displays on page 3.

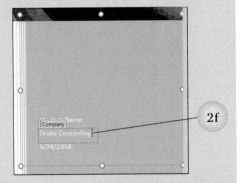

2f

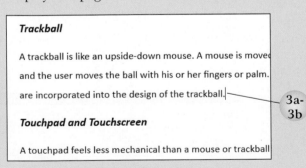

3a-3b

4. Save **4-CompDevices.docx**.

Check Your Work

Inserting and Removing Page Numbers

Word, by default, does not print page numbers on pages. To insert page numbers in a document, use the Page Number button in the Header & Footer group on the Insert tab. Click the Page Number button and a drop-down list displays with options for specifying the location of the page number. Point to an option in this list and a drop-down list displays a number of predesigned page number formats. Scroll through the options in the drop-down list and then click an option.

To change the format of page numbering in a document, double-click the page number, select the page number text, and then apply the formatting. Remove page numbers from a document by clicking the Page Number button and then clicking *Remove Page Numbers* at the drop-down list. Many of the predesigned page number formats insert page numbers in a header or footer pane. As explained in the next section of this chapter, a header pane contains text, such as a page number, that prints at the top of each page and a footer pane contains text that prints at the bottom of each page. If a page number is inserted in a header or footer pane, close the pane by clicking the Close Header and Footer button on the Header & Footer Tools Design tab or by double-clicking in the document, outside the header or footer pane.

Quick Steps

Insert Page Numbers
1. Click Insert tab.
2. Click Page Number button.
3. Click option at drop-down list.

[Page Number icon]

Project 3c Inserting Predesigned Page Numbers

Part 3 of 3

1. With **4-CompDevices.docx** open, insert page numbering by completing the following steps:
   a. Move the insertion point so it is positioned anywhere in the title *COMPUTER INPUT DEVICES*.
   b. Click the Insert tab.
   c. Click the Page Number button in the Header & Footer group and then point to *Top of Page*.
   d. Scroll through the drop-down list and then click the *Brackets 2* option.
2. Click the Close Header and Footer button on the Header & Footer Tools Design tab.
3. Scroll through the document and notice the page numbering that displays at the top of each page except the cover page. (The cover page and text are divided by a page break. Word does not include the cover page when numbering pages.)
4. Remove the page numbering by clicking the Insert tab, clicking the Page Number button, and then clicking *Remove Page Numbers* at the drop-down list.
5. Click the Page Number button, point to *Bottom of Page*, scroll down the drop-down list, and then click the *Accent Bar 2* option.
6. Click the Close Header and Footer button on the Header & Footer Tools Design tab.
7. Save, print, and then close **4-CompDevices.docx**.

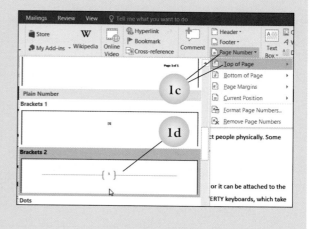

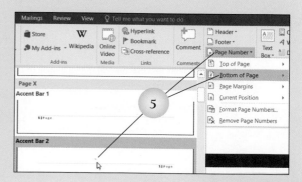

Check Your Work

Project 4 **Add Elements to a Report on the Writing Process**   **3 Parts**

You will open a document containing information on the process of writing effectively, insert a predesigned header and footer, remove a header, and format and delete header and footer elements.

Preview Finished Project

Tutorial

Inserting and Removing a Predesigned Header and Footer

 Header

Quick Steps

Insert Predesigned Header or Footer
1. Click Insert tab.
2. Click Header button or Footer button.
3. Click option at drop-down list.
4. Type text in specific placeholders in header or footer.
5. Click Close Header and Footer button.

Inserting Predesigned Headers and Footers

Text that appears in the top margin of a page is called a *header* and text that appears in the bottom margin of a page is referred to as a *footer*. Headers and footers are common in manuscripts, textbooks, reports, and other publications.

Insert a predesigned header in a document by clicking the Insert tab and then clicking the Header button in the Header & Footer group. This displays the Header button drop-down list. At this list, click a predesigned header option and the header is inserted in the document. Headers and footers are visible in Print Layout view but not Draft view.

A predesigned header or footer may contain location placeholders for entering specific information. For example, a header might contain the *[Document title]* placeholder. Click the placeholder and all the placeholder text is selected. With the placeholder text selected, type the personalized text. Delete a placeholder by clicking the placeholder to select it, clicking the placeholder tab, and then pressing the Delete key.

To return to the document after inserting a header or footer, double-click in the document outside the header or footer pane or click the Close Header and Footer button on the Header & Footer Tools Design tab.

Project 4a   Inserting a Predesigned Header in a Document   Part 1 of 3

1. Open **WritingProcess.docx** and then save it with the name **4-WritingProcess**.
2. Press Ctrl + End to move the insertion point to the end of the document.
3. Move the insertion point to the beginning of the heading *REFERENCES* and then insert a page break by clicking the Insert tab and then clicking the Page Break button in the Pages group.

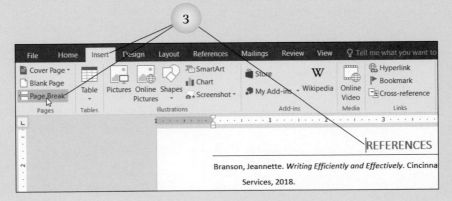

4. Press Ctrl + Home to move the insertion point to the beginning of the document and then insert a header by completing the following steps:

a. If necessary, click the Insert tab.

b. Click the Header button in the Header & Footer group.

c. Scroll to the bottom of the drop-down list and then click the *Sideline* option.

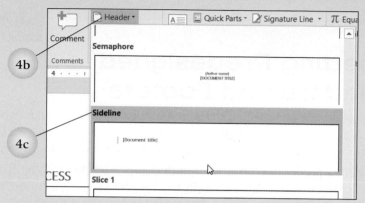

d. Click the *[Document title]* placeholder and then type The Writing Process.

e. Double-click in the document text. (This makes the document text active and dims the header.)

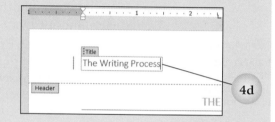

5. Scroll through the document to see how the header will print.

6. Save and then print **4-WritingProcess.docx**.

Check Your Work

 Footer

Insert a predesigned footer in the same manner as inserting a header. Click the Footer button in the Header & Footer group on the Insert tab and a drop-down list displays that is similar to the Header button drop-down list. Click a footer and the predesigned footer is inserted in the document.

Removing a Header or Footer

Remove a header from a document by clicking the Insert tab and then clicking the Header button in the Header & Footer group. At the drop-down list, click the *Remove Header* option. Complete similar steps to remove a footer.

1. With **4-WritingProcess.docx** open, press Ctrl + Home to move the insertion point to the beginning of the document.
2. Remove the header by clicking the Insert tab, clicking the Header button in the Header & Footer group, and then clicking the *Remove Header* option at the drop-down list.
3. Insert a footer in the document by completing the following steps:
   a. Click the Footer button in the Header & Footer group.
   b. Scroll down the drop-down list and then click *Ion (Light)*.

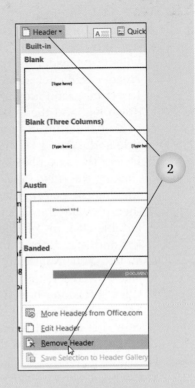

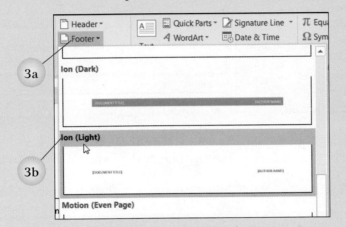

   c. Notice that Word inserted the document title at the left side of the footer. (Word remembered the document title you entered in the header.) Word also inserted your name at the right side of the footer. If the document title does not display, click the *[DOCUMENT TITLE]* placeholder and then type THE WRITING PROCESS. If your name does not display, click the *[AUTHOR NAME]* placeholder and then type your first and last names.
   d. Click the Close Header and Footer button on the Header & Footer Tools Design tab to close the Footer pane and return to the document.
4. Scroll through the document to see how the footer will print.
5. Save and then print **4-WritingProcess.docx**.

Check Your Work

Editing a Predesigned Header or Footer

Predesigned headers and footers contain elements such as page numbers, a title, and an author's name. The formatting of an element can be changed by clicking the element and then applying formatting. Delete an element from a header or footer by selecting the element and then pressing the Delete key.

1. With **4-WritingProcess.docx** open, remove the footer by clicking the Insert tab, clicking the Footer button, and then clicking *Remove Footer* at the drop-down list.
2. Insert and then format a header by completing the following steps:
   a. Click the Header button in the Header & Footer group on the Insert tab, scroll down the drop-down list, and then click *Grid*. (This header inserts the document title and a date placeholder.)
   b. Delete the date placeholder by clicking the *[Date]* placeholder, clicking the placeholder tab, and then pressing the Delete key.
   c. Double-click in the document text.
3. Insert and then format a footer by completing the following steps:
   a. Click the Insert tab.
   b. Click the Footer button, scroll down the drop-down list, and then click *Retrospect*.
   c. Select the name in the author placeholder at the left side of the footer and then type your first and last names.
   d. Select your name and the page number, apply bold formatting, and then change the font size to 10 point.
   e. Click the Close Header and Footer button.
4. Scroll through the document to see how the header and footer will print.
5. Save, print, and then close **4-WritingProcess.docx**.

Check Your Work

Project 5 **Format a Report on Desirable Employee Qualities**   **2 Parts**

You will open a document containing information on desirable employee qualities and then insert a watermark, change the page background color, and insert a page border.

Preview Finished Project

Quick Steps
Insert a Watermark
1. Click Design tab.
2. Click Watermark button.
3. Click option.

Quick Steps
Apply Page Background Color
1. Click Design tab.
2. Click Page Color button.
3. Click option.

Formatting the Page Background

The Page Background group on the Design tab contains three buttons for customizing the page background. Click the Watermark button and choose a predesigned watermark from options at the drop-down list. If a document is going to be viewed on-screen or on the Web, consider adding a page background color. Chapter 3 covered how to apply borders and shading to text at the Borders and Shading dialog box. This dialog box also contains options for inserting a page border. Display the Borders and Shading dialog box with the Page Border tab selected by clicking the Page Borders button in the Page Background group.

Inserting a Watermark

A watermark is a lightened image that displays behind the text in a document. Use a watermark to add visual appeal or to identify a document as a draft, sample, or confidential document. Word provides a number of predesigned watermarks. Display these watermarks by clicking the Watermark button in the Page Background group on the Design tab. Scroll through the list of watermarks and then click an option.

Applying Page Background Color

Use the Page Color button in the Page Background group to apply a background color to a document. This background color is intended for viewing a document on-screen or on the web. The color is visible on the screen but does not print. Insert a page color by clicking the Page Color button and then clicking a color at the drop-down color palette.

Project 5a Inserting a Watermark and Applying a Page Background Color

Part 1 of 2

1. Open **EmpQualities.docx** and then save it with the name **4-EmpQualities**.
2. Insert a watermark by completing the following steps:
   a. With the insertion point positioned at the beginning of the document, click the Design tab.
   b. Click the Watermark button in the Page Background group.
   c. At the drop-down list, click the *CONFIDENTIAL 1* option.
3. Scroll through the document and notice how the watermark displays behind the text.
4. Remove the watermark and insert a different one by completing the following steps:
   a. Click the Watermark button in the Page Background group and then click *Remove Watermark* at the drop-down list.
   b. Click the Watermark button and then click the *DO NOT COPY 1* option at the drop-down list.
5. Scroll through the document and notice how the watermark displays.
6. Move the insertion point to the beginning of the document.
7. Click the Page Color button in the Page Background group and then click the *Tan, Background 2* color option (third column, first row in the *Theme Colors* section).
8. Save **4-EmpQualities.docx**.

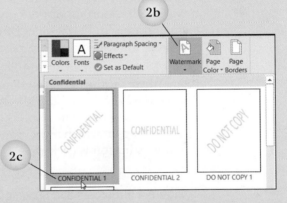

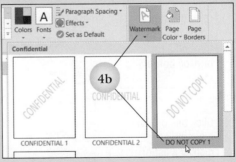

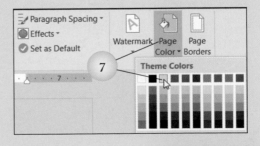

Check Your Work

Inserting a Page Border

To improve the visual appeal of a document, consider inserting a page border. When a page border is inserted in a multiple-page document, it prints on each page. To insert a page border, click the Page Borders button in the Page Background group on the Design tab. This displays the Borders and Shading dialog box with the Page Border tab selected, as shown in Figure 4.5. At this dialog box, specify the border style, color, and width.

The dialog box contains an option for inserting a page border containing an art image. To display the images available, click the *Art* option box arrow, scroll through the drop-down list, and then click an image.

Changing Page Border Options

By default, a page border displays and prints 24 points from the top, left, right, and bottom edges of the page. Some printers, particularly inkjet printers, have a nonprinting area around the outside edges of the page that can interfere with the printing of a border. Before printing a document with a page border, click the File tab and then click the *Print* option. Look at the preview of the page at the right side of the Print backstage area and determine whether the entire border is visible. If a portion of the border is not visible in the preview page (generally at the bottom and right sides of the page), consider changing measurements at the Border and Shading Options dialog box, shown in Figure 4.6.

Display the Border and Shading Options dialog box by clicking the Design tab and then clicking the Page Borders button. At the Borders and Shading dialog box with the Page Border tab selected, click the Options button in the lower right corner of the dialog box. The options at the Border and Shading Options dialog box change depending on whether the Borders tab or the Page Border tab is selected when the Options button is clicked.

Figure 4.5 Borders and Shading Dialog Box with Page Border Tab Selected

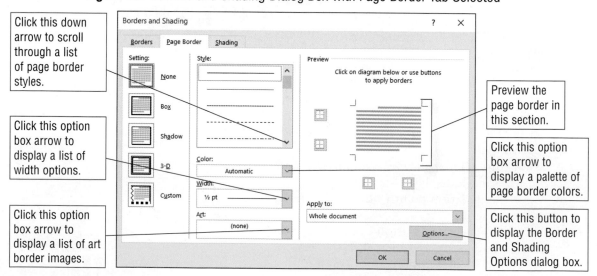

Figure 4.6 Border and Shading Options Dialog Box

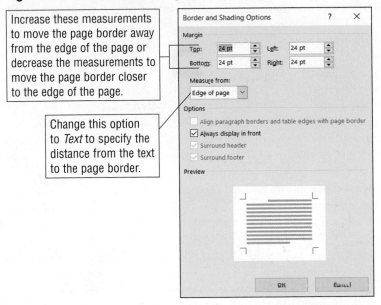

Increase these measurements to move the page border away from the edge of the page or decrease the measurements to move the page border closer to the edge of the page.

Change this option to *Text* to specify the distance from the text to the page border.

If a printer contains a nonprinting area and the entire page border will not print, consider increasing the spacing from the page border to the edge of the page. Do this with the *Top*, *Left*, *Bottom*, and/or *Right* measurement boxes. The *Measure from* option box has a default setting of *Edge of page*. This option can be changed to *Text*, which changes the top and bottom measurements to *1 pt* and the left and right measurements to *4 pt* and moves the page border into the page. Use the measurement boxes to specify the distances the page border should display and print from the edges of the text in the document.

Project 5b Inserting a Page Border

Part 2 of 2

1. With **4-EmpQualities.docx** open, remove the page color by clicking the Page Color button in the Page Background group on the Design tab and then clicking the *No Color* option.
2. Insert a page border by completing the following steps:
   a. Click the Page Borders button in the Page Background group on the Design tab.
   b. Click the *Box* option in the *Setting* section.
   c. Scroll down the list of line styles in the *Style* list box until the last line style displays and then click the third line from the end.
   d. Click the *Color* option box arrow and then click the *Dark Red, Accent 2* color option (sixth column, first row in the *Theme Colors* section).
   e. Click OK to close the dialog box.

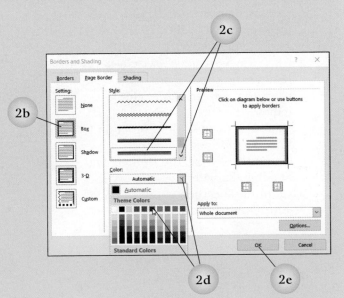

3. Increase the spacing from the page border to the edges of the page by completing the following steps:

   a. Click the Page Borders button in the Page Background group on the Design tab.

   b. At the Borders and Shading dialog box with the Page Border tab selected, click the Options button in the lower right corner.

   c. At the Border and Shading Options dialog box, click the *Top* measurement box up arrow until *31 pt* displays. (This is the maximum measurement allowed.)

   d. Increase the measurements in the *Left, Bottom,* and *Right* measurement boxes to *31 pt*.

   e. Click OK to close the Border and Shading Options dialog box.

   f. Click OK to close the Borders and Shading dialog box.

4. Save **4-EmpQualities.docx** and then print page 1.

5. Insert an image page border and change the page border spacing options by completing the following steps:

   a. Click the Page Borders button in the Page Background group on the Design tab.

   b. Click the *Art* option box arrow and then click the border image shown at the right (approximately one-third of the way down the drop-down list).

   c. Click the Options button in the lower right corner of the Borders and Shading dialog box.

   d. At the Border and Shading Options dialog box, click the *Measure from* option box arrow and then click *Text* at the drop-down list.

   e. Click the *Top* measurement box up arrow until *10 pt* displays.

   f. Increase the measurement in the *Bottom* measurement box to *10 pt* and the measurements in the *Left* and *Right* measurement boxes to *14 pt*.

   g. Click the *Surround header* check box to remove the check mark.

   h. Click the *Surround footer* check box to remove the check mark.

   i. Click OK to close the Border and Shading Options dialog box.

   j. Click OK to close the Borders and Shading dialog box.

6. Save, print, and then close **4-EmpQualities.docx**.

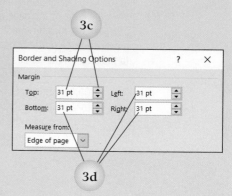

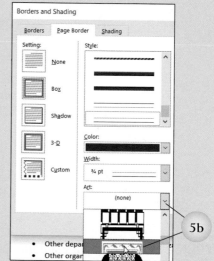

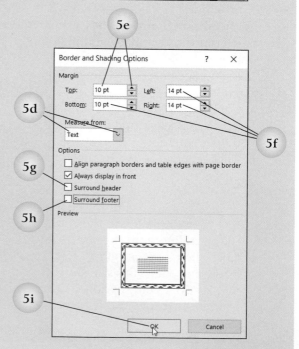

Check Your Work

Project 6 **Format a Lease Agreement**   **4 Parts**

You will open a lease agreement, search for specific text and replace it with other text, and then search for specific formatting and replace it with other formatting.

Finding and Replacing Text and Formatting

🔍 Find

ab⤷ac Replace

The Editing group on the Home tab contains the Find button and the Replace button. Use the Find button to search for specific text or formatting in a document and use the Replace button to search for and then replace specific text or formatting.

Tutorial

Finding Text

Finding Text

Click the Find button in the Editing group on the Home tab (or press the keyboard shortcut Ctrl + F) and the Navigation pane displays at the left side of the screen with the Results tab selected. With this tab selected, type search text in the search text box and any occurrence of the text in the document is highlighted. A fragment of the text surrounding the search text also displays in a thumbnail in the Navigation pane. For example, search for *Lessee* in **4-LeaseAgrmnt.docx** and the screen displays as shown in Figure 4.7. Any occurrence of *Lessee* displays highlighted in yellow in the document and the Navigation pane displays thumbnails of the text surrounding the occurrences of *Lessee*.

Quick Steps

Find Text
1. Click Find button.
2. Type search text.
3. Click Next button.

Figure 4.7 Navigation Pane Showing Search Results

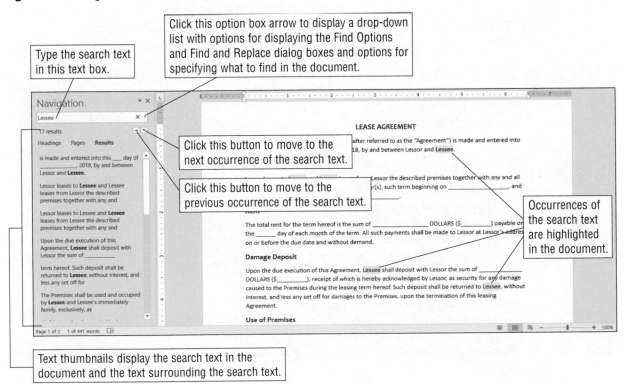

Type the search text in this text box.

Click this option box arrow to display a drop-down list with options for displaying the Find Options and Find and Replace dialog boxes and options for specifying what to find in the document.

Click this button to move to the next occurrence of the search text.

Click this button to move to the previous occurrence of the search text.

Occurrences of the search text are highlighted in the document.

Text thumbnails display the search text in the document and the text surrounding the search text.

Click a text thumbnail in the Navigation pane and the occurrence of the search text is selected in the document. Hover the mouse over a text thumbnail in the Navigation pane and the page number location displays in a small box near the mouse pointer. Move to the next occurrence of the search text by clicking the Next button (contains a down-pointing arrow) below and to the right of the search text box. Click the Previous button (contains an up-pointing arrow) to move to the previous occurrence of the search text.

Click the down arrow at the right side of the search text box and a drop-down list displays. It shows options for displaying dialog boxes, such as the Find Options dialog box and the Find and Replace dialog box. It also shows options for specifying what should be found in the document, such as figures, tables, and equations.

The search text in a document can be highlighted with options at the Find and Replace dialog box with the Find tab selected. Display this dialog box by clicking the Find button arrow in the Editing group on the Home tab and then clicking *Advanced Find* at the drop-down list. Another method for displaying the Find and Replace dialog box is to click the down arrow at the right side of the search text box in the Navigation pane and then click the *Advanced Find* option at the drop-down list. To highlight found text, type the search text in the *Find what* text box, click the Reading Highlight button, and then click *Highlight All* at the drop-down list. All occurrences of the text in the document are highlighted. To remove highlighting, click the Reading Highlight button and then click *Clear Highlighting* at the drop-down list.

Project 6a Finding and Highlighting Text

Part 1 of 4

1. Open **LeaseAgrmnt.docx** and then save it with the name **4-LeaseAgrmnt**.
2. Find all occurrences of *lease* by completing the following steps:
   a. Click the Find button in the Editing group on the Home tab.
   b. If necessary, click the Results tab in the Navigation pane.
   c. Type lease in the search text box in the Navigation pane.
   d. After a moment, all occurrences of *lease* in the document are highlighted and text thumbnails display in the Navigation pane. Click a couple of the text thumbnails in the Navigation pane to select the text in the document.
   e. Click the Previous button (contains an up-pointing arrow) to select the previous occurrence of *lease* in the document.
3. Use the Find and Replace dialog box with the Find tab selected to highlight all occurrences of *Premises* in the document by completing the following steps:
   a. Click in the document and press Ctrl + Home to move the insertion point to the beginning of the document.
   b. Click the search option box arrow in the Navigation pane and then click *Advanced Find* at the drop-down list.

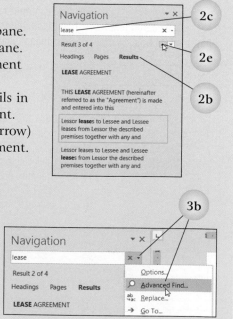

c. At the Find and Replace dialog box with the Find tab selected (and *lease* selected in the *Find what* text box), type Premises.
d. Click the Reading Highlight button and then click *Highlight All* at the drop-down list.
e. Click in the document to make it active and then scroll through the document and notice the occurrences of highlighted text.
f. Click in the dialog box to make it active.
g. Click the Reading Highlight button and then click *Clear Highlighting* at the drop-down list.
h. Click the Close button to close the Find and Replace dialog box.
4. Close the Navigation pane by clicking the Close button in the upper right corner of the pane.

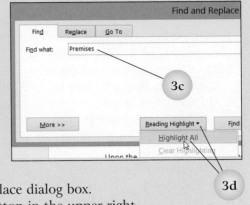

Tutorial

Finding and Replacing Text

Finding and Replacing Text

To find and replace text, click the Replace button in the Editing group on the Home tab or use the keyboard shortcut Ctrl + H. This displays the Find and Replace dialog box with the Replace tab selected, as shown in Figure 4.8. Type the search text in the *Find what* text box, press the Tab key, and then type the replacement text in the *Replace with* text box.

The Find and Replace dialog box contains several command buttons. Click the Find Next button to tell Word to find the next occurrence of the text. Click the Replace button to replace the text and find the next occurrence. If all occurrences of the text in the *Find what* text box are to be replaced with the text in the *Replace with* text box, click the Replace All button.

Quick Steps

Find and Replace Text
1. Click Replace button.
2. Type search text.
3. Press Tab key.
4. Type replacement text.
5. Click Replace or Replace All button.

Figure 4.8 Find and Replace Dialog Box with the Replace Tab Selected

Hint If the Find and Replace dialog box is in the way of specific text, drag it to a different location.

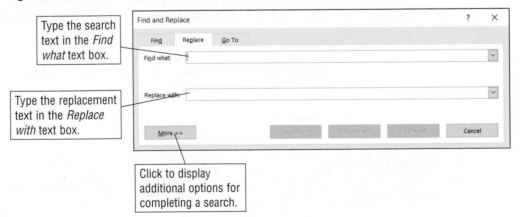

1. With **4-LeaseAgrmnt.docx** open, make sure the insertion point is positioned at the beginning of the document.
2. Find all occurrences of *Lessor* and replace them with *Tracy Hartford* by completing the following steps:

   a. Click the Replace button in the Editing group on the Home tab.

   b. At the Find and Replace dialog box with the Replace tab selected, type Lessor in the *Find what* text box.

   c. Press the Tab key to move the insertion point to the *Replace with* text box.

   d. Type Tracy Hartford.

   e. Click the Replace All button.

   f. At the message stating that 11 replacements were made, click OK. (Do not close the Find and Replace dialog box.)

3. With the Find and Replace dialog box still open, complete steps similar to those in Step 2 to find all occurrences of *Lessee* and replace them with *Michael Iwami*.
4. Click the Close button to close the Find and Replace dialog box.
5. Save **4-LeaseAgrmnt.docx**.

Check Your Work

Defining Search Parameters

The Find and Replace dialog box contains a variety of check boxes with options for completing a search. To display these options, click the More button in the lower left corner of the dialog box. This causes the Find and Replace dialog box to expand, as shown in Figure 4.9. Each option and what will occur if it is selected

Figure 4.9 Expanded Find and Replace Dialog Box

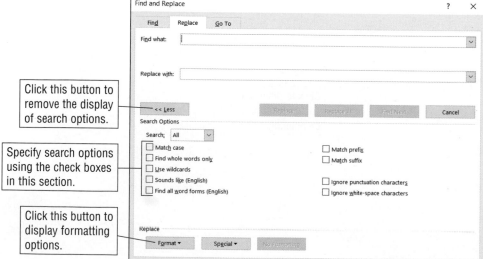

Click this button to remove the display of search options.

Specify search options using the check boxes in this section.

Click this button to display formatting options.

is described in Table 4.2. To remove the display of options, click the Less button. (The Less button was previously the More button.) If a mistake was made when replacing text, close the Find and Replace dialog box and then click the Undo button on the Quick Access Toolbar.

Table 4.2 Options at the Expanded Find and Replace Dialog Box

Choose this option	To
Match case	Exactly match the case of the search text. For example, search for *Book* and select the *Match case* option and Word will stop at *Book* but not *book* or *BOOK*.
Find whole words only	Find a whole word, not a part of a word. For example, search for *her* without selecting *Find whole words only* and Word will stop at *there*, *here*, *hers*, and so on.
Use wildcards	Use special characters as wildcards to search for specific text.
Sounds like (English)	Match words that sound alike but are spelled differently, such as *know* and *no*.
Find all word forms (English)	Find all forms of the word entered in the *Find what* text box. For example, enter *hold* and Word will stop at *held* and *holding*.
Match prefix	Find only those words that begin with the letters in the *Find what* text box. For example, enter *per* and Word will stop at words such as *perform* and *perfect* but skip words such as *super* and *hyperlink*.
Match suffix	Find only those words that end with the letters in the *Find what* text box. For example, enter *ly* and Word will stop at words such as *accurately* and *quietly* but skip words such as *catalyst* and *lyre*.
Ignore punctuation characters	Ignore punctuation within characters. For example, enter *US* in the *Find what* text box and Word will stop at *U.S.*
Ignore white-space characters	Ignore spaces between letters. For example, enter *F B I* in the *Find what* text box and Word will stop at *FBI*.

Project 6c Finding and Replacing Word Forms and Suffixes

Part 3 of 4

1. With **4-LeaseAgrmnt.docx** open, make sure the insertion point is positioned at the beginning of the document.
2. Find all word forms of the word *lease* and replace them with *rent* by completing the following steps:
   a. Click the Replace button in the Editing group on the Home tab.

b. At the Find and Replace dialog box with the Replace tab selected, type lease in the *Find what* text box.

c. Press the Tab key and then type rent in the *Replace with* text box.

d. Click the More button.

e. Click the *Find all word forms (English)* check box. (This inserts a check mark in the check box.)

f. Click the Replace All button.

g. At the message stating that Replace All is not recommended with Find All Word Forms, click OK.

h. At the message stating that six replacements were made, click OK.

i. Click the *Find all word forms* check box to remove the check mark.

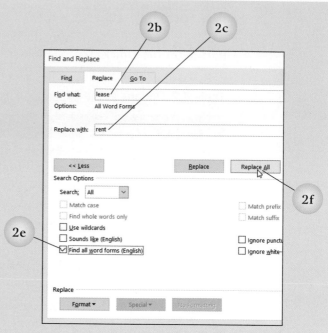

3. Find the word *less* and replace it with the word *minus* and specify that you want Word to find only those words that end in *less* by completing the following steps:

a. At the expanded Find and Replace dialog box, select the text in the *Find what* text box and then type less.

b. Select the text in the *Replace with* text box and then type minus.

c. Click the *Match suffix* check box to insert a check mark (telling Word to find only words that end in *less*).

d. Click the Replace All button.

e. Click OK at the message stating that two replacements were made.

f. Click the *Match suffix* check box to remove the check mark.

g. Click the Less button.

h. Close the Find and Replace dialog box.

4. Save **4-LeaseAgrmnt.docx**.

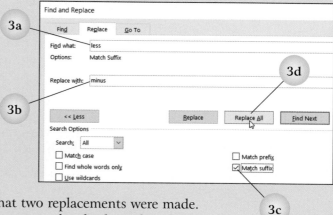

Check Your Work

Tutorial

Finding and Replacing Formatting

Finding and Replacing Formatting

Use options at the Find and Replace dialog box with the Replace tab selected to search for characters containing specific formatting and replace them with other characters or formatting. With the insertion point positioned in the *Find what* text box, specify formatting to be found in the document by clicking the More button, clicking the Format button in the lower left corner of the dialog box, and then clicking the type of formatting at the pop-up list. Click in the *Replace with* text box and then complete similar steps.

1. With **4-LeaseAgrmnt.docx** open, make sure the insertion point displays at the beginning of the document.
2. Find text set in 12-point Candara bold, in the standard dark red color and replace it with text set in 14-point Calibri bold, in the standard dark blue color by completing the following steps:

   a. Click the Replace button in the Editing group on the Home tab.

   b. At the Find and Replace dialog box, press the Delete key. (This deletes any text in the *Find what* text box.)

   c. Click the More button. (If a check mark displays in any of the check boxes, click the option to remove it.)

   d. With the insertion point positioned in the *Find what* text box, click the Format button in the lower left corner of the dialog box and then click *Font* at the pop-up list.

   e. At the Find Font dialog box, choose the *Candara* font and change the font style to *Bold*, the size to *12*, and the font color to *Dark Red* (first color option in the *Standard Colors* section).

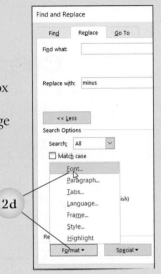

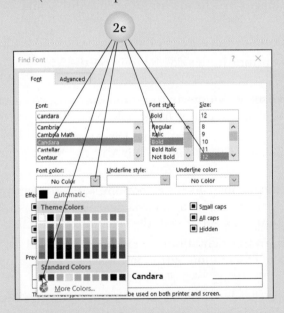

   f. Click OK to close the Find Font dialog box.

   g. At the Find and Replace dialog box, click in the *Replace with* text box and then delete any text that displays.

   h. Click the Format button in the lower left corner of the dialog box and then click *Font* at the pop-up list.

   i. At the Replace Font dialog box, choose the *Calibri* font and change the font style to *Bold*, the size to *14*, and the font color to *Dark Blue* (ninth color option in the *Standard Colors* section).

   j. Click OK to close the Replace Font dialog box.

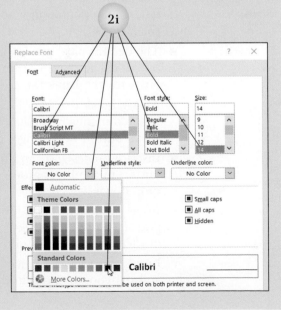

k. At the Find and Replace dialog box, click the Replace All button.
l. Click OK at the message stating that eight replacements were made.
m. Click in the *Find what* text box and then click the No Formatting button.
n. Click in the *Replace with* text box and then click the No Formatting button.
o. Click the Less button.
p. Close the Find and Replace dialog box.
3. Save, print, and then close **4-LeaseAgrmnt.docx**.

Check Your Work

Chapter Summary

- Change the document view with buttons in the view area on the Status bar or with options in the Views group on the View tab.

- Print Layout is the default view but this can be changed to other views, such as Draft view and Read Mode view.

- Draft view displays the document in a format for efficient editing and formatting.

- Read Mode view displays a document in a format for easy viewing and reading.

- Use the Zoom slider bar or buttons in the Zoom group on the View tab to change the display percentage.

- Use options at the Ribbon Display Options button drop-down list to specify if the Quick Access Toolbar, ribbon, and Status bar should be visible or hidden.

- Navigate in a document using the Navigation pane. Display the pane by inserting a check mark in the *Navigation Pane* check box in the Show group on the View tab.

- By default, a Word document contains 1-inch top, bottom, left, and right margins. Change margins with preset margin settings at the Margins button drop-down list or with options at the Page Setup dialog box with the Margins tab selected.

- The default page layout is portrait orientation, which can be changed to landscape orientation with the Orientation button in the Page Setup group on the Layout tab.

- The default page size is 8.5 inches by 11 inches, which can be changed with options at the Size button drop-down list or options at the Page Setup dialog box with the Paper tab selected.

- A page break that Word inserts automatically is a soft page break. A page break inserted manually is a hard page break. Insert a hard page break using the Page Break button in the Pages group on the Insert tab or by pressing Ctrl + Enter.

- Insert a predesigned and formatted cover page by clicking the Cover Page button in the Pages group on the Insert tab and then clicking an option at the drop-down list.

- Insert predesigned and formatted page numbering by clicking the Page Number button in the Header & Footer group on the Insert tab, specifying the location of the page number, and then clicking a page numbering option.

- Insert predesigned headers and footers in a document with the Header button and the Footer button in the Header & Footer group on the Insert tab.

- A watermark is a lightened image that displays behind the text in a document. Use the Watermark button in the Page Background group on the Design tab to insert a watermark.

- Insert a page background color in a document with the Page Color button in the Page Background group on the Design tab. The page background color is designed for viewing a document on screen and does not print.

- Click the Page Borders button in the Page Background group on the Design tab and the Borders and Shading dialog box with the Page Border tab selected displays. Use options at this dialog box to insert a page border or an art image page border in a document.

- Use the Find button in the Editing group on the Home tab to search for specific characters or formatting. Use the Replace button to search for specific characters or formatting and replace them with other characters or formatting.

- At the Find and Replace dialog box, click the Find Next button to find the next occurrence of the characters and/or formatting. Click the Replace button to replace the characters or formatting and find the next occurrence or click the Replace All button to replace all occurrences of the characters or formatting.

- Click the More button at the Find and Replace dialog box to display additional options for defining search parameters.

Commands Review

FEATURE	RIBBON TAB, GROUP	BUTTON, OPTION	KEYBOARD SHORTCUT
blank page	Insert, Pages		
Borders and Shading dialog box with Page Border tab selected	Design, Page Background		
Border and Shading Options dialog box	Design, Page Background	, Options	
cover page	Insert, Pages		
Draft view	View, Views		
Find and Replace dialog box with Find tab selected	Home, Editing	, *Advanced Find*	
Find and Replace dialog box with Replace tab selected	Home, Editing	ab↔ac	Ctrl + H
footer	Insert, Header & Footer		
header	Insert, Header & Footer		
margins	Layout, Page Setup		
Navigation pane	View, Show	*Navigation Pane*	Ctrl + F
orientation	Layout, Page Setup		
page break	Insert, Pages		Ctrl + Enter

FEATURE	RIBBON TAB, GROUP	BUTTON, OPTION	KEYBOARD SHORTCUT
page background color	Design, Page Background		
page numbering	Insert, Header & Footer		
Page Setup dialog box with Margins tab selected	Layout, Page Setup	, *Custom Margins* OR	
Page Setup dialog box with Paper tab selected	Layout, Page Setup	, *More Paper Sizes*	
paper size	Layout, Page Setup		
Print Layout view	View, Views		
Read Mode view	View, Views		
ribbon display options			
watermark	Design, Page Background		

Workbook

Chapter study tools and assessment activities are available in the *Workbook* ebook. These resources are designed to help you further develop and demonstrate mastery of the skills learned in this chapter.

Unit assessment activities are also available in the *Workbook*. These activities are designed to help you demonstrate mastery of the skills learned in this unit.

Microsoft

Word Level 1

Unit 2

Enhancing and Customizing Documents

Microsoft®
Word

Applying Formatting and Inserting Objects

Performance Objectives

Upon successful completion of Chapter 5, you will be able to:

1 Insert section breaks

2 Create and format text in columns

3 Hyphenate words automatically and manually

4 Create a drop cap

5 Insert symbols, special characters, and the date and time

6 Use the Click and Type feature

7 Vertically align text

8 Insert, format, and customize images, text boxes, shapes, and WordArt

9 Create and customize a screenshot

Precheck

Check your current skills to help focus your study.

To apply page or document formatting to only a portion of the document, insert a continuous section break or a section break that begins a new page. A section break is useful when formatting text in columns. The hyphenation feature hyphenates words at the ends of lines, creating a less ragged right margin. Use buttons in the Text and Symbols groups on the Insert tab to insert symbols, special characters, the date and time, text boxes, and WordArt. Word includes the Click and Type feature for positioning the insertion point at a particular location in the document and changing the paragraph alignment. Use the *Vertical alignment* option at the Page Setup dialog box with the Layout tab selected to specify how text is aligned vertically on the page. In addition to learning these features, you will learn how to increase the visual appeal of a document by inserting and customizing graphics, such as images, text boxes, shapes, WordArt, and screenshots.

Data Files

Before beginning chapter work, copy the WL1C5 folder to your storage medium and then make WL1C5 the active folder.

SNAP

If you are a SNAP user, launch the Precheck and Tutorials from your Assignments page.

Tutorial

Inserting and Deleting a Section Break

Breaks

Quick Steps

Insert a Section Break
1. Click Layout tab.
2. Click Breaks button.
3. Click section break type in drop-down list.

Hint When you delete a section break, the text that follows takes on the formatting of the text preceding the break.

Inserting a Section Break

Insert a section break in a document to change the layout and formatting of specific portions. For example, a section break can be inserted in the document and then the margins can be changed for the text between the section break and the end of the document or to the next section break.

Insert a section break in a document by clicking the Layout tab, clicking the Breaks button in the Page Setup group, and then clicking the desired option in the *Section Breaks* section of the drop-down list. A section break can be inserted that begins a new page or a continuous section break can be inserted. A continuous section break separates the document into sections but does not insert a page break.

A section break inserted in a document is not visible in Print Layout view. Change to Draft view or click the Show/Hide ¶ button on the Home tab to turn on the display of nonprinting characters and a section break displays in the document as a double row of dots with the words *Section Break* in the middle. Word will identify the type of section break. For example, if a continuous section break is inserted, the words *Section Break (Continuous)* display in the middle of the row of dots. To delete a section break, change to Draft view, click anywhere on the section break, and then press the Delete key. Another option is to click the Show/Hide ¶ button to turn on the display of nonprinting characters, click anywhere on the section break, and then press the Delete key.

Project 1a **Inserting a Continuous Section Break**　　　**Part 1 of 8**

1. Open **InputDevices.docx** and then save it with the name **5-InputDevices**.
2. Insert a continuous section break by completing the following steps:
   a. Move the insertion point to the beginning of the *Keyboard* heading.
   b. Click the Layout tab.
   c. Click the Breaks button in the Page Setup group and then click *Continuous* in the *Section Breaks* section of the drop-down list.
3. Click the Home tab, click the Show/Hide ¶ button in the Paragraph group, and then notice the section break at the end of the first paragraph of text.
4. Click the Show/Hide ¶ button to turn off the display of nonprinting characters.

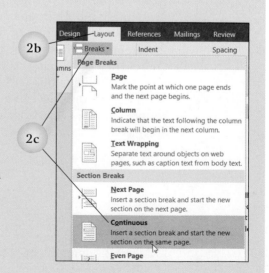

5. With the insertion point positioned at the beginning of the *Keyboard* heading, change the left and right margins to 1.5 inches. (The margin changes affect only the text after the continuous section break.)
6. Save and then print **5-InputDevices.docx**.

Check Your Work

Tutorial

Formatting Text into Columns

Formatting Text into Columns

When preparing a document containing text, an important point to consider is its readability. Readability refers to the ease with which a person can read and understand groups of words. The line length of text in a document can enhance or detract from its readability. If the line length is too long, the reader may lose his or her place and have a difficult time moving to the next line below.

To improve the readability of documents such as newsletters and reports, consider formatting the text in columns. One common type is the newspaper column, which is typically used for text in newspapers, newsletters, and magazines. Newspaper columns contain text in vertical columns.

 Columns

Quick Steps

Create Columns
1. Click Layout tab.
2. Click Columns button.
3. Click number of columns.

Create newspaper columns with the Columns button in the Page Setup group on the Layout tab or with options at the Columns dialog box. Using the Columns button creates columns of equal width. Use the Columns dialog box to create columns with varying widths. A document can include as many columns as will fit the space available on the page. Word determines how many columns can be included on the page based on the page width, the margin widths, and the size and spacing of the columns. Columns must be at least 0.5 inch in width. Changing column widths affects the entire document or the section of the document in which the insertion point is positioned.

Project 1b Formatting Text into Columns   **Part 2 of 8**

1. With **5-InputDevices.docx** open, make sure the insertion point is positioned below the section break and then change the left and right margins back to 1 inch.
2. Delete the section break by completing the following steps:
   a. Click the Show/Hide ¶ button in the Paragraph group on the Home tab to turn on the display of nonprinting characters.
   b. Click anywhere on *Section Break (Continuous)* at the end of the first paragraph below the title in the document. (This moves the insertion point to the beginning of the section break.)

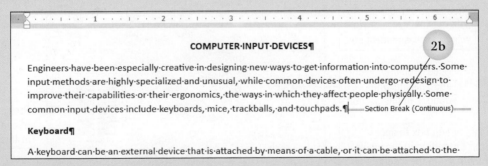

   c. Press the Delete key.
   d. Click the Show/Hide ¶ button to turn off the display of nonprinting characters.

3. Move the insertion point to the beginning of the first paragraph of text below the title and then insert a continuous section break.

4. Format the text into columns by completing the following steps:
   a. Make sure the insertion point is positioned below the section break.
   b. If necessary, click the Layout tab.
   c. Click the Columns button in the Page Setup group.
   d. Click *Two* at the drop-down list.

5. Save **5-InputDevices.docx**.

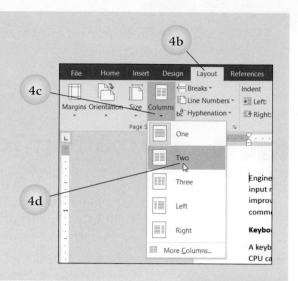

Check Your Work

Creating Columns with the Columns Dialog Box

Use the Columns dialog box to create newspaper columns that are equal or unequal in width. To display the Columns dialog box, shown in Figure 5.1, click the Columns button in the Page Setup group on the Layout tab and then click *More Columns* at the drop-down list.

With options at the Columns dialog box, specify the style and number of columns, enter specific column measurements, create unequal columns, and insert a line between columns. By default, column formatting is applied to the whole document. This can be changed to *This point forward* with the *Apply to* option box at the bottom of the Columns dialog box. With the *This point forward* option, a section break is inserted and the column formatting is applied to text from the location of the insertion point to the end of the document or until another column format is encountered. The *Preview* section of the dialog box displays an example of how the columns will appear in the document.

Figure 5.1 Columns Dialog Box

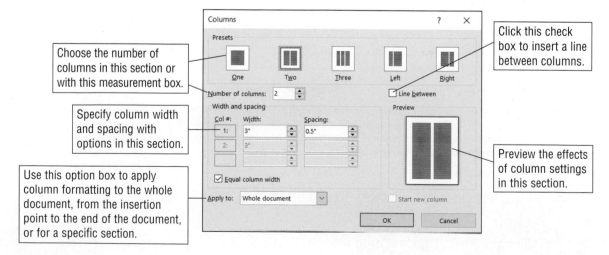

Choose the number of columns in this section or with this measurement box.

Specify column width and spacing with options in this section.

Use this option box to apply column formatting to the whole document, from the insertion point to the end of the document, or for a specific section.

Click this check box to insert a line between columns.

Preview the effects of column settings in this section.

Removing Column Formatting

To remove column formatting using the Columns button, position the insertion point in the section containing columns, click the Layout tab, click the Columns button, and then click *One* at the drop-down list. Column formatting can also be removed at the Columns dialog box by selecting the *One* option in the *Presets* section.

Inserting a Column Break

Hint You can also insert a column break with the keyboard shortcut Ctrl + Shift + Enter.

When formatting text into columns, Word automatically breaks the columns to fit the page. At times, automatic column breaks may appear in undesirable locations. Insert a manual column break by positioning the insertion point where the column is to end, clicking the Layout tab, clicking the Breaks button, and then clicking *Column* at the drop-down list.

Project 1c **Formatting Columns at the Columns Dialog Box** **Part 3 of 8**

1. With **5-InputDevices.docx** open, delete the section break by completing the following steps:
   a. Click the View tab and then click the Draft button in the Views group.
   b. Click anywhere on *Section Break (Continuous)* and then press the Delete key.
   c. Click the Print Layout button in the Views group on the View tab.
2. Remove column formatting by clicking the Layout tab, clicking the Columns button in the Page Setup group, and then clicking *One* at the drop-down list.
3. Format text in columns by completing the following steps:
   a. Position the insertion point at the beginning of the first paragraph of text below the title.
   b. Click the Columns button in the Page Setup group and then click *More Columns* at the drop-down list.
   c. At the Columns dialog box, click *Two* in the *Presets* section.
   d. Click the *Spacing* measurement box down arrow until *0.3"* displays.
   e. Click the *Line between* check box to insert a check mark.
   f. Click the *Apply to* option box arrow and then click *This point forward* at the drop-down list.
   g. Click OK to close the dialog box.

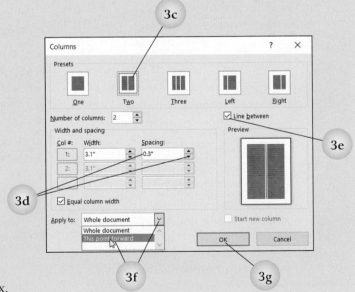

---

4. Insert a column break by completing the
   following steps:
   a. Position the insertion point at the beginning
      of the heading *Mouse*.
   b. Click the Breaks button in the Page Setup
      group and then click *Column* at the drop-
      down list.
5. Save and then print **5-InputDevices.docx**.

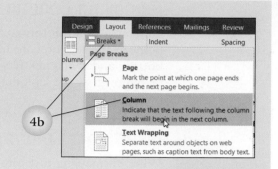

4b

Check Your Work

Balancing Columns on a Page

In a document containing text formatted into columns, Word automatically lines
up (balances) the last lines of text at the bottoms of the columns, except on the
last page. Text in the first column of the last page may flow to the end of the page,
while the text in the second column may end far short of the end of the page.
Balance columns by inserting a continuous section break at the end of the text.

Project 1d Formatting and Balancing Columns of Text

Part 4 of 8

1. With **5-InputDevices.docx** open, delete the column break by positioning the insertion
   point at the beginning of the heading *Mouse* and then pressing the Backspace key.
2. Select the entire document and then change the font to 12-point Constantia.
3. Move the insertion point to the end of the document and then balance the columns by
   clicking the Layout tab, clicking the Breaks button, and then clicking *Continuous* at the
   drop-down list.

> A touchscreen allows the user to choose
> options by pressing the appropriate part of
> the screen. Touchscreens are widely used
>
> in bank ATMs and in kiosks at retail
> outlets and in tourist areas.

3

4. Apply the Green, Accent 6, Lighter 60% paragraph shading (last column, third row) to the
   title *COMPUTER INPUT DEVICES*.
5. Apply the Green, Accent 6, Lighter 80% paragraph shading (last column, second row) to
   each heading in the document.
6. Insert page numbering that prints at the bottom center of each page using the Plain
   Number 2 option.
7. Double-click in the document to make it active.
8. Save **5-InputDevices.docx**.

Check Your Work

Hyphenating Words

Tutorial

Hyphenating
Words

In some Word documents, especially those with left and right margins wider than 1 inch or those with text set in columns, the right margin may appear quite ragged. Improve the display of the text by making line lengths more uniform using the hyphenation feature to hyphenate long words that fall at the ends of lines. Use the hyphenation feature to automatically or manually hyphenate words.

Automatically Hyphenating Words

bc Hyphenation

To automatically hyphenate words in a document, click the Layout tab, click the Hyphenation button in the Page Setup group, and then click *Automatic* at the drop-down list. Scroll through the document and check to see if hyphens display in appropriate locations within the words. To remove all the hyphens after hyphenating words in a document, immediately click the Undo button on the Quick Access Toolbar.

Hint Avoid dividing words at the ends of more than two consecutive lines.

Manually Hyphenating Words

Quick Steps

Automatically Hyphenate a Document
1. Click Layout tab.
2. Click Hyphenation button.
3. Click *Automatic*.

Manually Hyphenate a Document
1. Click Layout tab.
2. Click Hyphenation button.
3. Click *Manual*.
4. Click Yes or No to hyphenate indicated words.
5. When complete, click OK.

To control where hyphens appear in words during hyphenation, choose manual hyphenation. To do this, click the Layout tab, click the Hyphenation button in the Page Setup group, and then click *Manual* at the drop-down list. This displays the Manual Hyphenation dialog box, as shown in Figure 5.2. (The word in the *Hyphenate at* text box will vary.)

At this dialog box, click Yes to hyphenate the word as indicated in the *Hyphenate at* text box, click No if the word should not be hyphenated, or click Cancel to cancel hyphenation. The hyphenation can be repositioned in the *Hyphenate at* text box. Word displays the word with syllable breaks indicated by hyphens. Each place the word will be hyphenated displays as a blinking black bar. To hyphenate the word at a different place, position the blinking black bar where the word is to be hyphenated and then click Yes. Continue clicking Yes or No at the Manual Hyphenation dialog box.

Be careful with words ending in *-ed*. Several two-syllable words can be divided before that final syllable—for example, *noted*. However, one-syllable words ending in *-ed* should not be hyphenated. An example is *served*. Watch for this type of occurrence and click No to cancel the hyphenation. At the hyphenation complete message, click OK.

Figure 5.2 Manual Hyphenation Dialog Box

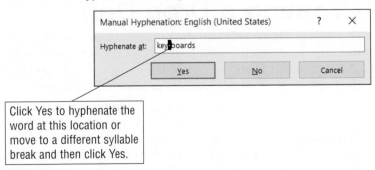

Click Yes to hyphenate the word at this location or move to a different syllable break and then click Yes.

Remove all hyphens in a document by immediately clicking the Undo button on the Quick Access Toolbar. To delete a few but not all the optional hyphens inserted during hyphenation, use the Find and Replace dialog box. To do this, display the Find and Replace dialog box with the Replace tab selected, insert an optional hyphen symbol in the *Find what* text box (to do this, click the More button, click the Special button, and then click *Optional Hyphen* at the pop-up list), and make sure the *Replace with* text box is empty. Complete the find and replace, clicking the Replace button to replace the hyphen with nothing or clicking the Find Next button to leave the hyphen in the document.

Project 1e Automatically and Manually Hyphenating Words

Part 5 of 8

1. With **5-InputDevices.docx** open, hyphenate words automatically by completing the following steps:
   a. Press Ctrl + Home.
   b. Click the Layout tab.
   c. Click the Hyphenation button in the Page Setup group and then click *Automatic* at the drop-down list.
2. Scroll through the document and notice the hyphenation.
3. Click the Undo button to remove the hyphens.
4. Manually hyphenate words by completing the following steps:
   a. Click the Hyphenation button in the Page Setup group and then click *Manual* at the drop-down list.
   b. At the Manual Hyphenation dialog box, make one of the following choices:
      • Click Yes to hyphenate the word as indicated in the *Hyphenate at* text box.
      • Move the hyphen in the word to a more desirable location and then click Yes.
      • Click No if the word should not be hyphenated.
   c. Continue clicking Yes or No at the Manual Hyphenation dialog box.
   d. At the message indicating that hyphenation is complete, click OK.
5. Save **5-InputDevices.docx**.

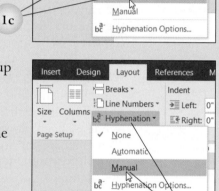

Creating a Drop Cap

 Drop Cap

Use a drop cap to enhance the appearance of text. A drop cap is the first letter of the first word of a paragraph that is set into the paragraph with formatting that differentiates it from the rest of the paragraph. Drop caps can be used to identify the beginnings of major sections or parts of a document.

Create a drop cap with the Drop Cap button in the Text group on the Insert tab. The drop cap can be set in the paragraph or in the margin. At the Drop Cap dialog box, specify a font, the number of lines the letter should drop, and the distance the letter should be positioned from the text of the paragraph. Add a drop cap to the entire first word of a paragraph by selecting the word and then clicking the Drop Cap button.

Quick Steps
Create a Drop Cap
1. Click Insert tab.
2. Click Drop Cap button.
3. Click drop cap option.

1. With **5-InputDevices.docx** open, create a drop cap by completing the following steps:
   a. Position the insertion point on the first word of the first paragraph below the title (*Engineers*).
   b. Click the Insert tab.
   c. Click the Drop Cap button in the Text group.
   d. Click *In margin* at the drop-down gallery.
2. Looking at the drop cap, you decide that you do not like it positioned in the margin and want it to be a little smaller. To change the drop cap, complete the following steps:
   a. With the *E* in the word *Engineers* selected, click the Drop Cap button in the Text group and then click *None* at the drop-down gallery.
   b. Click the Drop Cap button and then click *Drop Cap Options* at the drop-down gallery.
   c. At the Drop Cap dialog box, click *Dropped* in the *Position* section.
   d. Click the *Font* option box arrow, scroll up the drop-down list, and then click *Cambria*.
   e. Click the *Lines to drop* measurement box down arrow to change the number to *2*.
   f. Click OK to close the dialog box.
   g. Click outside the drop cap to deselect it.
3. Save **5-InputDevices.docx**.

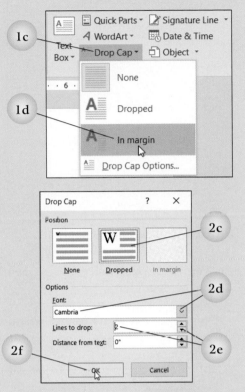

Check Your Work

Inserting Symbols and Special Characters

Use the Symbol button on the Insert tab to insert special symbols in a document. Click the Symbol button in the Symbols group on the Insert tab and a drop-down list displays the most recently inserted symbols along with a *More Symbols* option. Click one of the symbols in the list to insert it in the document or click the *More Symbols* option to display the Symbol dialog box, as shown in Figure 5.3. At the Symbol dialog box, double-click the desired symbol and then click Close or click the symbol, click the Insert button, and then click the Close button. Another method for selecting a symbol at the Symbol dialog box is to type the symbol code in the *Character code* text box.

At the Symbol dialog box with the Symbols tab selected, the font can be changed with the *Font* option box. When the font is changed, different symbols display in the dialog box. Click the Special Characters tab at the Symbol dialog box and a list of special characters displays along with keyboard shortcuts for creating them.

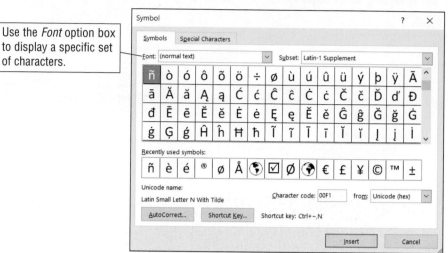

Quick Steps

Insert a Symbol
1. Click Insert tab.
2. Click Symbol button.
3. Click symbol.
OR
1. Click Insert tab.
2. Click Symbol button.
3. Click *More Symbols*.
4. Double-click symbol.
5. Click Close.

Figure 5.3 Symbol Dialog Box with Symbols Tab Selected

Use the *Font* option box to display a specific set of characters.

Project 1g Inserting Symbols and Special Characters

Part 7 of 8

1. With **5-InputDevices.docx** open, press Ctrl + End to move the insertion point to the end of the document.
2. Press the Enter key, type Prepared by:, and then press the spacebar.
3. Type the first name Matthew and then press the spacebar.
4. Insert the last name *Viña* by completing the following steps:
   a. Type Vi.
   b. If necessary, click the Insert tab.
   c. Click the Symbol button in the Symbols group.
   d. Click *More Symbols* at the drop-down list.
   e. At the Symbol dialog box, make sure the *Font* option box displays *(normal text)* and then double-click the ñ symbol (located in approximately the tenth through twelfth rows).
   f. Click the Close button.
   g. Type a.
5. Press Shift + Enter.
6. Insert the keyboard symbol (⌨) by completing the following steps:
   a. Click the Symbol button and then click *More Symbols*.
   b. At the Symbol dialog box, click the *Font* option box arrow and then click *Wingdings* at the drop-down list. (You will need to scroll down the list to display this option.)
   c. Select the current number in the *Character code* text box and then type 55.
   d. Click the Insert button and then click the Close button.
7. Type SoftCell Technologies.

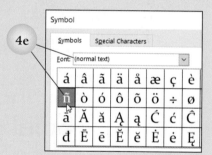

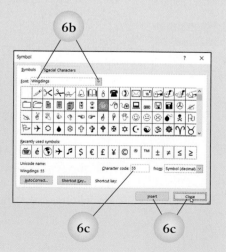

8. Insert the registered trademark symbol (®) by completing the following steps:
    a. Click the Symbol button and then click *More Symbols*.
    b. At the Symbol dialog box, click the Special Characters tab.
    c. Double-click the ® symbol (tenth option from the top).
    d. Click the Close button.
    e. Press Shift + Enter.
9. Select the keyboard symbol (⌨) and then change the font size to 18 points.
10. Save **5-InputDevices.docx**.

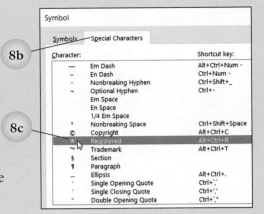

Check Your Work

Inserting the Date and Time

Tutorial

Inserting the Date and Time

 Date & Time

Quick Steps

Insert the Date and Time
1. Click Insert tab.
2. Click Date & Time button.
3. Click desired option in list box.
4. Click OK.

Use the Date & Time button in the Text group on the Insert tab to insert the current date and time in a document. Click this button and the Date and Time dialog box displays, as shown in Figure 5.4. (Your date will vary from what you see in the figure.) At the Date and Time dialog box, click the desired date and/or time format in the *Available formats* list box.

If the *Update automatically* check box does not contain a check mark, the date and/or time arc inserted in the document as text that can be edited in the normal manner. The date and/or time can also be inserted as a field. The advantage to using a field is that the date and time are updated when a document is reopened. Insert a check mark in the *Update automatically* check box to insert the date and/or time as a field. The date can also be inserted as a field using the keyboard shortcut Alt + Shift + D, and the time can be inserted as a field with the keyboard shortcut Alt + Shift + T.

A date or time field will automatically update when a document is reopened. The date and time can also be updated in the document by clicking the date or time field and then clicking the Update tab or pressing the F9 function key.

Figure 5.4 Date and Time Dialog Box

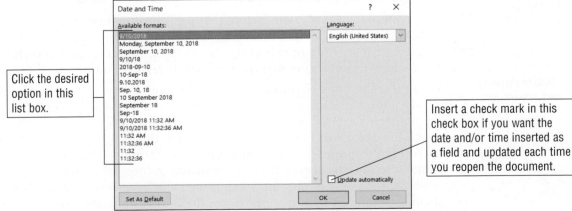

1. With **5-InputDevices.docx** open, press Ctrl + End and make sure the insertion point is positioned below the company name.

2. Insert the current date by completing the following steps:
   a. Click the Insert tab.
   b. Click the Date & Time button in the Text group.
   c. At the Date and Time dialog box, click the third option from the top in the *Available formats* list box. (Your date and time will vary from what you see in the image at the right.)
   d. Click in the *Update automatically* check box to insert a check mark.
   e. Click OK to close the dialog box.

3. Press Shift + Enter.

4. Insert the current time by pressing Alt + Shift + T.

5. Save **5-InputDevices.docx**.

6. Update the time by clicking the time and then pressing the F9 function key.

7. Save, print, and then close **5-InputDevices.docx**.

Check Your Work

Project 2 **Create an Announcement about Supervisory Training**   **4 Parts**

You will create an announcement about upcoming supervisory training in Australia and use the Click and Type feature to center and right-align text. You will vertically center the text on the page and insert and format an image and an online image to add visual appeal to the announcement.

Preview Finished Project

Tutorial

Using Click and Type

Ợuick Steps
Use Click and Type
1. Hover mouse at left margin, between left and right margins, or at right margin.
2. When horizontal lines display next to mouse pointer, double-click left mouse button.

Using the Click and Type Feature

Word contains a Click and Type feature that positions the insertion point at a specific location and alignment in the document. This feature can be used to position one or more lines of text as it is being typed rather than typing the text and then selecting and formatting the text, which requires multiple steps.

To use the Click and Type feature, make sure the document displays in Print Layout view and then hover the mouse pointer at the location the insertion point is to be positioned. As the mouse pointer moves, the pointer displays with varying horizontal lines representing the alignment. When the desired alignment lines display below the mouse pointer, double-click the left mouse button. If the horizontal lines do not display next to the mouse pointer when the mouse button is double-clicked, a left tab is set at the position of the insertion point. To change the alignment and not set a tab, make sure the horizontal lines display near the mouse pointer before double-clicking the mouse button.

1. At a blank document, create the centered text shown in Figure 5.5 by completing the following steps:
   a. Position the I-beam pointer between the left and right margins at about the 3.25-inch mark on the horizontal ruler and at the top of the vertical ruler.
   b. When the center alignment lines display below the I-beam pointer, double-click the left mouse button.
   c. Type the centered text shown in Figure 5.5. Press Shift + Enter to end each line except the last line. 
2. Change to right alignment by completing the following steps:
   a. Position the I-beam pointer near the right margin at approximately the 1-inch mark on the vertical ruler until the right alignment lines display at the left side of the I-beam pointer.
   b. Double-click the left mouse button.
   c. Type the right-aligned text shown in Figure 5.5. Press Shift + Enter to end the first line. 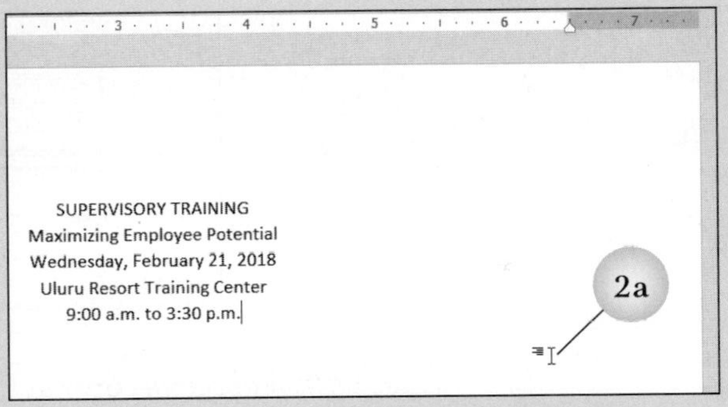
3. Select the centered text and then change the font to 14-point Candara bold and the line spacing to double spacing.
4. Select the right-aligned text, change the font to 10-point Candara bold, and then deselect the text.
5. Save the document and name it **5-Training**.

Check Your Work

Figure 5.5 Project 2a

SUPERVISORY TRAINING
Maximizing Employee Potential
Wednesday, February 21, 2018
Uluru Resort Training Center
9:00 a.m. to 3:30 p.m.

Sponsored by
Cell Systems

Tutorial

Vertically Aligning Data

Vertically Aligning Text

Text or items in a Word document are aligned at the top of the page by default. Change this alignment with the *Vertical alignment* option box at the Page Setup dialog box with the Layout tab selected, as shown in Figure 5.6. Display this dialog box by clicking the Layout tab, clicking the Page Setup group dialog box launcher, and then clicking the Layout tab at the Page Setup dialog box.

Figure 5.6 Page Setup Dialog Box with Layout Tab Selected

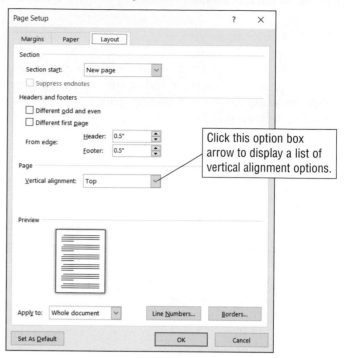

Click this option box arrow to display a list of vertical alignment options.

Quick Steps

Vertically Align Text
1. Click Layout tab.
2. Click Page Setup group dialog box launcher.
3. Click Layout tab.
4. Click *Vertical alignment* option box.
5. Click alignment.
6. Click OK.

The *Vertical alignment* option box in the *Page* section of the Page Setup dialog box contains four choices: *Top*, *Center*, *Justified*, and *Bottom*. The default setting is *Top*, which aligns text and items such as images at the top of the page. Choose *Center* to position the text in the middle of the page vertically. The *Justified* option aligns text between the top and bottom margins. The *Center* option positions text in the middle of the page vertically, while the *Justified* option adds space between paragraphs of text (not within) to fill the page from the top to the bottom margins. If the text is centered or justified, the text does not display centered or justified on the screen in Draft view but it does display centered or justified in Print Layout view. Choose the *Bottom* option to align text at the bottom of the page.

Project 2b Vertically Centering Text

Part 2 of 4

1. With **5-Training.docx** open, click the Layout tab and then click the Page Setup group dialog box launcher.
2. At the Page Setup dialog box, click the Layout tab.
3. Click the *Vertical alignment* option box arrow and then click *Center* at the drop-down list.
4. Click OK to close the dialog box.
5. Save and then print **5-Training.docx**.

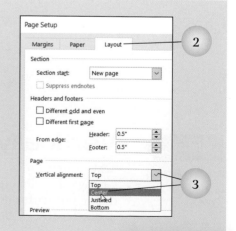

Check Your Work

Tutorial

Inserting, Sizing, and Positioning an Image

Inserting and Formatting Images

Insert an image, such as a picture or piece of clip art, in a Word document with buttons in the Illustrations group on the Insert tab. Click the Pictures button to display the Insert Picture dialog box containing the image file or click the Online Pictures button and search online for images, such as pictures and clip art.

Inserting an Image

 Pictures

To insert an image in a document, click the Insert tab and then click the Pictures button in the Illustrations group. At the Insert Picture dialog box, navigate to the folder containing the image and then double-click the image file.

Tutorial

Formatting an Image

Customizing and Formatting an Image

Quick Steps

Insert an Image
1. Click Insert tab.
2. Click Pictures button.
3. Double-click image file in Insert Picture dialog box.

 Crop

When an image is inserted in a document the Picture Tools Format tab is active. Use buttons on this tab to format and customize the image. Use options in the Adjust group on the Picture Tools Format tab to remove unwanted portions of the image, correct the brightness and contrast, change the image color, apply artistic effects, compress the size of the image file, change to a different image, and reset the image to the original formatting. Use buttons in the Picture Styles group to apply a predesigned style to the image, change the image border, and apply other picture effects to the image. With options in the Arrange group, position the image on the page, specify how text will wrap around it, align the image with other elements in the document, and rotate the image. Use the Crop button in the Size group to remove any unnecessary parts of the image and specify the image size with the *Shape Height* and *Shape Width* measurement boxes.

An image can also be customized and formatted with options at the shortcut menu. Display this menu by right-clicking the image. Use options at the shortcut menu to replace the image with another image, insert a caption, specify text wrapping, size and position the image, and display the Format Picture task pane.

 Position

 Wrap Text

 Layout Options

To move an image, apply a text wrapping style with the Position button or the Wrap Text button on the Picture Tools Format tab and with options from the Layout Options button side menu. The Layout Options button displays just outside the upper right corner of the selected image. Click this button to display a side menu with wrapping options. Click the <u>See more</u> hyperlink text at the bottom of the side menu to display the Layout dialog box containing additional options for positioning the image on the page. Close the Layout Options button side menu by clicking the button or clicking the Close button in the upper right corner of the side menu.

Sizing an Image

Hint Size a selected image horizontally, vertically, or diagonally from the center outward by pressing and holding down the Ctrl key and then dragging a sizing handle.

Change the size of an image with the *Shape Height* and *Shape Width* measurement boxes in the Size group on the Picture Tools Format tab or with the sizing handles that display around a selected image. To change the image size with a sizing handle, position the mouse pointer on a sizing handle until the pointer turns into a double-headed arrow and then click and hold down the left mouse button. Drag the sizing handle in or out to decrease or increase the size of the image and then release the mouse button. Use the middle sizing handles at the left and right sides of the image to make the image wider or thinner. Use the middle sizing handles at the top and bottom of the image to make the image taller or shorter. Use the sizing handles at the corners of the image to change both the width and height at the same time.

Moving an Image

Move an image to a specific location on the page with options at the Position button drop-down gallery in the Arrange group on the Picture Tools Format tab. Choose an option from this gallery and the image is moved to the specified location and square text wrapping is applied to it.

The image can also be moved by dragging it to the new location. Before dragging an image, specify how the text will wrap around it by clicking the Wrap Text button in the Arrange group and then clicking the desired wrapping style at the drop-down list. After choosing a wrapping style, move the image by positioning the mouse pointer on the image border until the mouse pointer displays with a four-headed arrow attached. Click and hold down the left mouse button, drag the image to the new location, and then release the mouse button. As an image is moved to the top, left, right, or bottom margin or to the center of the document, green alignment guides display. Use these guides to help position the image on the page. Gridlines can be turned on to help position an image precisely. Do this by clicking the Align Objects button in the Arrange group on the Picture Tools Format tab and then clicking *View Gridlines*.

Align Objects

Rotate the image by positioning the mouse pointer on the round rotation handle (circular arrow) above the image until the pointer displays with a black circular arrow attached. Click and hold down the left mouse button, drag in the desired direction, and then release the mouse button. An image can also be rotated with options at the Rotate Objects button drop-down gallery. For example, the image can be rotated left or right or flipped horizontally or vertically.

Rotate Objects

Project 2c Inserting and Customizing an Image

Part 3 of 4

1. With **5-Training.docx** open, return the vertical alignment to top alignment by completing the following steps:
   a. Click the Layout tab.
   b. Click the Page Setup group dialog box launcher.
   c. At the Page Setup dialog box, make sure the Layout tab is selected.
   d. Click the *Vertical alignment* option box arrow and then click *Top* at the drop-down list.
   e. Click OK to close the dialog box.
2. Select and then delete the text *Sponsored by* and *Cell Systems*.
3. Select the remaining text and change the line spacing to single spacing.
4. Move the insertion point to the beginning of the document, press the Enter key, and then move the insertion point back to the beginning of the document.
5. Insert an image by completing the following steps:
   a. Click the Insert tab and then click the Pictures button in the Illustrations group.
   b. At the Insert Picture dialog box, navigate to your WL1C5 folder.
   c. Double-click *Uluru.jpg* in the Content pane.
6. Crop the image by completing the following steps:
   a. Click the Crop button in the Size group on the Picture Tools Format tab.

b. Position the mouse pointer on the bottom middle crop handle (which displays as a short black line) until the pointer turns into the crop tool (which displays as a small black T).

c. Click and hold down the left mouse button, drag up to just below the rock (as shown at the right), and then release the mouse button.

d. Click the Crop button in the Size group to turn the feature off.

7. Change the size of the image by clicking in the *Shape Height* measurement box in the Size group, typing 3.1, and then pressing the Enter key.

8. Move the image behind the text by clicking the Layout Options button outside the upper right corner of the image and then clicking the *Behind Text* option at the side menu (second column, second row in the *With Text Wrapping* section). Close the side menu by clicking the Close button in the upper right corner of the side menu.

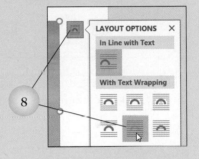

9. Rotate the image by clicking the Rotate Objects button in the Arrange group and then clicking *Flip Horizontal* at the drop-down gallery.

10. Change the image color by clicking the Color button in the Adjust group and then clicking *Saturation: 300%* (sixth option in the *Color Saturation* section).

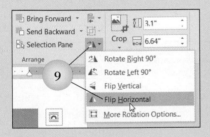
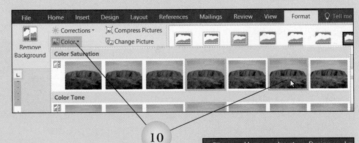

11. Apply an artistic effect by clicking the Artistic Effects button in the Adjust group and then clicking the *Watercolor Sponge* option (second column, third row).

12. Apply a picture effect by clicking the Picture Effects button in the Picture Styles group, pointing to Bevel, and then clicking the *Circle* option (first column, first row in the *Bevel* section).

13. After looking at the new color and artistic effect, you decide to return to the original color and artistic effect and remove the bevel effect by clicking the Reset Picture button in the Adjust group on the Picture Tools Format tab.

14. Sharpen the image by clicking the Corrections button in the Adjust group and then clicking the *Sharpen: 25%* option (fourth option in the *Sharpen/Soften* section).

15. Change the contrast of the image by clicking the Corrections button in the Adjust group and then clicking the *Brightness: 0% (Normal) Contrast: +40%* option (third column, bottom row in the *Brightness/Contrast* section).

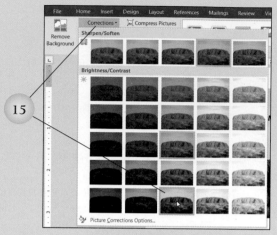

16. Apply a picture style by clicking the More Picture Styles button in the Picture Styles group and then clicking the *Simple Frame, Black* option.

17. Compress the image file by completing the following steps:
   a. Click the Compress Pictures button in the Adjust group.
   b. At the Compress Pictures dialog box, make sure check marks display in both options in the *Compression options* section and then click OK.

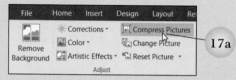

18. Position the mouse pointer on the border of the selected image until the pointer displays with a four-headed arrow attached. Click and hold down the left mouse button, drag the image up and slightly to the left until you

see green alignment guides at the top margin and the center of the page, and then release the mouse button. If the green alignment guides do not display, turn on the guides by clicking the Align button in the Arrange group on the Picture Tools Format tab and then clicking the *Use Alignment Guides* option.

19. Save and then print **5-Training.docx**.
20. With the image selected, remove the background by completing the following steps:
   a. Click the Remove Background button in the Adjust group on the Picture Tools Format tab.
   b. Using the left middle sizing handle, drag the left border to the left border line of the image.
   c. Drag the right middle sizing handle to the right border line of the image.
   d. Drag the bottom middle sizing handle to the bottom border of the image, which displays as a dashed line.
   e. Drag the top middle sizing handle down to just above the top of the rock.

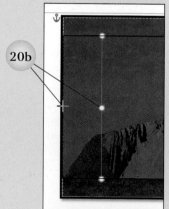

f. Click the Keep Changes button in the Close group on the Background Removal tab. (The image should now display with the sky removed.)

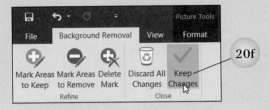

20f

21. Save **5-Training.docx**.

Check Your Work

Inserting an Online Image

Online Pictures

Use the Bing Image Search feature to search for specific images online. To use this feature, click the Insert tab and then click the Online Pictures button. This displays the Insert Pictures window, shown in Figure 5.7. Click in the search text box, type the search term or topic, and then press the Enter key. Images that match the search term or topic display in the window.

To insert an image, click the image and then click the Insert button or double-click the image. This downloads the image to the document. Customize the image with options and buttons on the Picture Tools Format tab.

When selecting online images to use in documents, be aware that many images are copyrighted and thus may not be available for use without permission. By default, Bing will limit search results to those licensed under Creative Commons. Usually, these images are free to use, but an image may have limitations for its use. For example, it may be necessary to credit the source. Always review the specific license for any image you want to use to ensure you can comply with the specific requirements for that image.

Quick Steps

Insert an Online Image
1. Click Insert tab.
2. Click Online Pictures button.
3. Type search word or topic.
4. Press Enter.
5. Double-click image.

Figure 5.7 Insert Pictures Window

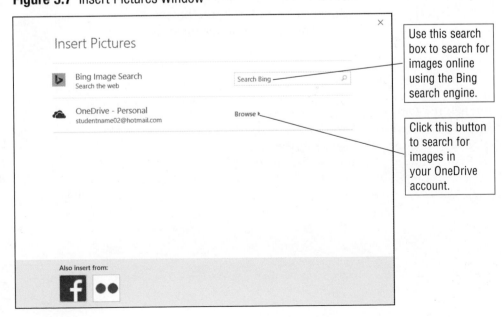

Use this search box to search for images online using the Bing search engine.

Click this button to search for images in your OneDrive account.

1. With **5-Training.docx** open, insert an image of Australia (with the Northern Territory highlighted) by completing the following steps:
   a. Click the Insert tab.
   b. Click the Online Pictures button in the Illustrations group.
   c. At the Insert Pictures window, type northern territory australia and then press the Enter key.
   d. Double-click the Australia image shown below. (If this image is not available online, click the Pictures button on the Insert tab. At the Insert Picture dialog box, navigate to your WL1C5 folder and then double-click the file *NT-Australia.png*.)

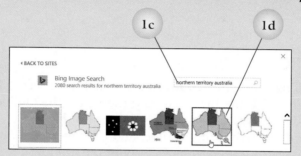

2. Size and position the image by completing the following steps:
   a. Click the Position button in the Arrange group.
   b. Click the *Position in Top Right with Square Text Wrapping* option (third column, first row in the *With Text Wrapping* section).
   c. Click the Wrap Text button.
   d. Click the *Behind Text* option at the drop-down gallery.
   e. Click in the *Shape Height* measurement box in the Size group, type 1, and then press the Enter key.

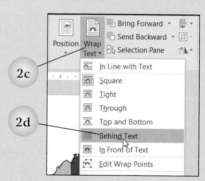

3. Make the white background of the image transparent by completing the following steps:
   a. Click the Color button in the Adjust group.
   b. Click the *Set Transparent Color* option at the bottom of the drop-down list. (The mouse pointer turns into a dropper tool.)
   c. Position the dropper tool on the white background of the image and then click the left mouse button.
4. Click the Color button in the Adjust group and then click the *Orange, Accent color 2 Light* option (third column, third row in the *Recolor* section).
5. Click outside the image to deselect it.
6. Save, print, and then close **5-Training.docx**.

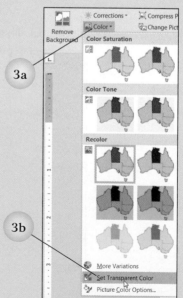

Check Your Work

Inserting a Text Box

Add interest or create a location in a document for text by inserting or drawing a text box. Click the Insert tab and then click the Text Box button and a drop-down list displays with predesigned text boxes and the *Draw Text Box* option. Choose one of the predesigned text boxes, which already contain formatting, or draw a text box and then customize or apply formatting to it with options and buttons on the Drawing Tools Format tab.

Inserting a Predesigned Text Box

One use for a text box in a document is to insert a pull quote. A pull quote is a quote from the text that is "pulled out" and enlarged and positioned in an attractive location on the page. Some advantages of using pull quotes are that they reinforce important concepts, summarize the message, and break up text blocks to make them easier to read. If a document contains multiple pull quotes, keep them in the order in which they appear in the text to ensure clear comprehension by readers.

A text box for a pull quote can be drawn in a document or a predesigned text box can be inserted in the document. To insert a predesigned text box, click the Insert tab, click the Text Box button, and then click the predesigned text box at the drop-down list.

Formatting a Text Box

When a text box is selected, the Drawing Tools Format tab is active. This tab contains buttons for formatting and customizing the text box. Use options in the Insert Shapes group on the Drawing Tools Format tab to insert a shape in the document. Click the Edit Shape button in the Insert Shapes group and a drop-down list displays. Click the *Change Shape* option to change the shape of the selected text box. Click the *Edit Points* option and small black squares display at points around the text box. Use the mouse to drag these points to increase or decrease specific points around the text box.

Apply predesigned styles to a text box and change the shape fill, outline, and effects with options in the Shape Styles group. Change the formatting of the text in the text box with options in the WordArt Styles group. Click the More WordArt Styles button in the WordArt Styles group and then click a style at the drop-down gallery. Customize text in the text box with the Text Fill, Text Outline, and Text Effects buttons in the Text group. Use options in the Arrange group to position the text box on the page, specify text wrapping in relation to the text box, align the text box with other objects in the document, and rotate the text box. Specify the text box size with the *Shape Height* and *Shape Width* measurement boxes in the Size group.

1. Open **Robots.docx** and then save it with the name **5-Robots**.
2. Insert a predesigned text box by completing the following steps:
   a. Click the Insert tab.
   b. Click the Text Box button in the Text group.
   c. Scroll down the drop-down list and then click the *Ion Quote (Dark)* option.
3. Type the following text in the text box: "The task of creating a humanlike body has proven incredibly difficult."
4. Delete the line and the source placeholder in the text box by pressing the F8 function key (which turns on the Selection Mode), pressing Ctrl + End (which selects text from the location of the insertion point to the end of the text box), and then pressing the Delete key.

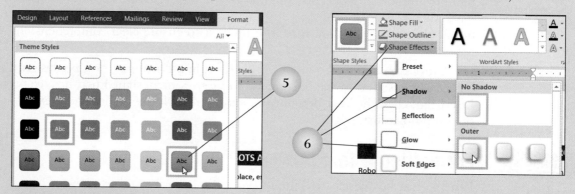

5. With the Drawing Tools Format tab active, click the More Shape Styles button in the Shape Styles group and then click the *Subtle Effect - Blue, Accent 5* option (sixth column, fourth row in the *Theme Styles* section).
6. Click the Shape Effects button in the Shape Styles group, point to *Shadow*, and then click the *Offset Diagonal Bottom Right* option (first column, first row in the *Outer* section).

7. Position the mouse pointer on the border of the selected text box until the pointer turns into a four-headed arrow and then drag the text box so it is positioned as shown at the right.
8. Click outside the text box to deselect it.
9. Save **5-Robots.docx**.

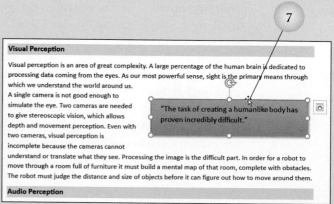

Check Your Work

Drawing and Formatting a Text Box

Quick Steps

Draw a Text Box
1. Click Insert tab.
2. Click Text Box button.
3. Click *Draw Text Box.*
4. Click or drag in document to create box.

In addition to the built-in text boxes provided by Word, a text box can be drawn in a document. To draw a text box, click the Insert tab, click the Text Box button in the Text group, and then click *Draw Text Box* at the drop-down list. With the mouse pointer displaying as crosshairs (a plus [+] symbol), click in the document to insert the text box or position the crosshairs in the document and then drag to create the text box. When a text box is selected, the Drawing Tools Format tab is active. Use buttons on this tab to format drawn text boxes in the same manner as built-in text boxes.

Project 3b Inserting and Formatting a Text Box

Part 2 of 2

1. With **5-Robots.docx** open, press Ctrl + End to move the insertion point to the end of the document.
2. Insert a text box by completing the following steps:
   a. Click the Insert tab.
   b. Click the Text Box button and then click the *Draw Text Box* option.
   c. Position the mouse pointer (displays as crosshairs) immediately right of the insertion point and then click the left mouse button. (This inserts the text box in the document.)
3. Change the text box height and width by completing the following steps:
   a. Click in the *Shape Height* measurement box in the Size group, type 1.2, and then press the Enter key.
   b. Click in the *Shape Width* measurement box in the Size group, type 4.5, and then press the Enter key.
4. Center the text box by clicking the Align button and then clicking *Align Center* at the drop-down list.
5. Apply a shape style by clicking the More Shape Styles button in the Shape Styles group and then clicking the *Subtle Effect - Blue, Accent 1* option (second column, fourth row in the *Theme Styles* section).
6. Apply a bevel shape effect by clicking the Shape Effects button, pointing to the *Bevel* option, and then clicking the *Soft Round* option at the side menu (second column, second row in the *Bevel* section).
7. Apply a 3-D shape effect by clicking the Shape Effects button, pointing to *3-D Rotation*, and then clicking the *Perspective Above* option (first column, second row in the *Perspective* section).

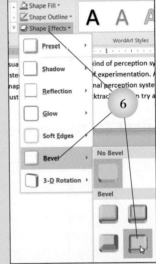

8. Insert and format text in the text box by completing the following steps:
   a. Press the Enter key two times. (The insertion point should be positioned in the text box.)
   b. Click the Home tab.
   c. Change the font size to 14 points, apply bold formatting, and change the font color to standard *Dark Blue*.
   d. Click the Center button in the Paragraph group.
   e. Type International Conference on Artifical Intelligence Summer 2019.
   f. Click outside the text box to deselect it. (Your text box should appear as shown at the right.)
9. Save, print, and then close **5-Robots.docx**.

International Conference on Artificial Intelligence Summer 2019

8f

Check Your Work ▶

Project 4 Prepare a Company Flyer   **2 Parts**

You will prepare a company flyer by inserting and customizing shapes and WordArt.

Preview Finished Project

Tutorial

Inserting, Sizing, and Positioning a Shape and Line

Tutorial

Formatting a Shape and Line

 Shapes

Quick Steps

Draw a Shape
1. Click Insert tab.
2. Click Shapes button.
3. Click shape.
4. Click or drag in document to create shape.

Hint To draw a square, choose the Rectangle shape and then press and hold down the Shift key while drawing.

Drawing Shapes

Use the Shapes button on the Insert tab to draw shapes in a document, including lines, basic shapes, block arrows, flow chart shapes, stars and banners, and callouts. Click a shape and the mouse pointer displays as crosshairs. Position the crosshairs in the document where the shape is to be inserted and then click the left mouse button or click and hold down the left mouse button, drag to create the shape, and then release the mouse button. The shape is inserted in the document and the Drawing Tools Format tab is active.

A shape selected from the *Lines* section of the drop-down list and then drawn in the document is considered a line drawing. A shape selected from another section of the drop-down list and then drawn in the document is considered an enclosed object. When drawing an enclosed object, maintain the proportions of the shape by pressing and holding down the Shift key while dragging with the mouse to create the shape.

Copying Shapes

To copy a shape, select the shape and then click the Copy button in the Clipboard group on the Home tab. Position the insertion point at the location where the copied shape is to be inserted and then click the Paste button. A selected shape can also be copied by pressing and holding down the Ctrl key while dragging a copy of the shape to the new location.

Project 4a Drawing Arrow Shapes   Part 1 of 2

1. At a blank document, press the Enter key two times and then draw an arrow shape by completing the following steps:
   a. Click the Insert tab.
   b. Click the Shapes button in the Illustrations group and then click the *Striped Right Arrow* shape (fifth column, second row) in the *Block Arrows* section.
   c. Position the mouse pointer (which displays as crosshairs) immediately right of the insertion point and then click the left mouse button. (This inserts the arrow shape in the document.)
2. Format the arrow by completing the following steps:
   a. Click in the *Shape Height* measurement box in the Size group, type 2.4, and then press the Enter key.
   b. Click in the *Shape Width* measurement box in the Size group, type 4.5, and then press the Enter key.

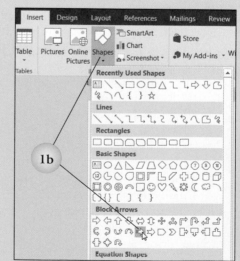

c. Horizontally align the arrow by clicking the Align button in the Arrange group and then clicking *Distribute Horizontally* at the drop-down list.

d. Click the More Shape Styles button in the Shape Styles group and then click the *Intense Effect - Green, Accent 6* option (last option at the drop-down gallery).

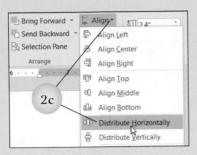

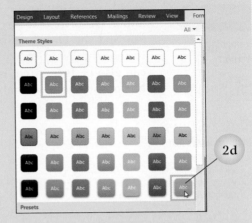

e. Click the Shape Effects button in the Shape Styles group, point to *Bevel*, and then click the *Angle* option (first column, second row in the *Bevel* section).

f. Click the Shape Outline button arrow in the Shape Styles group and then click the *Dark Blue* option (ninth option in the *Standard Colors* section).

3. Copy the arrow by completing the following steps:

   a. With the mouse pointer positioned in the arrow (mouse pointer displays with a four-headed arrow attached), press and hold down the Ctrl key and click and hold down the left mouse button. Drag down until the copied arrow displays just below the top arrow, release the mouse button, and then release the Ctrl key.

   b. Click in the document to deselect the arrows and then click the second arrow to select it.

   c. Copy the selected arrow by pressing and holding down the Ctrl key and clicking and holding down the left mouse button and then dragging the copied arrow just below the second arrow.

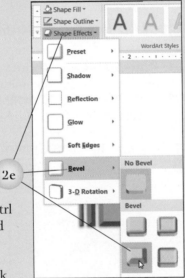

4. Flip the middle arrow by completing the following steps:

   a. Click in the document to deselect the arrows and then click the middle arrow to select it.

   b. Click the Rotate button in the Arrange group on the Drawing Tools Format tab and then click the *Flip Horizontal* option at the drop-down gallery.

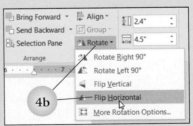

5. Insert the text *Financial* in the top arrow by completing the following steps:

   a. Click the top arrow to select it.

   b. Type Financial.

   c. Select *Financial*.

   d. Click the Home tab.

   e. Change the font size to 16 points, apply bold formatting, and change the font color to standard *Dark Blue* (ninth option in the *Standard Colors* section).

6. Complete steps similar to those in Step 5 to insert the word *Direction* in the middle arrow.

7. Complete steps similar to those in Step 5 to insert the word *Retirement* in the bottom arrow.

8. Save the document and name it **5-FinConsult**.

9. Print the document.

Check Your Work

Tutorial

Inserting, Sizing,
and Positioning
WordArt

Tutorial

Formatting
WordArt

A WordArt

Creating and Formatting WordArt

Use the WordArt feature to distort or modify text to conform to a variety of shapes. This is useful for creating company logos, letterheads, flyer titles, and headings.

To insert WordArt in a document, click the Insert tab and then click the WordArt button in the Text group. At the drop-down list, click the desired option and a WordArt text box is inserted in the document containing the words *Your text here* and the Drawing Tools Format tab is active. Type the WordArt text and then format the WordArt with options on the Drawing Tools Format tab. Existing text can also be formatted as WordArt. To do this, select the text, click the WordArt button on the Insert tab and then click the WordArt option at the drop-down list.

Quick Steps

Create WordArt Text
1. Click Insert tab.
2. Click WordArt button.
3. Click option.
4. Type WordArt text.

Project 4b Inserting and Modifying WordArt

Part 2 of 2

1. With **5-FinConsult.docx** open, press Ctrl + Home to move the insertion point to the beginning of the document.
2. Insert WordArt text by completing the following steps:
   a. Type Miller Financial Services and then select *Miller Financial Services*.
   b. Click the Insert tab.
   c. Click the WordArt button in the Text group and then click the *Fill - Orange, Accent 2, Outline - Accent 2* option (third column, first row).

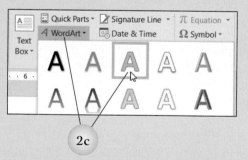

2c

3. Format the WordArt text by completing the following steps:
   a. Make sure the WordArt text border displays as a solid line.
   b. Click the Text Fill button arrow in the WordArt Styles group on the Drawing Tools Format tab and then click the *Light Green* color option (fifth option in the *Standard Colors* section).
   c. Click the Text Outline button arrow in the WordArt Styles group and then click the *Green, Accent 6, Darker 50%* option (last option in *Theme Colors* section).

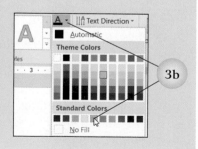

3b

d. Click the Text Effects button in the WordArt Styles group, point to *Glow*, and then click the *Blue, 5 pt glow, Accent color 1* option (first option in the *Glow Variations* section).

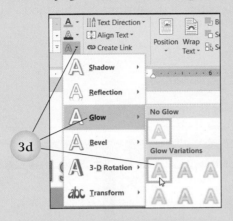

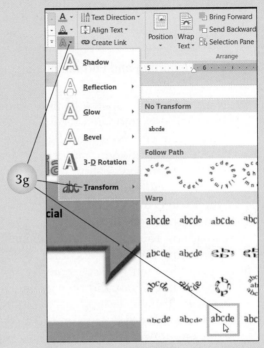

e. Click in the *Shape Height* measurement box in the Size group and then type 1.
f. Click in the *Shape Width* measurement box in the Size group, type 6, and then press the Enter key.
g. Click the Text Effects button in the WordArt Styles group, point to *Transform*, and then click the *Can Up* option (third column, fourth row in the *Warp* section).
h. Click the Position button in the Arrange group and then click the *Position in Top Center with Square Text Wrapping* option (second column, first row in the *With Text Wrapping* section).

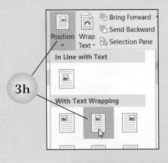

4. Click outside the WordArt to deselect it.
5. Move the arrows as needed to ensure they do not overlap the WordArt or each other and that they all fit on one page.
6. Save, print, and then close **5-FinConsult.docx**.

Check Your Work

Project 5 **Create and Format Screenshots**   **2 Parts**

You will create screenshots of the Print and Export backstage areas, screen clippings of cover pages, and a sample cover page document.

Preview Finished Project

Tutorial

Inserting and Formatting Screenshot and Screen Clipping Images

Creating and Inserting a Screenshot

The Illustrations group on the Insert tab contains a Screenshot button, which captures the contents of a screen as an image or captures a portion of a screen. To capture the entire screen, open a new document, click the Insert tab, click the Screenshot button in the Illustrations group, and then click the desired screen thumbnail at the drop-down list. The currently active document does not display

Screenshot

as a thumbnail at the drop-down list—only other documents or files that are open. Click the specific thumbnail in the drop-down list and a screenshot of the screen is inserted as an image in the open document. The screenshot image is selected and the Picture Tools Format tab is active. Use buttons on this tab to customize the screenshot image.

Project 5a Inserting and Formatting Screenshots

Part 1 of 2

1. Press Ctrl + N to open a blank document.
2. Press Ctrl + N to open a second blank document, type Print Backstage Area at the left margin, and then press the Enter key.
3. Save the document and name it **5-BackstageAreas**.
4. Point to the Word button on the taskbar and then click the thumbnail representing the blank document.

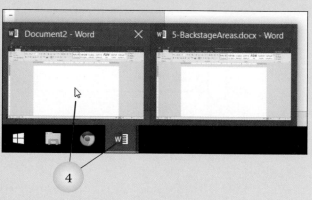

5. Display the Print backstage area by clicking the File tab and then clicking the *Print* option.
6. Point to the Word button on the taskbar and then click the thumbnail representing **5-BackstageAreas.docx**.
7. Insert and format a screenshot of the Print backstage area by completing the following steps:
   a. Click the Insert tab.
   b. Click the Screenshot button in the Illustrations group and then click the thumbnail in the drop-down list. (This inserts a screenshot of the Print backstage area in the document.)

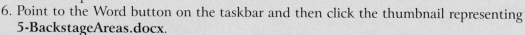

   c. With the screenshot image selected, click the *Drop Shadow Rectangle* picture style option (fourth option in the picture styles gallery).
   d. Select the measurement in the *Shape Width* measurement box in the Size group, type 5.5, and then press the Enter key.
8. Press Ctrl + End and then press the Enter key. (The insertion point should be positioned below the screenshot image.)
9. Type Export Backstage Area at the left margin and then press the Enter key.
10. Point to the Word button on the taskbar and then click the thumbnail representing the blank document.
11. At the backstage area, click the *Export* option. (This displays the Export backstage area.)
12. Point to the Word button on the taskbar and then click the thumbnail representing **5-BackstageAreas.docx**.
13. Insert and format a screenshot of the Export backstage area by completing steps similar to those in Step 7.
14. Press Ctrl + Home to move the insertion point to the beginning of the document.
15. Save, print, and then close **5-BackstageAreas.docx**.
16. At the Export backstage area, press the Esc key to redisplay the blank document.
17. Close the blank document.

Check Your Work

Not only can a screenshot be made of an entire screen, but a screenshot can also be made of a specific portion of a screen by clicking the *Screen Clipping* option at the Screenshot button drop-down list. Click this option and the other open document, file, or Windows Start screen or desktop displays in a dimmed manner and the mouse pointer displays as crosshairs. Using the mouse, draw a border around the specific area of the screen to be captured. The area identified is inserted in the other document as an image, the image is selected, and the Picture Tools Format tab is active.

Project 5b   **Creating and Formatting a Screen Clipping**   **Part 2 of 2**

1. Open **NSSLtrhd.docx** and then save it with the name **5-NSSCoverPages**.
2. Type the text Sample Cover Pages and then press the Enter key two times.
3. Select the text you just typed, change the font to 18-point Copperplate Gothic Bold, and then center the text.
4. Press Ctrl + End to move the insertion point below the text.
5. Open **NSSCoverPg01.docx** and then change the zoom to 40% by clicking six times on the Zoom Out button at the left side of the Zoom slider bar on the Status bar.
6. Point to the Word button on the taskbar and then click the thumbnail representing **5-NSSCoverPages.docx**.
7. Insert and format a screen clipping image by completing the following steps:
   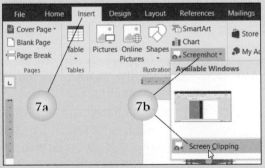
   a. Click the Insert tab.
   b. Click the Screenshot button in the Illustrations group and then click the *Screen Clipping* option.
   c. When **NSSCoverPg01.docx** displays in a dimmed manner, position the mouse crosshairs in the upper left corner of the cover page, click and hold down the left mouse button, drag down to the lower right corner of the cover page, and then release the mouse button. (See the image below and to the right.)
   d. With the cover page screen clipping image inserted in **5-NSSCoverPages.docx**, make sure the image is selected. (The sizing handles should display around the cover page image.)
   e. Click the Wrap Text button in the Arrange group on the Picture Tools Format tab and then click *Square* at the drop-down gallery.
   f. Select the current measurement in the *Shape Width* measurement box in the Size group, type 3, and then press the Enter key.

8. Point to the Word button on the Taskbar and then click the thumbnail representing **NSSCoverPg01.docx**.
9. Close **NSSCoverPg01.docx**.
10. Open **NSSCoverPg02.docx** and then, if neccessary, change the zoom to 40%.

11. Point to the Word button on the Taskbar and then click the thumbnail representing **5-NSSCoverPages.docx**.
12. Insert and format a screen clipping image of the cover page by completing steps similar to those in Step 7.
13. If necessary, position the two cover page screenshot images side by side in the document.
14. Save, print, and then close **5-NSSCoverPages.docx**.
15. Close **NSSCoverPg02.docx**.

Check Your Work

Chapter Summary

- Apply formatting to a portion of a document by inserting a continuous section break or a section break that begins a new page. Turn on the display of nonprinting characters or change to Draft view to display section breaks; they are not visible in Print Layout view.

- Set text in columns to improve the readability of documents such as newsletters and reports. Format text in columns using the Columns button in the Page Setup group on the Layout tab or with options at the Columns dialog box.

- Remove column formatting with the Columns button on the Layout tab or at the Columns dialog box. Balance column text on the last page of a document by inserting a continuous section break at the end of the text.

- Improve the display of text by hyphenating long words that fall at the ends of lines. Use the hyphenation feature to hyphenate words automatically or manually.

- To enhance the appearance of text, use drop caps to identify the beginnings of major sections or paragraphs. Create drop caps with the Drop Cap button in the Text group on the Insert tab.

- Insert symbols with options at the Symbol dialog box with the Symbols tab selected, and insert special characters with options at the Symbol dialog box with the Special Characters tab selected.

- Click the Date & Time button in the Text group on the Insert tab to display the Date and Time dialog box. Insert the date or time with options at this dialog box or with keyboard shortcuts. If the date or time is inserted as a field, update the field with the Update tab or the F9 function key.

- Use the Click and Type feature to center, right-align, and left-align text.

- Vertically align text in a document with the *Vertical alignment* option at the Page Setup dialog box with the Layout tab selected.

- Insert an image such as a picture or clip art with buttons in the Illustrations group on the Insert tab.

- To insert an image from a folder on the computer's hard drive or removable drive, click the Insert tab and then click the Pictures button. At the Insert Picture dialog box, navigate to the specific folder and then double-click the image file.

- To insert an online image, click the Insert tab and then click the Online Pictures button. At the Insert Pictures window, type the search text or topic, press the Enter key, and then double-click the image.

- Customize and format an image with options and buttons on the Picture Tools Format tab. Size an image with the *Shape Height* and *Shape Width* measurement boxes in the Size group or with the sizing handles that display around a selected image.

- Move an image using options from the Position button drop-down gallery on the Picture Tools Format tab, or by choosing a text wrapping style and then moving the image by dragging it with the mouse.

- Insert a predesigned text box using options from the Text Box button drop-down gallery on the Insert tab. A predesigned text box or drawn text box can be used to create a pull quote, which is a quote that is pulled from the document text.

- Draw a text box by clicking the Text Box button in the Text group on the Insert tab, clicking the *Draw Text Box* option at the drop-down list, and then clicking or dragging in the document.

- Customize a text box with buttons on the Drawing Tools Format tab.

- Draw shapes in a document by clicking the Shapes button in the Illustrations group on the Insert tab, clicking a shape at the drop-down list, and then clicking or dragging in the document to draw the shape. Customize a shape with options on the Drawing Tools Format tab.

- Copy a shape by pressing and holding down the Ctrl key while dragging the selected shape.

- Use WordArt to distort or modify text to conform to a variety of shapes. Customize WordArt with options on the Drawing Tools Format tab.

- Use the Screenshot button in the Illustrations group on the Insert tab to capture the contents of a screen or a portion of a screen. Use buttons on the Picture Tools Format tab to customize a screenshot image.

Commands Review

FEATURE	RIBBON TAB, GROUP	BUTTON, OPTION	KEYBOARD SHORTCUT
Column break	Layout, Page Setup	, Columns	Ctrl + Shift + Enter
columns	Layout, Page Setup		
Columns dialog box	Layout, Page Setup	, More Columns	
continuous section break	Layout, Page Setup	, Continuous	
Date and Time dialog box	Insert, Text		
drop cap	Insert, Text		
hyphenate words automatically	Layout, Page Setup	, Automatic	
insert date as field			Alt + Shift + D
Insert Picture dialog box	Insert, Illustrations		
Insert Pictures window	Insert, Illustrations		
insert time as field			Alt + Shift + T
Manual Hyphenation dialog box	Layout, Page Setup	, Manual	
Page Setup dialog box	Layout, Page Setup		
predesigned text box	Insert, Text		
screenshot	Insert, Illustrations		
shapes	Insert, Illustrations		
Symbol dialog box	Insert, Symbols	, More Symbols	
text box	Insert, Text		
update field			F9
WordArt	Insert, Text		

Workbook

Chapter study tools and assessment activities are available in the *Workbook* ebook. These resources are designed to help you further develop and demonstrate mastery of the skills learned in this chapter.

Microsoft®

Word

Maintaining Documents and Printing Envelopes and Labels

Performance Objectives

Upon successful completion of Chapter 6, you will be able to:

1 Create and rename a folder

2 Select, delete, copy, move, rename, and print documents

3 Save documents in different file formats

4 Open, close, arrange, maximize, minimize, and restore documents

5 Split a window, view documents side by side, and open a new window

6 Insert a file into an open document

7 Preview and print specific text and pages in a document

8 Print envelopes and labels

9 Create a document using a template

Almost every company that conducts business maintains a filing system. The system may consist of documents, folders, and cabinets or it may be a computerized filing system, where information is stored on the computer's hard drive or another storage medium. Whatever type of filing system a business uses, daily maintenance of files is important to its operation. In this chapter, you will learn to maintain files (documents) in Word, performing such activities as creating additional folders and copying, moving, and renaming documents. You will also learn how to create and print documents, envelopes, and labels and create a document using a Word template.

Project 1 Manage Documents

8 Parts

You will perform a variety of file management tasks, including creating and renaming a folder; selecting and then deleting, copying, cutting, pasting, and renaming documents; deleting a folder; opening multiple documents; and saving a document in a different format.

Preview Finished Project

Maintaining Documents

Hint Display the Open dialog box with the keyboard shortcut Ctrl + F12.

Many file (document) management tasks can be completed at the Open dialog box (and some at the Save As dialog box). These tasks can include copying, moving, printing, and renaming documents; opening multiple documents; and creating new folders and renaming existing folders.

Directions and projects in this chapter assume that you are managing documents and folders on a USB flash drive or your computer's hard drive. If you are using your OneDrive account, some of the document and folder management tasks may vary.

Using Print Screen

Keyboards contain a Print Screen key that will capture the contents of the screen and insert the image in temporary memory. The image can then be inserted in a Word document. Press the Print Screen key to capture the entire screen as an image or press Alt + Print Screen to capture only the dialog box or window open on the screen. The Print Screen feature is useful for file management because the folder contents can be printed to help keep track of documents and folders.

To use the Print Screen key, display the desired information on the screen and then press the Print Screen key on the keyboard (generally located in the top row) or press Alt + Print Screen to capture the dialog box or window open on the screen. When the Print Screen key or Alt + Print Screen is pressed, nothing seems to happen, but in fact, the screen image is captured and inserted in the Clipboard. To insert this image in a document, display a blank document and then click the Paste button in the Clipboard group on the Home tab. The image can also be pasted by right-clicking in a blank location in a document and then clicking the *Paste* option at the shortcut menu.

Tutorial

Managing Folders

Creating a Folder

Word documents, like paper documents, should be grouped logically and placed in folders. The main folder on a storage medium is called the *root folder* and additional folders can be created within it. At the Open or Save As dialog box, documents display in the Content pane preceded by document icons and folders display preceded by folder icons.

New folder

New folder

Create a new folder by clicking the New folder button on the dialog box toolbar. This inserts a folder in the Content pane that contains the text *New folder*. Type a name for the folder (the typed name replaces *New folder*) and then press the Enter key. A folder name can contain a maximum of 255 characters. Folder names can use numbers, spaces, and symbols, except those symbols explained in the *Naming a Document* section on page 8 in Chapter 1.

Quick Steps

Create a Folder
1. Display Open dialog box.
2. Click New folder button.
3. Type folder name.
4. Press Enter.

To make the new folder active, double-click the folder name in the Open dialog box Content pane. The current folder path displays in the Address bar and includes the current folder and any previous folders. If the folder is located on an external storage device, the drive letter and name may display in the path. A right-pointing triangle displays to the right of each folder name in the Address bar. Click this right-pointing triangle and a drop-down list displays the names of any subfolders within the folder.

Project 1a Creating a Folder

Part 1 of 8

1. Open a blank document and then press Ctrl + F12 to display the Open dialog box.
2. In the *This PC* list in the Navigation pane, click the drive containing your storage medium. (You may need to scroll down the list to display the drive.)
3. Double-click the *WL1C6* folder in the Content pane.
4. Click the New folder button on the dialog box toolbar.
5. Type Correspondence and then press the Enter key.
6. Capture the Open dialog box as an image and insert the image in a document by completing the following steps:
   a. With the Open dialog box displayed, hold down the Alt key and then press the Print Screen key on your keyboard (generally located in the top row).
   b. Close the Open dialog box.
   c. At the blank document, click the Paste button in the Clipboard group on the Home tab. (If a blank document does not display on your screen, press Ctrl + N to open a blank document.)
   d. With the print screen image inserted in the document, print the document by clicking the File tab, clicking the *Print* option, and then clicking the Print button at the Print backstage area.
7. Close the document without saving it.
8. Display the Open dialog box and make WL1C6 the active folder.

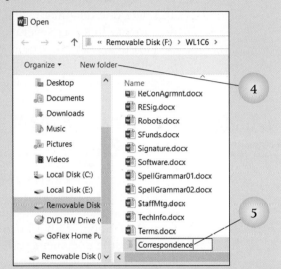

Check Your Work

Renaming a Folder

Organize ▾

Organize

Quick Steps

Rename a Folder
1. Display Open dialog box.
2. Right-click folder.
3. Click *Rename*.
4. Type new name.
5. Press Enter.

When organizing files and folders, a folder may need to be renamed. Rename a folder using the Organize button on the toolbar in the Open or Save As dialog box or using a shortcut menu. To rename a folder using the Organize button, display the Open or Save As dialog box, click the folder to be renamed, click the Organize button on the toolbar in the dialog box, and then click *Rename* at the drop-down list. This selects the folder name and inserts a border around it. Type the new name for the folder and then press the Enter key. To rename a folder using a shortcut menu, display the Open dialog box, right-click the folder name in the Content pane, and then click *Rename* at the shortcut menu. Type a new name for the folder and then press the Enter key.

1. With the Open dialog box open, right-click the *Correspondence* folder name in the Content pane.
2. Click *Rename* at the shortcut menu.
3. Type ComputerDocs and then press the Enter key.

Selecting Documents

Complete document management tasks on one document or selected documents. To select one document, display the Open dialog box and then click the desired document. To select several adjacent documents (documents that display next to each other), click the first document, hold down the Shift key, and then click the last document. To select documents that are not adjacent, click the first document, hold down the Ctrl key, click any other documents, and then release the Ctrl key.

Tutorial

Managing Documents

Quick Steps

Delete a Folder or Document
1. Display Open dialog box.
2. Click folder or document name.
3. Click Organize button.
4. Click *Delete*.
5. Click Yes.

Hint Remember to empty the Recycle Bin on a regular basis.

Deleting Documents

Deleting documents is part of document maintenance. To delete a document, display the Open or Save As dialog box, select the document, click the Organize button on the toolbar, and then click *Delete* at the drop-down list. If documents are being deleted from an external drive, such as a USB flash drive, click the Yes button at the confirmation message. This message does not display if a document is being deleted from the computer's hard drive. To delete a document using the shortcut menu, right-click the document name in the Content pane and then click *Delete* at the shortcut menu. If a confirmation message displays, click Yes.

Documents deleted from the hard drive are automatically sent to the Recycle Bin. If a document is accidentally sent to the Recycle Bin, it can be easily restored. To free space on the drive, empty the Recycle Bin on a periodic basis. Restoring a document from or emptying the contents of the Recycle Bin is completed at the Windows desktop (not in Word). To display the Recycle Bin, minimize the Word window, display the Windows desktop, and then double-click the *Recycle Bin* icon on the Windows desktop. At the Recycle Bin, files can be restored and the Recycle Bin can be emptied.

1. Open **FutureHardware.docx** and save it with the name **6-FutureHardware**.
2. Close **6-FutureHardware.docx**.
3. Delete **6-FutureHardware.docx** by completing the following steps:
   a. Display the Open dialog box.
   b. Click *6-FutureHardware.docx* to select it.
   c. Click the Organize button on the toolbar and then click *Delete* at the drop-down list.
   d. At the question asking if you want to delete **6-FutureHardware.docx**, click Yes. (This question will not display if you are deleting the file from your computer's hard drive.)
4. Delete selected documents by completing the following steps:
   a. At the Open dialog box, click *CompCareers.docx*.
   b. Hold down the Shift key and then click *CompEthics.docx*.
   c. Position the mouse pointer on a selected document and then click the right mouse button.
   d. At the shortcut menu, click *Delete*.
   e. At the question asking if you want to delete the items, click Yes.

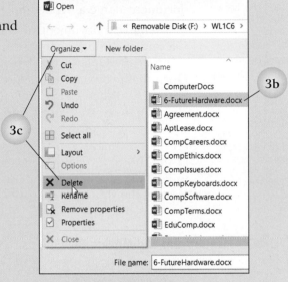

5. Open **CompKeyboards.docx** and save it with the name **6-CompKeyboards**.
6. Save a copy of the **6-CompKeyboards.docx** file in the ComputerDocs folder by completing the following steps:
   a. With **6-CompKeyboards.docx** open, press the function key F12 to display the Save As dialog box.
   b. At the Save As dialog box, double-click the *ComputerDocs* folder at the top of the Content pane. (Folders are listed before documents.)
   c. Click the Save button in the lower right corner of the dialog box.
7. Close **6-CompKeyboards.docx**.
8. Press Ctrl + F12 to display the Open dialog box and then click *WL1C6* in the Address bar.

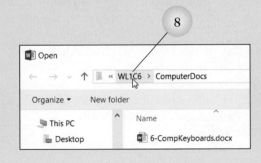

Copying and Moving Documents

Copy a Document
1. Display Open dialog box.
2. Right-click document name.
3. Click *Copy*.
4. Navigate to folder.
5. Right-click blank area in Content pane.
6. Click *Paste*.

Move a Document
1. Display Open dialog box.
2. Right-click document name.
3. Click *Cut*.
4. Navigate to folder.
5. Right-click blank area in Content pane.
6. Click *Paste*.

A document can be copied to another folder without opening the document first. To do this, use the *Copy* and *Paste* options from the Organize button drop-down list or the shortcut menu at the Open dialog box or the Save As dialog box. A document or selected documents also can be copied into the same folder. When a document is copied a second time into the same folder, Word adds to the document name a hyphen followed by the word *Copy*.

Remove a document from one folder and insert it in another folder using the *Cut* and *Paste* options from the Organize button drop-down list or the shortcut menu at the Open dialog box. To do this with the Organize button, display the Open dialog box, select the document to be removed (cut), click the Organize button, and then click *Cut* at the drop-down list. Navigate to the desired folder, click the Organize button, and then click *Paste* at the drop-down list. To do this with the shortcut menu, display the Open dialog box, position the arrow pointer on the document to be removed, click the right mouse button, and then click *Cut* at the shortcut menu. Navigate to the desired folder, position the arrow pointer in a blank area in the Content pane, click the right mouse button, and then click *Paste* at the shortcut menu.

Project 1d Copying and Moving Documents

Note: If you are using your OneDrive account, the steps for copying and moving files will vary from the steps in this project. Check with your instructor.

1. At the Open dialog box with WL1C6 the active folder, copy a document to another folder by completing the following steps:
   a. Click **CompTerms.docx** in the Content pane, click the Organize button, and then click *Copy* at the drop-down list.
   b. Navigate to the ComputerDocs folder by double-clicking *ComputerDocs* at the top of the Content pane.
   c. Click the Organize button and then click *Paste* at the drop-down list.
2. Change back to the WL1C6 folder by clicking *WL1C6* in the Address bar.
3. Copy several documents to the ComputerDocs folder by completing the following steps:
   a. Click **IntelProp.docx**. (This selects the document.)
   b. Hold down the Ctrl key, click **Robots.docx**, click **TechInfo.docx**, and then release the Ctrl key. (You may need to scroll down the Content pane to display the three documents and then select the documents.)
   c. Position the arrow pointer on one of the selected documents, click the right mouse button, and then click *Copy* at the shortcut menu.
   d. Double-click the *ComputerDocs* folder.
   e. Position the arrow pointer in any blank area in the Content pane, click the right mouse button, and then click *Paste* at the shortcut menu.
4. Click *WL1C6* in the Address bar.

5. Move **CompIssues.docx** to the ComputerDocs folder by completing the following steps:
   a. Position the arrow pointer on ***CompIssues.docx***, click the right mouse button, and then click *Cut* at the shortcut menu.
   b. Double-click *ComputerDocs* to make it the active folder.
   c. Position the arrow pointer in any blank area in the Content pane, click the right mouse button, and then click *Paste* at the shortcut menu.
6. Capture the Open dialog box as an image and insert the image in a document by completing the following steps:
   a. With the Open dialog box displayed, press Alt + Print Screen.
   b. Close the Open dialog box.
   c. At a blank document, click the Paste button in the Clipboard group on the Home tab. (If a blank document does not display on your screen, press Ctrl + N to open a blank document.)
   d. With the print screen image inserted in the document, print the document.
7. Close the document without saving it.
8. Display the Open dialog box and make WL1C6 the active folder.

Check Your Work

Renaming Documents

Quick Steps
Rename a Document
1. Display Open dialog box.
2. Click document name.
3. Click Organize button and then click *Rename*.
4. Type new name.
5. Press Enter.

At the Open dialog box, use the *Rename* option from the Organize button drop-down list to give a document a different name. The *Rename* option changes the name of the document and keeps it in the same folder. To rename a document, display the Open dialog box, click the document to be renamed, click the Organize button, and then click *Rename* at the drop-down list. This selects the name and displays a black border around the document name. Type the new name and then press the Enter key. A document can also be renamed by right-clicking the document name at the Open dialog box and then clicking *Rename* at the shortcut menu. Type the new name for the document and then press the Enter key.

Deleting a Folder

As explained earlier in this chapter, a document or selected documents can be deleted. Delete a folder and all of its contents in the same manner as deleting a document.

Hint Open a recently opened document by clicking the File tab, clicking the *Open* option, and then clicking the document in the *Recent* option list.

Opening Multiple Documents

To open more than one document, select the documents in the Open dialog box and then click the Open button. Multiple documents can also be opened by positioning the arrow pointer on one of the selected documents, clicking the right mouse button, and then clicking *Open* at the shortcut menu.

Changing Dialog Box View

Use options in the Change your view button drop-down list at the Open or Save As dialog box to customize the display of folders and documents in the Content pane. Click the Change your view button arrow and a drop-down list displays with options for displaying folders and documents as icons, a list, with specific details, as tiles, or in content form. Change the view by clicking an option at the drop-down list or by clicking the Change your view button until the dialog box displays in the desired view.

1. Rename a document in the ComputerDocs folder by completing the following steps:
   a. At the Open dialog box with the WL1C6 folder open, double-click the *ComputerDocs* folder to make it active.
   b. Click **Robots.docx** to select it.
   c. Click the Organize button.
   d. Click *Rename* at the drop-down list.
   e. Type Androids and then press the Enter key.
2. Capture the Open dialog box as an image and insert the image in a document by completing the following steps:
   a. Press Alt + Print Screen.
   b. Close the Open dialog box.
   c. At a blank document, click the Paste button in the Clipboard group on the Home tab. (If a blank document does not display on your screen, press Ctrl + N to open a blank document.)
   d. With the print screen image inserted in the document, print the document.
3. Close the document without saving it.
4. Display the Open dialog box and make WL1C6 the active folder.
5. Change the dialog box view by clicking the Change your view button arrow and then clicking *Large icons* at the drop-down list.
6. Change the view again by clicking the Change your view button arrow and then clicking *Content* at the drop-down list.
7. Change the view back to a list by clicking the Change your view button and then clicking *List* at the drop-down list.
8. At the Open dialog box, click the *ComputerDocs* folder to select it.
9. Click the Organize button and then click *Delete* at the drop-down list.
10. If a message displays asking if you want to remove the folder and its contents, click Yes.
11. Select **CompKeyboards.docx**,**CompSoftware.docx**, and **CompTerms.docx**.
12. Click the Open button in the lower right corner of the dialog box.
13. Close the open documents.

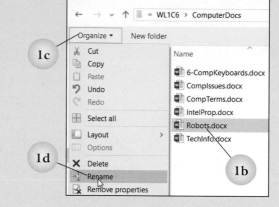

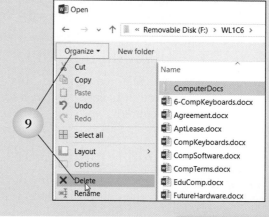

Check Your Work

Tutorial

Saving in a Different Format

Saving in a Different Format

When a document is saved, it is saved as a Word document with the .docx file extension. If the document is to be shared with someone who is using a different word processing program or a different version of Word, consider saving the document in another format. At the Export backstage area, click the *Change File Type* option and the backstage area displays, as shown in Figure 6.1.

Quick Steps

Save in a Different Format
1. Click File tab.
2. Click *Export* option.
3. Click *Change File Type* option.
4. Click format in *Document File Types* or *Other File Types* section.
5. Click Save As button.

Saving in Different Document File Types Use options in the *Document File Types* section, which is below the *Change File Type* heading, to save the Word document with the default file format, in a previous version of Word, in the OpenDocument Text format, or as a template. The OpenDocument Text format is an XML-based file format for displaying, storing, and editing files, such as word processing, spreadsheet, and presentation files. OpenDocument Text format is free from any licensing, royalty payments, or other restrictions. Since technology changes at a rapid pace, saving a document in the OpenDocument Text format ensures that the information in it can be accessed, retrieved, and used now and in the future.

Saving in Other File Types Additional file types are available in the *Other File Types* section. If a document is being sent to a user who does not have access to Microsoft Word, consider saving the document in plain text or rich text file format. Use the *Plain Text (*.txt)* option to save the document with all the formatting stripped, which is good for universal file exchange. Use the *Rich Text Format (*.rtf)* option to save the document with most of the character formatting applied to the text in the document, such as bold, italic, underline, bullets, and fonts, as well as some paragraph formatting. Before the widespread use of Adobe's portable document format (PDF), rich text format was the most portable file format used to exchange files. With the *Single File Web Page (*.mht, *.mhtml)* option, a document can be saved as a single-page web document. Click the *Save as Another File Type* option and the Save As dialog box displays. Click the *Save as type* option box and a drop-down list displays with a variety of available file type options.

Figure 6.1 Export Backstage Area with *Change File Type* Option Selected

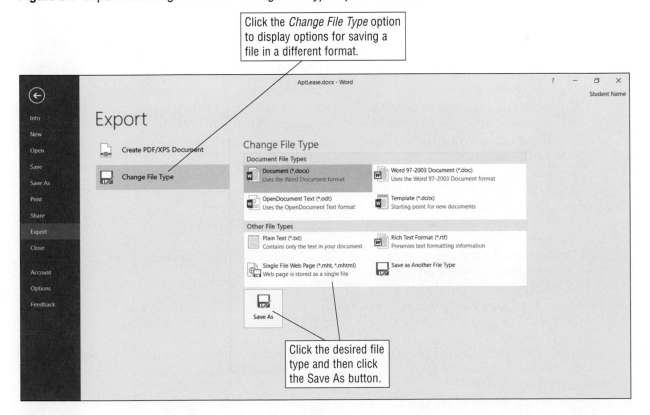

1. Open **AptLease.docx** and then save it in Word 97-2003 format by completing the following steps:
   a. Click the File tab and then click the *Export* option.
   b. At the Export backstage area, click the *Change File Type* option.
   c. Click the *Word 97-2003 Document (*.doc)* option in the *Document File Types* section and then click the Save As button.

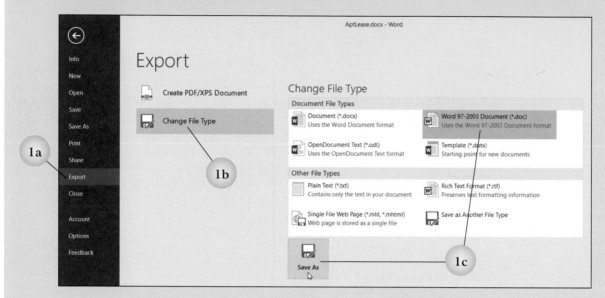

   d. At the Save As dialog box with the *Save as type* option changed to *Word 97-2003 Document (*.doc)*, type 6-AptLease-Word97-2003 in the *File name* text box and then press the Enter key.
2. At the document, notice that the title bar displays *[Compatibility Mode]* after the document name.
3. Click the Design tab and notice that the Themes, Colors, and Fonts buttons are dimmed. (This is because the themes features were not available in Word 97 through 2003.)
4. Close **6-AptLease-Word97-2003.doc**.
5. Open **AptLease.docx**.
6. Save the document in plain text format by completing the following steps:
   a. Click the File tab and then click the *Export* option.
   b. At the Export backstage area, click the *Change File Type* option.
   c. Click the *Plain Text (*.txt)* option in the *Other File Types* section and then click the Save As button.
   d. At the Save As dialog box, type 6-AptLease-PlainTxt and then press the Enter key.
   e. At the File Conversion dialog box, click OK.
7. Close **6-AptLease-PlainTxt.txt**.
8. Display the Open dialog box and, if necessary, display all the files. To do this, click the file type button at the right side of the *File name* text box and then click *All Files (*.*)* at the drop-down list.
9. Double-click ***6-AptLease-PlainTxt.txt***. (If a File Conversion dialog box displays, click OK. Notice that the character and paragraph formatting have been removed from the document.)
10. Close **6-AptLease-PlainTxt.txt**.

Check Your Work

Quick Steps

Save in a Different Format at the Save As Dialog Box
1. Press F12 to display Save As dialog box.
2. Type document name.
3. Click *Save as type* option box.
4. Click format.
5. Click Save button.

Saving in a Different File Type at the Save As Dialog Box In addition to saving a document using options in the Export backstage area with the *Change File Type* option selected, a document can be saved in a different format using the *Save as type* option box at the Save As dialog box. Click the *Save as type* option box and a drop-down list displays containing all the available file formats for saving a document. Click the desired format and then click the Save button.

Project 1g Saving in a Different Format at the Save As Dialog Box

Part 7 of 8

1. Open **AptLease.docx**.
2. Save the document in rich text format by completing the following steps:
   a. Press the function key F12 to display the Save As dialog box.
   b. At the Save As dialog box, type 6-AptLease-RichTxt in the *File name* text box.
   c. Click the *Save as type* option box.
   d. Click *Rich Text Format (*.rtf)* at the drop-down list.
   e. Click the Save button.
3. Close the document.
4. Display the Open dialog box and, if necessary, display all the files.
5. Double-click *6-AptLease-RichTxt.rtf*. (Notice that the formatting has been retained in the document.)
6. Close the document.

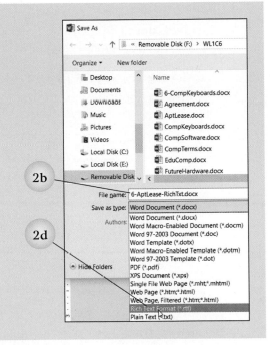

Tutorial

Saving and Opening a Document in PDF Format

Saving in PDF/XPS Format A Word document can be saved in PDF or XPS file format. PDF stands for *portable document format* and is a file format that preserves fonts, formatting, and images in a printer-friendly version that looks the same on most computers. A person who receives a Word file saved in PDF format does not need to have the Word application on his or her computer to open, read, and print the file. Exchanging PDF files is a popular method for collaborating, since this file type has cross-platform compatibility, allowing users to open PDF files on Windows-based personal computers, Macintosh computers, tablets, and smartphones. The XML paper specification (XPS) format, which was developed by Microsoft, is a fixed-layout format with all the formatting preserved (similar to PDF).

To save a document in PDF or XPS format, click the File tab, click the *Export* option, and then click the Create PDF/XPS button. This displays the Publish as PDF or XPS dialog box with the *PDF (*.pdf)* option selected in the *Save as type* option box. To save the document in XPS format, click the *Save as type* option box and then click *XPS Document (*.xps)* at the drop-down list. At the Save As dialog box, type a name in the *File name* text box and then click the Publish button.

A PDF file will open in Adobe Acrobat Reader, Microsoft Edge, and Word 2016. An XPS file will open in Internet Explorer and XPS Viewer. One method for opening a PDF or XPS file is to open File Explorer navigate, to the folder containing the file, right-click the file, and then point to *Open with*. This displays a side menu with the programs that can be used to open the file. A PDF file can be opened and edited in Word but an XPS file cannot.

Project 1h   Saving in PDF Format and Editing a PDF File in Word

Part 8 of 8

1. Open **NSS.docx** and then save the document in PDF format by completing the following steps:
   a. Click the File tab and then click the *Export* option.
   b. At the Export backstage area, click the Create PDF/XPS button.
   c. At the Publish as PDF or XPS dialog box, make sure that *PDF (*.pdf)* is selected in the *Save as type* option box and that the *Open file after publishing* check box contains a check mark. After confirming both selections, click the Publish button.

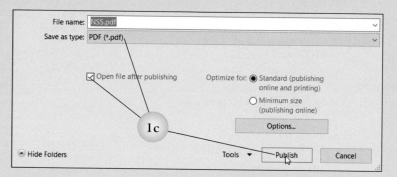

2. Scroll through the document in Adobe Acrobat Reader and then close Acrobat Reader by clicking the Close button in the upper right corner of the window.
3. Close **NSS.docx**.
4. In Word, open the **NSS.pdf** file you saved to your WL1C6 folder. At the message telling you that Word will convert the file to an editable Word document, click the OK button.
5. Notice that the formatting of the text is slightly different from the original formatting and that the graphic has been moved to the second page. Edit the file by completing the following steps:
   a. Click the Design tab and then click the *Lines (Distinctive)* style set.
   b. Delete the text *We are* in the text below the first heading and replace it with Northland Security Systems is.
6. Save the file with Save As and name it **6-NSS**. (The file will be saved in the .docx file format.)
7. Print and then close **6-NSS.docx**.
8. Display the Open dialog box, capture the Open dialog box as an image, and then close the Open dialog box. Press Ctrl + N to open a blank document, paste the image in the document, print the document, and then close the document without saving it.

Check Your Work

<table>
<tr><td>

Project 2 **Manage Multiple Documents**   **7 Parts**

You will arrange, maximize, restore, and minimize windows; move selected text between split windows; compare formatting of documents side by side; and print specific text, pages, and multiple copies.

</td></tr>
</table>

Working with Windows

Tutorial

Working with Windows

Multiple documents can be opened in Word. The insertion point can be moved between the documents and information can be moved or copied from one document and pasted into another. When a new document is opened, it displays on top of any previously opened document. With multiple documents open, the window containing each document can be resized to see all or a portion of it on the screen.

💡 **Hint** Press Ctrl + F6 to switch between open documents.

When a document is open, a Word button displays on the taskbar. Hover the mouse pointer over this button and a thumbnail of the document displays above the button. If more than one document is open, another Word button displays behind the first button in a cascading manner with only a portion of the button displaying at the right side of the first button. If multiple documents are open, hovering the mouse pointer on the Word button or clicking the Word button on the taskbar will display thumbnails of all the documents above the buttons. To make a change to a document, click the thumbnail that represents the document.

💡 **Hint** Press Ctrl + W or Ctrl + F4 to close the active document window.

 Switch Windows

Another method for determining what documents are open is to click the View tab and then click the Switch Windows button in the Window group. The document name in the list with the check mark in front of it is the active document. The active document contains the insertion point. To make a different document active, click the document name. To switch to another document using the keyboard, type the number shown in front of the desired document.

Arranging Windows

Quick Steps

Arrange Windows
1. Open documents.
2. Click View tab.
3. Click Arrange All button.

 Arrange All

If several documents are open, they can be arranged so a portion of each displays. The portion that displays includes the title (if present) and the opening paragraph of each document. To arrange a group of open documents, click the View tab and then click the Arrange All button in the Window group.

Maximizing, Restoring, and Minimizing Documents

Use the Maximize and Minimize buttons in the upper right corner of the active document to change the size of the window. The two buttons are at the left of the Close button. (The Close button is in the upper right corner of the screen and contains an X.)

 Maximize

 Minimize

🔲 Restore

If all of the open documents are arranged on the screen, clicking the Maximize button in the active document causes that document to expand to fill the screen. In addition, the Maximize button changes to the Restore button. To return the active document back to its original size, click the Restore button. Click the Minimize button in the active document and the document is reduced and a button displays on the taskbar representing it. To maximize a document that has been minimized, click the button on the taskbar representing it.

Note: If you are using Word on a network system that contains a virus checker, you may not be able to open multiple documents at once. Continue by opening each document individually.

1. Open the following documents: **AptLease.docx**, **CompSoftware.docx**, **IntelProp.docx**, and **NSS.docx**.
2. Arrange the windows by clicking the View tab and then clicking the Arrange All button in the Window group.

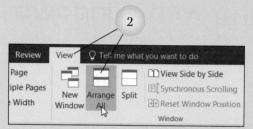

3. Make **AptLease.docx** the active document by clicking the Switch Windows button in the Window group on the View tab of the document at the top of your screen and then clicking *AptLease.docx* at the drop-down list.
4. Close **AptLease.docx**.
5. Make **IntelProp.docx** active and then close it.
6. Make **CompSoftware.docx** active and minimize it by clicking the Minimize button in the upper right corner of the active window.

7. Maximize **NSS.docx** by clicking the Maximize button immediately left of the Close button.
8. Close **NSS.docx**.
9. Restore **CompSoftware.docx** by clicking the button on the taskbar that represents the document.
10. Maximize **CompSoftware.docx**.

Splitting a Window

A window can be split into two panes, which is helpful for viewing different parts of a document at one time. For example, display an outline for a report in one pane and the part of the report to be edited in the other pane. The original window is split into two panes that extend horizontally across the screen.

Split a window by clicking the View tab and then clicking the Split button in the Window group. This splits the window in two with a split bar and another horizontal ruler. The location of the split bar can be changed by positioning the mouse pointer on the split bar until it displays as an up-and-down-pointing arrow with two small lines in the middle, holding down the left mouse button, dragging to the new location, and then releasing the mouse button.

When a window is split, the insertion point is positioned in the bottom pane. To move the insertion point to the other pane with the mouse, position the I-beam pointer in the other pane and then click the left mouse button. To remove the split bar from the document, click the View tab and then click the Remove Split button in the Window group. The split bar can also be double-clicked or dragged to the top or bottom of the screen.

Project 2b Moving Selected Text between Split Windows

Part 2 of 7

1. With **CompSoftware.docx** open, save the document and name it **6-CompSoftware**.
2. Click the View tab and then click the Split button in the Window group.

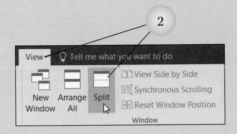

3. Move the first section below the second section by completing the following steps:
   a. Click in the top pane and then click the Home tab.
   b. Select the section *SECTION 1: PERSONAL-USE SOFTWARE* from the title to right above *SECTION 2: GRAPHICS AND MULTIMEDIA SOFTWARE*.
   c. Click the Cut button in the Clipboard group in the Home tab.
   d. Click in the bottom pane and then move the insertion point to the end of the document.
   e. Click the Paste button in the Clipboard group on the Home tab.
   f. Reverse the numbers in the two titles to *SECTION 1: GRAPHICS AND MULTIMEDIA SOFTWARE* and *SECTION 2: PERSONAL-USE SOFTWARE*.
4. Remove the split from the window by clicking the View tab and then clicking the Remove Split button in the Window group.
5. Press Ctrl + Home to move the insertion point to the beginning of the document.
6. Save **6-CompSoftware.docx**.

Check Your Work

Viewing Documents Side by Side

View Side by Side

Synchronous Scrolling

Öuick Steps
View Documents Side by Side
1. Open two documents.
2. Click View tab.
3. Click View Side by Side button.

The contents of two documents can be compared on screen by opening both documents, clicking the View tab, and then clicking the View Side by Side button in the Window group. Both documents are arranged on the screen side by side, as shown in Figure 6.2. By default, synchronous scrolling is active. With this feature active, scrolling in one document causes the same scrolling in the other document. This feature is useful for comparing the text, formatting, or another feature between documents. To scroll in one document and not the other, click the Synchronous Scrolling button in the Window group to turn it off.

Figure 6.2 Viewing Documents Side by Side

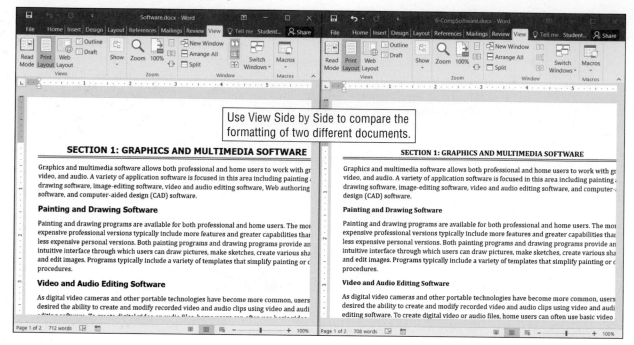

Use View Side by Side to compare the formatting of two different documents.

Project 2c Viewing Documents Side by Side

Part 3 of 7

1. With **6-CompSoftware.docx** open, open **Software.docx**.
2. Click the View tab and then click the View Side by Side button in the Window group.
3. Scroll through both documents simultaneously. Notice the difference between the two documents. (The titles and headings are set in different fonts and colors.) Select and then format the title and headings in **6-CompSoftware. docx** so they match the formatting in **Software.docx**. *Hint: Use the Format Painter button to copy the formats.*
4. Turn off synchronous scrolling by clicking the Synchronous Scrolling button in the Window group on the View tab.
5. Scroll through the document and notice that no scrolling occurs in the other document.
6. Make **Software.docx** the active document and then close it.
7. Save **6-CompSoftware.docx**.

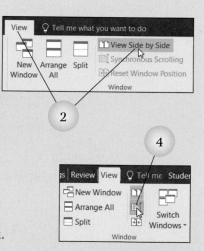

Check Your Work

Quick Steps

Open a New Window
1. Open document.
2. Click View tab.
3. Click New Window button.

 New Window

Opening a New Window

In addition to splitting a document to view two locations of the same document, a new window can be opened that contains the same document. When a new window is opened, the document name in the Title bar displays followed by *:2*. The document name in the original window displays followed by *:1*. Any change made to the document in one window is reflected in the document in the other window.

1. With **6-CompSoftware.docx** open, open a new window by clicking the New Window button in the Window group on the View tab. (Notice that the document name in the Title bar displays followed by *:2*.)
2. Click the View tab and then click the View Side by Side button in the Window group.
3. Click the Synchronous Scrolling button to turn off synchronous scrolling.
4. With the **6-CompSoftware.docx:2** window active, look at the first paragraph of text and notice the order in which the software is listed in the last sentence (painting and drawing software, image-editing software, video and audio editing software, and computer-aided design [CAD] software).
5. Click in the **6-CompSoftware.docx:1** window and then cut and paste the headings and text so the software displays in the order listed in the paragraph.
6. Click the Save button on the Quick Access Toolbar.
7. Close the second version of the document by clicking the Word buttons on the taskbar and then clicking the Close button in the upper right corner of the **6-CompSoftware. docx:2** thumbnail (above the Word button on the taskbar).

Check Your Work

Tutorial

Inserting a File

Object

Inserting a File

The contents of one document can be inserted into another using the Object button in the Text group on the Insert tab. Click the Object button arrow and then click *Text from File* and the Insert File dialog box displays. This dialog box contains similar features as the Open dialog box. Navigate to the desired folder and then double-click the document to be inserted in the open document.

Quick Steps
Insert a File
1. Click Insert tab.
2. Click Object button arrow.
3. Click *Text from File*.
4. Navigate to folder.
5. Double-click document.

1. With **6-CompSoftware.docx** open, move the insertion point to the end of the document.
2. Insert a file into the open document by completing the following steps:
   a. Click the Insert tab.
   b. Click the Object button arrow in the Text group and then click *Text from File* at the drop-down list.
   c. At the Insert File dialog box, navigate to the WL1C6 folder and then double-click *EduComp.docx*.
3. Save **6-CompSoftware.docx**.

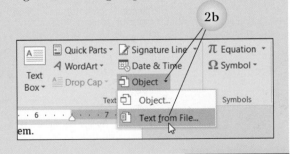

Check Your Work

Previewing and Printing

Use options at the Print backstage area, shown in Figure 6.3, to specify what is to be printed and to preview pages before printing them. To display the Print backstage area, click the File tab and then click the *Print* option.

Previewing Pages

Hint Display the Print backstage area with the keyboard shortcut Ctrl + P.

Zoom to Page

At the Print backstage area, a preview of the page where the insertion point is positioned displays at the right side (see Figure 6.3). Click the Next Page button (right-pointing triangle) below and to the left of the page, to view the next page in the document and click the Previous Page button (left-pointing triangle) to display the previous page in the document. Use the Zoom slider bar to increase or decrease the size of the page and click the Zoom to Page button to fit the page in the viewing area in the Print backstage area.

Figure 6.3 Print Backstage Area

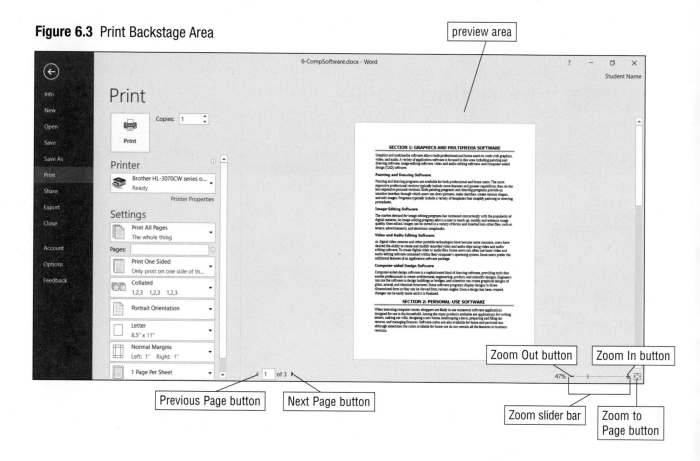

1. With **6-CompSoftware.docx** open, press Ctrl + Home to move the insertion point to the beginning of the document.
2. Preview the document by clicking the File tab and then clicking the *Print* option.
3. Click the Zoom In button (plus symbol) at the right side of the Zoom slider bar two times. (This increases the size of the preview page.)
4. At the Print backstage area, click the Next Page button below and to the left of the preview page. (This displays page 2 in the preview area.)
5. Click the Zoom Out button (minus [-] symbol) at the left side of the Zoom slider bar, until two pages of the document display in the preview area.
6. Change the zoom at the Zoom dialog box by completing the following steps:
   a. Click the percentage number at the left side of the Zoom slider bar.
   b. At the Zoom dialog box, click the *Many pages* option in the *Zoom to* section.
   c. Click OK to close the dialog box. (Notice that all pages in the document display as thumbnails in the preview area.)
7. Click the Zoom to Page button at the right side of the Zoom slider bar. (This returns the page to the default size.)
8. Click the Back button to return to the document.

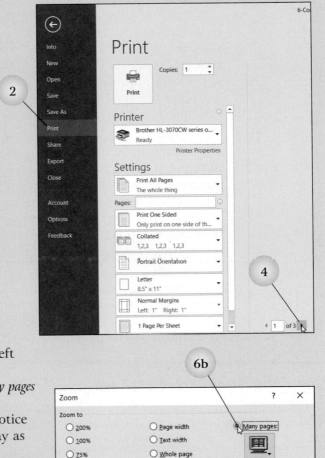

Printing Specific Text and Pages

💡 **Hint** Save a document before printing it.

Control what prints in a document with options at the Print backstage area. Click the first gallery in the *Settings* category and a drop-down list displays with options for printing all the pages in the document, selected text, the current page, or a custom range of pages.

Print a portion of a document by selecting the text and then choosing the *Print Selection* option at the Print backstage area. With this option, only the selected text in the document prints. (This option is dimmed unless text is selected in the document.) Click the *Print Current Page* option to print only the page on which the insertion point is located. Use the *Custom Print* option to identify a specific page, multiple pages, or a range of pages to print. To print specific pages, use a comma (,) to indicate *and* and use a hyphen (-) to indicate *through*. For example, to print pages 2 and 5, type 2,5 in the *Pages* text box and to print pages 6 through 10, type 6-10.

With the other galleries available in the *Settings* category of the Print backstage area, specify whether to print on one or both sides of the page, change the page orientation (portrait or landscape), specify how the pages are collated, choose a paper size, and specify margins of a document. The last gallery contains options for printing 1, 2, 4, 6, 8, or 16 pages of a multiple-page document on one sheet of paper. This gallery also contains the *Scale to Paper Size* option. Click this option and then use the side menu to choose the paper size to scale the document.

To print more than one copy of a document, use the *Copies* measurement box to the right of the Print button. If several copies of a multiple-page document are printed, Word collates the pages as they print. For example, if two copies of a three-page document are printed, pages 1, 2, and 3 print and then the pages print a second time. Printing collated pages is helpful for assembling them but takes more printing time. To reduce printing time, tell Word *not* to print collated pages by clicking the *Collated* gallery in the *Settings* category and then clicking *Uncollated*.

To send a document directly to the printer without displaying the Print backstage area, consider adding the Quick Print button to the Quick Access Toolbar. To do this, click the Customize Quick Access Toolbar button at the right side of the toolbar, and then click *Quick Print* at the drop-down gallery. Click the Quick Print button and all the pages of the active document print.

Project 2g Printing Specific Text and Pages

1. With **6-CompSoftware.docx** open, print selected text by completing the following steps:
   a. Select the heading *Painting and Drawing Software* and the paragraph of text that follows it.
   b. Click the File tab and then click the *Print* option.
   c. At the Print backstage area, click the first gallery in the *Settings* category (displays with *Print All Pages*) and then click *Print Selection* at the drop-down list.
   d. Click the Print button.
2. Change the margins and page orientation and then print only the first page by completing the following steps:
   a. Press Ctrl + Home to move the insertion point to the beginning of the document.

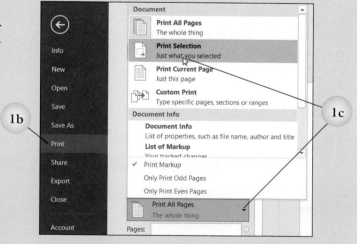

b. Click the File tab and then click the *Print* option.

c. At the Print backstage area, click the fourth gallery (displays with *Portrait Orientation)* in the *Settings* category and then click *Landscape Orientation* at the drop-down list.

d. Click the sixth gallery (displays with *Normal Margins*) in the *Settings* category and then click *Narrow* at the drop-down list.

e. Click the first gallery (displays with *Print All Pages*) in the *Settings* category and then click *Print Current Page* at the drop-down list.

f. Click the Print button. (The first page of the document prints in landscape orientation with 0.5-inch margins.)

3. Print all the pages as thumbnails on one page by completing the following steps:

a. Click the File tab and then click the *Print* option.

b. At the Print backstage area, click the bottom gallery (displays with *1 Page Per Sheet*) in the *Settings* category and then click *4 Pages Per Sheet* at the drop-down list.

c. Click the first gallery (displays with *Print Current Page*) in the *Settings* category and then click *Print All Pages* at the drop-down list.

d. Click the Print button.

4. Select the entire document, change the line spacing to 1.5 lines, and then deselect the text.

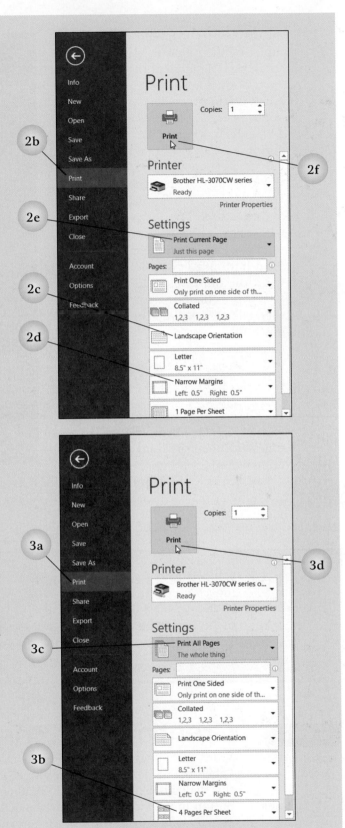

5. Print two copies of specific pages by completing the following steps:
   a. Click the File tab and then click the *Print* option.
   b. Click the fourth gallery (displays with *Landscape Orientation*) at the *Settings* category and then click *Portrait Orientation* in the drop-down list.
   c. Click in the *Pages* text box below the first gallery in the *Settings* category, and then type 1,3.
   d. Click the *Copies* measurement box up arrow (located to the right of the Print button) to display *2*.
   e. Click the third gallery (displays with *Collated*) in the *Settings* category and then click *Uncollated* at the drop-down list.
   f. Click the bottom gallery (displays with *4 Pages Per Sheet*) in the *Settings* category and then click *1 Page Per Sheet* at the drop-down list.
   g. Click the Print button. (The first page of the document will print two times and then the third page will print two times.)
6. Save and then close **6-CompSoftware.docx**.

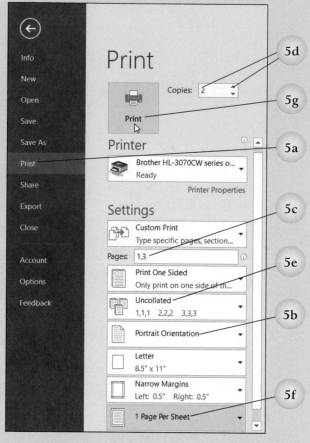

Check Your Work

Project 3 Create and Print Envelopes

2 Parts

You will create an envelope document and type the return address and delivery address using envelope addressing guidelines issued by the United States Postal Service. You will also open a letter document and then create an envelope using the inside address.

Preview Finished Project

Tutorial

Preparing an Envelope

 Envelopes

Creating and Printing Envelopes

Word automates the creation of envelopes with options at the Envelopes and Labels dialog box with the Envelopes tab selected, as shown in Figure 6.4. Display this dialog box by clicking the Mailings tab and then clicking the Envelopes button in the Create group. At the dialog box, type the delivery address in the *Delivery address* text box and the return address in the *Return address* text box. Send the envelope directly to the printer by clicking the Print button or insert the envelope in the current document by clicking the Add to Document button.

Figure 6.4 Envelopes and Labels Dialog Box with Envelopes Tab Selected

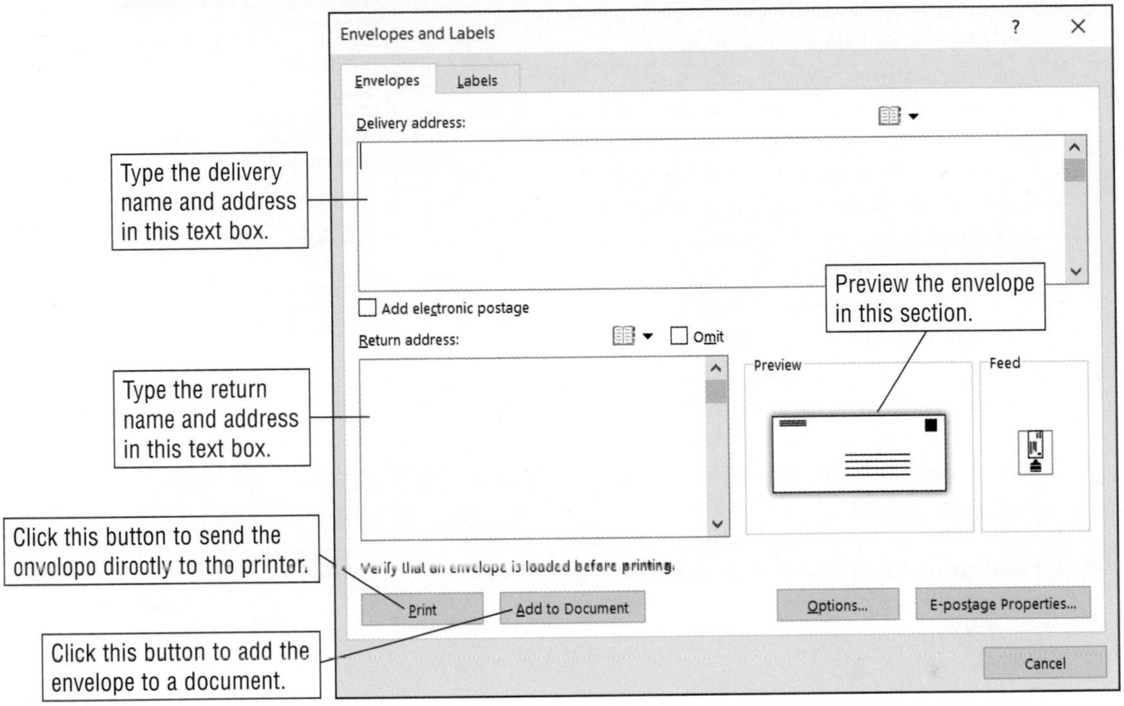

Type the delivery name and address in this text box.

Preview the envelope in this section.

Type the return name and address in this text box.

Click this button to send the envelope directly to the printer.

Click this button to add the envelope to a document.

Create an Envelope
1. Click Mailings tab.
2. Click Envelopes button.
3. Type delivery address.
4. Click in *Return address* text box.
5. Type return address.
6. Click Add to Document button or Print button.

If a return address is entered before printing the envelope, Word will display the question *Do you want to save the new return address as the default return address?* At this question, click Yes to save the current return address for future envelopes or click No if the return address should not be used as the default. By default, the return address in the *Return address* text box will print on the envelope. To omit the printing of the return address, insert a check mark in the *Omit* check box.

The Envelopes and Labels dialog box contains a *Preview* sample box and a *Feed* sample box. The *Preview* sample box shows how the envelope will appear when printed and the *Feed* sample box shows how the envelope should be inserted into the printer.

When addressing envelopes, consider following general guidelines issued by the United States Postal Service (USPS). The USPS guidelines suggest using all capital letters with no commas or periods for return and delivery addresses. Figure 6.5 shows envelope addresses that follow the USPS guidelines. Use abbreviations for street suffixes (such as *ST* for *Street* and *AVE* for *Avenue*). For a complete list of address abbreviations, visit the USPS.com website and then search for *Official USPS Abbreviations*.

Project 3a Printing an Envelope

Part 1 of 2

1. At a blank document, create an envelope that prints the delivery address and return address shown in Figure 6.5. Begin by clicking the Mailings tab.
2. Click the Envelopes button in the Create group.

3. At the Envelopes and Labels dialog box with the Envelopes tab selected, type the delivery address shown in Figure 6.5 (the one containing the name *GREGORY LINCOLN*). (Press the Enter key to end each line in the name and address.)
4. Click in the *Return address* text box. (If any text displays in the *Return address* text box, select and then delete it.)
5. Type the return address shown in Figure 6.5 (the one containing the name *WENDY STEINBERG*). (Press the Enter key to end each line in the name and address.)
6. Click the Add to Document button.
7. At the message *Do you want to save the new return address as the default return address?*, click No.
8. Save the document and name it **6-Env**.
9. Print and then close **6-Env.docx**. *Note: Manual feed of the envelope may be required. Please check with your instructor.*

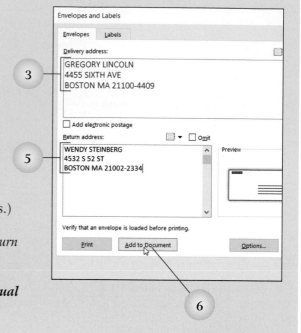

Check Your Work

Figure 6.5 Project 3a

```
WENDY STEINBERG
4532 S 52 ST
BOSTON MA 21002-2334




                    GREGORY LINCOLN
                    4455 SIXTH AVE
                    BOSTON MA 21100-4409
```

If the Envelopes and Labels dialog box opens in a document containing a name and address (each name and address line must end with a press of the Enter key and not Shift + Enter), the name and address are automatically inserted in the *Delivery address* text box in the dialog box. The name and address are inserted in the *Delivery address* text box as they appear in the document and may not conform to the USPS guidelines. The USPS guidelines for addressing envelopes are only suggestions, not requirements. Word automatically inserts the first name and address in a document in the *Delivery address* text box if the name and address lines end with a press of the Enter key. A different name and address in a document with each line ending in a press of the Enter key can be inserted in the *Delivery address* text box by selecting the name and address and then displaying the Envelopes and Labels dialog box.

1. Open **LAProg.docx**.
2. Click the Mailings tab.
3. Click the Envelopes button in the Create group.
4. At the Envelopes and Labels dialog box (with the Envelopes tab selected), make sure the delivery address displays properly in the *Delivery address* text box.
5. If any text displays in the *Return address* text box, insert a check mark in the *Omit* check box (located to the right of the *Return address* option). (This tells Word not to print the return address on the envelope.)
6. Click the Print button.
7. Close **LAProg.docx** without saving the changes.

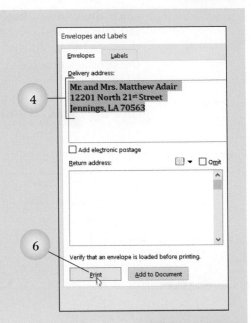

Check Your Work

Project 4 **Create Labels**   **2 Parts**

You will create mailing labels containing different names and addresses, labels with the same name and address, and labels with an image.

Preview Finished Project

Creating and Printing Labels

Use Word's labels feature to print text on mailing labels, file labels, disc labels, and other types of labels. Word includes a variety of predefined formats for the brands and sizes of labels that can be purchased at most office supply stores. Use the Labels feature to create a sheet of mailing labels with different names and addresses on each label or the same name and address or image on each label.

Tutorial

Creating Mailing Labels with Different Names and Addresses

 Labels

Creating Mailing Labels with Different Names and Addresses

To create a sheet of mailing labels with different names and addresses on each label, click the Labels button in the Create group on the Mailings tab. At the Envelopes and Labels dialog box with the Labels tab selected, as shown in Figure 6.6, leave the *Address* text box empty and then click the New Document button to insert the labels in a new document. The insertion point is positioned in the first label. Type the name and address in the label and then press the Tab key one or two times (depending on the label) to move the insertion point to the next label. Pressing Shift + Tab will move the insertion point to the preceding label.

Changing Label Options

Click the Options button at the Envelopes and Labels dialog box with the Labels tab selected and the Label Options dialog box displays, as shown in Figure 6.7. At the Label Options dialog box, choose the type of printer, the label product, and the product number. This dialog box also displays information about the selected label, such as type, height, width, and paper size. When a label is selected, Word automatically determines the label margins. To customize these default settings, click the Details button at the Label Options dialog box.

Figure 6.6 Envelopes and Labels Dialog Box with Labels Tab Selected

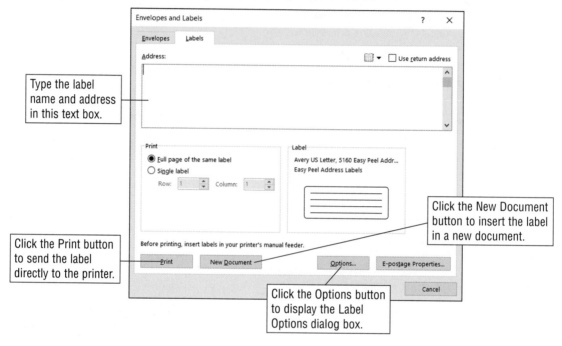

Type the label name and address in this text box.

Click the Print button to send the label directly to the printer.

Click the New Document button to insert the label in a new document.

Click the Options button to display the Label Options dialog box.

Figure 6.7 Label Options Dialog Box

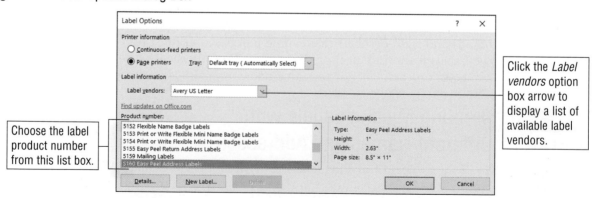

Click the *Label vendors* option box arrow to display a list of available label vendors.

Choose the label product number from this list box.

Project 4a Creating Mailing Labels with Different Names and Addresses

Part 1 of 2

1. At a blank document, click the Mailings tab.
2. Click the Labels button in the Create group.
3. At the Envelopes and Labels dialog box with the Labels tab selected, click the Options button.
4. At the Label Options dialog box, click the *Label vendors* option box arrow and then click *Avery US Letter* at the drop-down list.
5. Scroll down the *Product number* list box and then click *5160 Easy Peel Address Labels*.
6. Click OK or press the Enter key.
7. At the Envelopes and Labels dialog box, click the New Document button.
8. At the document screen, type the first name and address shown in Figure 6.8 in the first label.
9. Press the Tab key two times to move the insertion point to the next label and then type the second name and address shown in Figure 6.8.
10. Continue in this manner until all the names and addresses shown in Figure 6.8 have been typed. (After typing the third name and address, you only need to press the Tab key once to move the insertion point to the first label in the second row.)
11. Save the document and name it **6-Labels**.
12. Print and then close **6-Labels.docx**.
13. Close the blank document without saving changes.

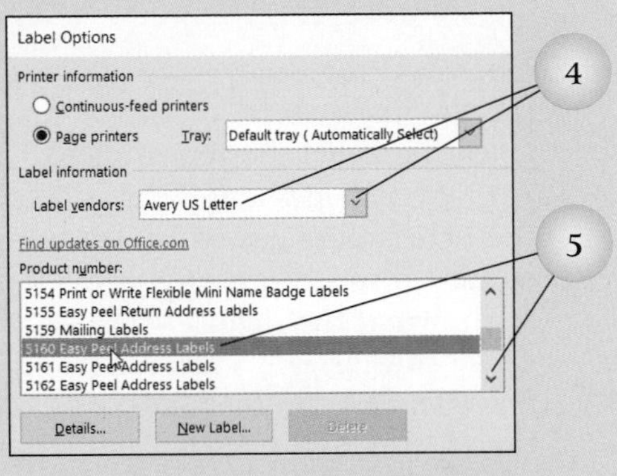

Check Your Work

Tutorial

Creating Mailing Labels with the Same Name and Address and an Image

Creating Mailing Labels with the Same Name and Address

To create labels with the same name and address on each label, open a document containing the desired name and address, click the Mailings tab, and then click the Labels button. At the Envelopes and Labels dialog box, make sure the desired label vendor and product number are selected and then click the New Document button. Another method for creating labels with the same name and address is to display the Envelopes and Labels dialog box with the Labels tab selected, type the name and address in the *Address* text box, and then click the New Document button.

Creating Mailing Labels with an Image

Labels can be created with a graphic image, such as a company's logo and address or a company's slogan. To create labels with an image, insert the image in a

Figure 6.8 Project 4a

DAVID LOWRY 12033 S 152 ST HOUSTON TX 77340	MARCELLA SANTOS 394 APPLE BLOSSOM FRIENDSWOOD TX 77533	KEVIN DORSEY 26302 PRAIRIE DR HOUSTON TX 77316
AL AND DONNA SASAKI 1392 PIONEER DR BAYTOWN TX 77903	JACKIE RHYNER 29039 107 AVE E HOUSTON TX 77302	MARK AND TINA ELLIS 607 FORD AVE HOUSTON TX 77307

document, select the image, click the Mailings tab. and then click the Labels button. At the Envelopes and Labels dialog box, make sure the desired label vendor and product number are selected and then click the New Document button.

Project 4b   Creating Mailing Labels with the Same Name and Address and an Image   Part 2 of 2

1. Open **LAProg.docx** and create mailing labels with the delivery address. Begin by clicking the Mailings tab.
2. Click the Labels button in the Create group.
3. At the Envelopes and Labels dialog box with the Labels tab selected, make sure the delivery address displays properly in the *Address* text box as shown at the right.
4. Make sure *Avery US Letter, 5160 Easy Peel Address Labels* displays in the *Label* section; if not, refer to Steps 3 through 6 of Project 4a to select the label type.
5. Click the New Document button.
6. Save the mailing label document and name it **6-LAProg.docx**.
7. Print and then close **6-LAProg.docx**.
8. Close **LAProg.docx**.
9. At a blank document, insert an image by completing the following steps:
   a. Click the Insert tab and then click the Pictures button in the Illustrations group.
   b. At the Insert Picture dialog box, make sure the WL1C6 folder on your storage medium is active and then double-click **BGCLabels.png**.
10. With the image selected in the document, click the Mailings tab and then click the Labels button.
11. At the Envelopes and Labels dialog box, make sure *Avery US Letter, 5160 Easy Peel Address Labels* displays in the *Label* section and then click the New Document button.
12. Save the document and name it **6-BGCLabels**.
13. Print and then close **6-BGCLabels.docx**.
14. Close the document containing the image without saving changes.

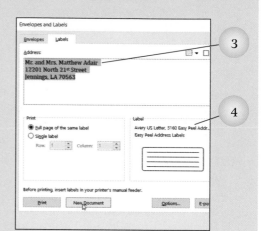

Check Your Work

Project 5   Use a Template to Create a Business Letter   1 Part

You will use a letter template provided by Word to create a business letter.

Preview Finished Project

Tutorial

Creating a Document Using a Template

Creating a Document Using a Template

Word includes a number of template documents that are formatted for specific uses. Each Word document is based on a template document and the Normal template is the default. Use Word templates to create a variety of documents with special formatting, such as letters, calendars, and awards.

Figure 6.9 New Backstage Area

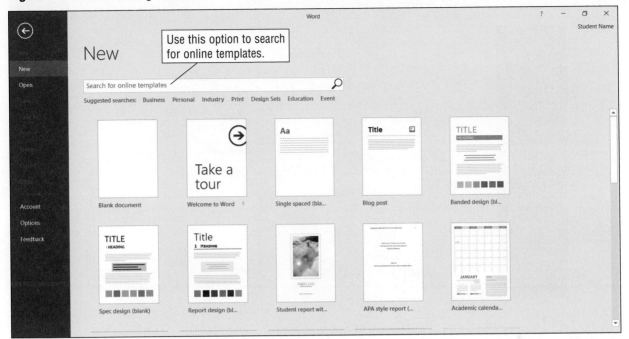

Display templates by clicking the File tab and then clicking the *New* option. This displays the New backstage area, as shown in Figure 6.9. Open one of the templates in the New backstage area by clicking the template. This opens a document based on the template, not the template file.

In addition to the templates that display at the New backstage area, templates can be downloaded from the Internet. To do this, click in the search text box, type the search text or category, and then press the Enter key. Templates that match the search text or category display in the New backstage area. Click the desired template and then click the Create button or double-click the template. This downloads the template and opens a document based on it. Locations for personalized text may display in placeholders in the document. Click the placeholder text and then type the personalized text.

If a template is used on a regular basis, consider pinning it to the New backstage area. To do this, search for the template, hover the mouse pointer over it, and then click the left-pointing stick pin (Pin to list) to the right of the template name. To unpin a template, click the down-pointing stick pin (Unpin from list).

Project 5 Creating a Letter Using a Template   Part 1 of 1

1. Click the File tab and then click the *New* option.
2. At the New backstage area, click in the search text box, type letter, and then press the Enter key.
3. When templates display that match *letter*, notice the *Category* list box at the right side of the New backstage area.
4. Click the *Business* option in the *Category* list box. (This displays only business letter templates.)

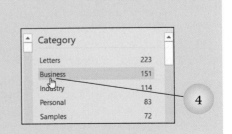

5. Scroll down the template list and then double-click the *Letter (Equity theme)* template.

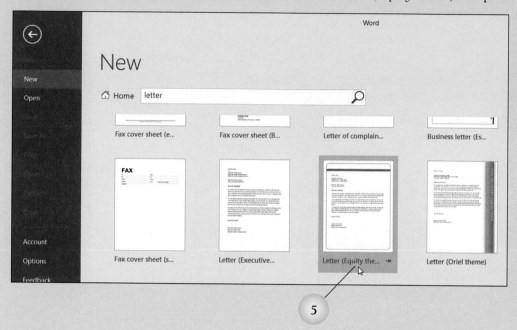

6. When the letter document displays on the screen, click the *[Pick the date]* placeholder, click the placeholder down arrow, and then click the Today button at the bottom of the calendar.

7. Click in the name below the date, select the name, and then type your first and last names.

8. Click the *[Type the sender company name]* placeholder and then type Sorenson Funds.

9. Click the *[Type the sender company address]* placeholder, type 6250 Aurora Boulevard, press the Enter key, and then type Baltimore, MD 20372.

10. Click the *[Type the recipient name]* placeholder and then type Ms. Jennifer Gonzalez.

11. Click the *[Type the recipient address]* placeholder, type 12990 Boyd Street, press the Enter key, and then type Baltimore, MD 20375.

12. Click the *[Type the salutation]* placeholder and then type Dear Ms. Gonzalez:.

13. Insert a file in the document by completing the following steps:
    a. Click anywhere in the three paragraphs of text in the body of the letter and then press the Delete key.
    b. Click the Insert tab.
    c. Click the Object button arrow in the Text group and then click *Text from File* at the drop-down list.
    d. At the Insert File dialog box, navigate to the WL1C6 folder on your storage medium and then double-click **SFunds.docx**.
    e. Press the Backspace key to delete a blank line.

14. Click the *[Type the closing]* placeholder and then type Sincerely,.

15. If your name does not display above the *[Type the sender title]* placeholder, select the name and then type your first and last names.

16. Click the *[Type the sender title]* placeholder and then type Financial Consultant.

17. Save the document and name it **6-SFunds**. (If a message displays notifying you that the document will be upgraded to the newest file format, click OK.)

18. Print and then close **6-SFunds.docx**.

Check Your Work

Chapter Summary

- Group Word documents logically into folders. Create a new folder at the Open or Save As dialog box.

- One document or several documents can be selected at the Open dialog box. Copy, move, rename, delete, or open a document or selected documents.

- Use the *Cut*, *Copy*, and *Paste* options from the Organize button drop-down list or the Open dialog box shortcut menu to move or copy a document from one folder to another.

- Delete documents and/or folders with the *Delete* option from the Organize button drop-down list or shortcut menu.

- Click the *Change File Type* option at the Export backstage area and options display for saving the document in a different file format. Documents can also be saved in different file formats with the *Save as type* option box at the Save As dialog box.

- Move among open documents by hovering the mouse pointer over the Word button on the taskbar and then clicking the thumbnail of the document or by clicking the View tab, clicking the Switch Windows button in the Window group, and then clicking the document name.

- View portions of all open documents by clicking the View tab and then clicking the Arrange All button in the Window group.

- Use the Minimize, Restore, and Maximize buttons in the upper right corner of the window to reduce or increase the size of the active window.

- Divide a window into two panes by clicking the View tab and then clicking the Split button in the Window group.

- View the contents of two open documents side by side by clicking the View tab and then clicking the View Side by Side button in the Window group.

- Open a new window containing the same document by clicking the View tab and then clicking the New Window button in the Window group.

- Insert a document into the open document by clicking the Insert tab, clicking the Object button arrow, and then clicking *Text from File* at the drop-down list. At the Insert File dialog box, double-click the document.

- Preview a document at the Print backstage area. Scroll through the pages in the document with the Next Page and the Previous Page buttons, which display below the preview page. Use the Zoom slider bar to increase or decrease the display size of the preview page.

- Use options at the Print backstage area to customize the print job by changing the page orientation, size, and margins; specify how many pages to print on one page; indicate the number of copies and whether to collate the pages; and specify the printer.

- Create and print an envelope at the Envelopes and Labels dialog box with the Envelopes tab selected.

- If the Envelopes and Labels dialog box is opened in a document containing a name and address (with each line ending with a press of the Enter key), that information is automatically inserted in the *Delivery address* text box in the dialog box.

- Use Word's labels feature to print text on mailing labels, file labels, disc labels, and other types of labels. Create labels at the Envelopes and Labels dialog box with the Labels tab selected.

- Available templates display in the New backstage area. Double-click a template to open a document based on it. Search for templates online by typing in the search text or category in the search text box and then pressing the Enter key.

Commands Review

FEATURE	RIBBON TAB, GROUP	BUTTON, OPTION	KEYBOARD SHORTCUT
arrange documents	View, Window		
Envelopes and Labels dialog box with Envelopes tab selected	Mailings, Create		
Envelopes and Labels dialog box with Labels tab selected	Mailings, Create		
Export backstage area	File, *Export*		
Insert File dialog box	Insert, Text	, *Text from File*	
maximize document			Ctrl + F10
minimize document			
New backstage area	File, *New*		
new window	View, Window		
Open dialog box	File, *Open*	*Browse*	Ctrl + F12
Print backstage area	File, *Print*		Ctrl + P
restore document to previous size			
Save As dialog box	File, *Save As*	*Browse*	F12
split window	View, Window		Alt + Ctrl + S
switch windows	View, Window		
synchronous scrolling	View, Window		
view documents side by side	View, Window		

Workbook

Chapter study tools and assessment activities are available in the *Workbook* ebook. These resources are designed to help you further develop and demonstrate mastery of the skills learned in this chapter.

Microsoft®
Word

Creating Tables and SmartArt

Performance Objectives

Upon successful completion of Chapter 7, you will be able to:

1   Create a table

2   Change the table design and layout

3   Convert text to a table and a table to text

4   Draw a table

5   Insert a Quick Table

6   Perform calculations on data in a table

7   Insert an Excel spreadsheet

8   Create, format, and modify a SmartArt graphic

Precheck

Check your current skills to help focus your study.

Some Word data can be organized in a table, which is a combination of columns and rows. Use the Tables feature to insert data in columns and rows. This data can consist of text, values, and formulas. In this chapter, you will learn how to create and format a table and insert and format data in it. Word also includes a SmartArt feature that provides a number of predesigned graphics. In this chapter, you will learn how to use these graphics to create diagrams and organizational charts.

Data Files

Before beginning chapter work, copy the WL1C7 folder to your storage medium and then make WL1C7 the active folder.

SNAP

If you are a SNAP user, launch the Precheck and Tutorials from your Assignments page.

Tutorial

Creating a Table

Table

Quick Steps

Create a Table
1. Click Insert tab.
2. Click Table button.
3. Point to create number of columns and rows.
4. Click mouse button.
OR
1. Click Insert tab.
2. Click Table button.
3. Click *Insert Table*.
4. Specify number of columns and rows.
5. Click OK.

Hint You can create a table within a table, creating a *nested* table.

Creating a Table

Use the Tables feature to create boxes of information called *cells*. A cell is the intersection between a row and a column. A cell can contain text, characters, numbers, data, graphics, or formulas. Create a table by clicking the Insert tab, clicking the Table button, moving the mouse pointer down and to the right in the drop-down grid until the correct numbers of rows and columns display, and then clicking the mouse button. A table can also be created with options at the Insert Table dialog box. Display this dialog box by clicking the Table button in the Tables group on the Insert tab and then clicking *Insert Table* at the drop-down list.

Figure 7.1 shows an example of a table with four columns and four rows. Various parts of the table are identified in Figure 7.1, such as the gridlines, move table column marker, end-of-cell marker, end-of-row marker, table move handle, and resize handle. In a table, nonprinting characters identify the ends of cells and the ends of rows. To view these characters, click the Show/Hide ¶ button in the Paragraph group on the Home tab. The end-of-cell marker displays inside each cell and the end-of-row marker displays at the end of each row of cells. These markers are identified in Figure 7.1.

When a table is created, the insertion point is positioned in the cell in the upper left corner of the table. Each cell in a table has a cell designation. Columns in a table are lettered from left to right beginning with *A*. Rows in a table are numbered from top to bottom beginning with *1*. The cell in the upper left corner of the table is cell A1. The cell to the right of A1 is B1, the cell to the right of B1 is C1, and so on.

When the insertion point is positioned in a cell in the table, move table column markers display on the horizontal ruler. These markers represent the ends of columns and are useful in changing the widths of columns. Figure 7.1 identifies a move table column marker.

Figure 7.1 Table with Nonprinting Characters Displayed

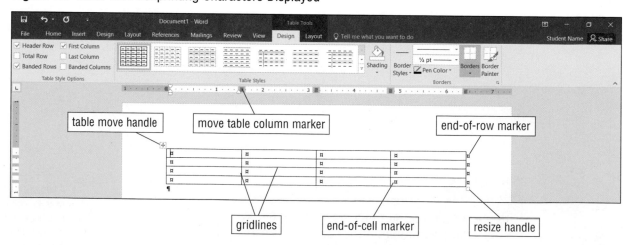

Entering Text in Cells

Hint Pressing the Tab key in a table moves the insertion point to the next cell. Pressing Ctrl + Tab moves the insertion point to the next tab within a cell.

With the insertion point positioned in a cell, type or edit text. Move the insertion point to another cell with the mouse by clicking in the cell. To move the insertion point to another cell using the keyboard, press the Tab key to move to the next cell or press Shift + Tab to move to the preceding cell.

If the text typed in a cell does not fit on one line, it wraps to the next line within the same cell, or if the Enter key is pressed within a cell, the insertion point moves to the next line within the same cell. The cell vertically lengthens to accommodate the text and all cells in that row also lengthen. Pressing the Tab key in a table causes the insertion point to move to the next cell in the table. To move the insertion point to a tab within a cell, press Ctrl + Tab. If the insertion point is in the last cell of the table, pressing the Tab key adds another row to the table. Insert a page break within a table by pressing Ctrl + Enter. The page break is inserted between rows, not within a row.

Moving the Insertion Point within a Table

To use the mouse to move the insertion point to a different cell within the table, click in the specific cell. To use the keyboard to move the insertion point to a different cell within the table, refer to the information shown in Table 7.1.

Table 7.1 Insertion Point Movement within a Table Using the Keyboard

To move the insertion point	Press
to next cell	Tab
to preceding cell	Shift + Tab
forward one character	Right Arrow key
backward one character	Left Arrow key
to previous row	Up Arrow key
to next row	Down Arrow key
to first cell in row	Alt + Home
to last cell in row	Alt + End
to top cell in column	Alt + Page Up
to bottom cell in column	Alt + Page Down

1. At a blank document, turn on bold formatting and then type the title CONTACT INFORMATION, as shown in Figure 7.2.
2. Turn off bold formatting and then press the Enter key.
3. Create the table shown in Figure 7.2 by completing the following steps:
   a. Click the Insert tab.
   b. Click the Table button in the Tables group.
   c. Move the mouse pointer down and to the right in the drop-down grid until the label above the grid displays as *3x5 Table* and then click the left mouse button.

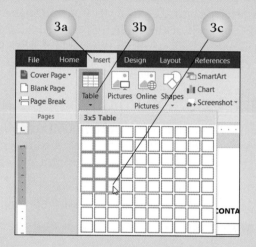

4. Type the text in the cells as indicated in Figure 7.2. Press the Tab key to move to the next cell and press Shift + Tab to move to the preceding cell. (If you accidentally press the Enter key within a cell, immediately press the Backspace key. Do not press the Tab key after typing the text in the last cell. If you do, another row is inserted in the table. If this happens, immediately click the Undo button on the Quick Access Toolbar.)
5. Save the table and name it **7-Tables**.

Check Your Work

Figure 7.2 Project 1a

CONTACT INFORMATION

Maggie Rivera	First Trust Bank	(203) 555-3440
Les Cromwell	Madison Trust	(602) 555-4900
Cecilia Nordyke	American Financial	(509) 555-3995
Regina Stahl	United Fidelity	(301) 555-1201
Justin White	Key One Savings	(360) 555-8963

Using the Insert Table Dialog Box

A table can also be created with options at the Insert Table dialog box, shown in Figure 7.3. To display this dialog box, click the Insert tab, click the Table button in the Tables group, and then click *Insert Table*. At the Insert Table dialog box, enter the numbers of columns and rows and then click OK.

Figure 7.3 Insert Table Dialog Box

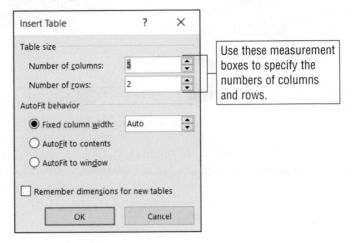

Use these measurement boxes to specify the numbers of columns and rows.

Project 1b **Creating a Table with the Insert Table Dialog Box**   **Part 2 of 8**

1. With **7-Tables.docx** open, press Ctrl + End to move the insertion point below the table.
2. Press the Enter key two times.
3. Turn on bold formatting and then type the title OPTIONAL PLAN PREMIUM RATES, as shown in Figure 7.4.
4. Turn off bold formatting and then press the Enter key.
5. Click the Insert tab, click the Table button in the Tables group, and then click *Insert Table* at the drop-down list.
6. At the Insert Table dialog box, type 3 in the *Number of columns* measurement box. (The insertion point is automatically positioned in this measurement box.)
7. Press the Tab key (this moves the insertion point to the *Number of rows* measurement box) and then type 5.
8. Click OK.
9. Type the text in the cells as indicated in Figure 7.4. Press the Tab key to move to the next cell and press Shift + Tab to move to the preceding cell. To indent the text in cells B2 through B5 and cells C2 through C5, press Ctrl + Tab to move the insertion point to a tab within a cell and then type the text.
10. Save **7-Tables.docx**.

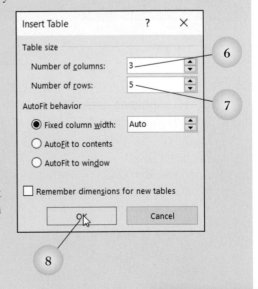

Check Your Work

Figure 7.4 Project 1b

OPTIONAL PLAN PREMIUM RATES

Waiting Period	Basic Plan Employees	Plan 2018 Employees
60 days	0.67%	0.79%
90 days	0.49%	0.59%
120 days	0.30%	0.35%
180 days	0.23%	0.26%

Changing the Table Design

When a table is created, the Table Tools Design tab is active. This tab contains a number of options for enhancing the appearance of the table, as shown in Figure 7.5. With options in the Table Styles group, apply a predesigned style that adds color and border lines to a table and shading to cells. Maintain further control over the predesigned style formatting applied to columns and rows with options in the Table Style Options group. For example, if the table contains a total row, insert a check mark in the *Total Row* check box. Apply a predesigned table style with options in the Table Styles group.

 Border Styles

Border Painter

Use options in the Borders group to customize the borders of cells in a table. Click the Border Styles button to display a drop-down list of predesigned border lines. Use other buttons in the Borders group to change the line style, width, and color; add or remove borders; and apply the same border style to other cells with the Border Painter button.

Figure 7.5 Table Tools Design Tab

Project 1c Applying Table Styles

Part 3 of 8

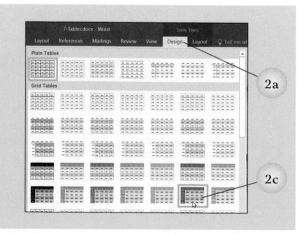

1. With **7-Tables.docx** open, click in any cell in the top table.
2. Apply a table style by completing the following steps:
   a. Make sure the Table Tools Design tab is active.
   b. Click the More Table Styles button in the table styles gallery in the Table Styles group.
   c. Click the *Grid Table 5 Dark - Accent 5* table style (sixth column, fifth row in the *Grid Tables* section).

3. After looking at the table, you realize that the first row is not a header row and the first column should not be formatted differently from the other columns. To format the first row and the first column in the same manner as the other rows and columns, click the *Header Row* check box and the *First Column* check box in the Table Style Options group to remove the check marks.

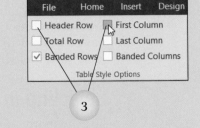

4. Click in any cell in the bottom table and then apply the List Table 6 Colorful - Accent 5 table style (sixth column, sixth row in the *List Tables* section).
5. Add color borders to the top table by completing the following steps:
   a. Click in any cell in the top table.
   b. Click the Pen Color button arrow in the Borders group on the Table Tools Design tab and then click the *Orange, Accent 2, Darker 50%* color option (sixth column, bottom row in the *Theme Colors* section).
   c. Click the *Line Weight* option box arrow in the Borders group and then click *1½ pt* at the drop-down list. (When you choose a line weight, the Border Painter button is automatically activated.)

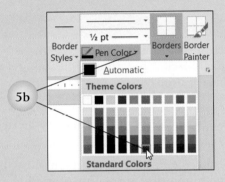
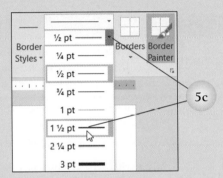

   d. Using the mouse (the mouse pointer displays as a pen), drag along all four sides of the table. (As you drag with the mouse, a thick brown line is inserted. If you make a mistake or the line does not display as you intended, click the Undo button and then continue drawing along each side of the table.)
6. Click the Border Styles button arrow and then click the *Double solid lines, 1/2 pt, Accent 2* option (third column, third row in the *Theme Borders* section).
7. Drag along all four sides of the bottom table.
8. Click the Border Painter button to turn off the feature.
9. Save **7-Tables.docx**.

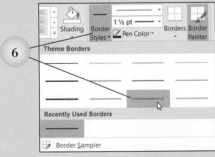

Check Your Work

Selecting Cells

Data within a table can be formatted in several ways. For example, the alignment of text within cells or rows can be changed, rows or columns can be selected and then moved or copied, and character formatting can be applied to text, such as bold, italic, and underlining. To format specific cells, rows, or columns, select the cells.

Selecting in a Table with the Mouse

Use the mouse pointer to select a cell, row, or column or to select an entire table. Table 7.2 describes methods for selecting in a table with the mouse. The left edge of each cell, between the left column border and the end-of-cell marker or first character in the cell, is called the cell selection bar. Position the mouse pointer in the cell selection bar and it turns into a small black arrow that points up and to the right. Each row in a table contains a row selection bar, which is the space just left of the left edge of the table. Position the mouse pointer in the row selection bar and the mouse pointer turns into a white arrow that points up and to the right.

Table 7.2 Selecting in a Table with the Mouse

To select this	Do this
cell	Position the mouse pointer in the cell selection bar at the left edge of the cell until it turns into a small black arrow that points up and to the right and then click the left mouse button.
row	Position the mouse pointer in the row selection bar at the left edge of the table until it turns into an arrow that points up and to the right and then click the left mouse button.
column	Position the mouse pointer on the uppermost horizontal gridline of the table in the appropriate column until it turns into a small black arrow that points down and then click the left mouse button.
adjacent cells	Position the mouse pointer in the first cell to be selected, click and hold down the left mouse button, drag the mouse pointer to the last cell to be selected, and then release the mouse button.
all cells in a table	Click the table move handle or position the mouse pointer in the row selection bar for the first row at the left edge of the table until it turns into an arrow that points up and to the right, click and hold down the left mouse button, drag down to select all the rows in the table, and then release the left mouse button.
text within a cell	Position the mouse pointer at the beginning of the text, click and hold down the left mouse button, and then drag the mouse across the text. (When a cell is selected, its background color changes to gray. When the text within a cell is selected, only those lines containing text are selected.)

Selecting in a Table with the Keyboard

In addition to the mouse, the keyboard can be used to select specific cells within a table. Table 7.3 displays the commands for selecting specific elements of a table.

To select only the text within a cell, rather than the entire cell, press the F8 function key to turn on the Extend mode and then move the insertion point with an arrow key. When a cell is selected, its background color changes to gray. When the text within a cell is selected, only those lines containing text are selected.

Table 7.3 Selecting in a Table with the Keyboard

To select	Press
next cell's contents	Tab
preceding cell's contents	Shift + Tab
entire table	Alt + 5 (on numeric keypad with Num Lock off)
adjacent cells	Press and hold down the Shift key and then press an arrow key repeatedly.
column	Position the insertion point in the top cell of the column, click and hold down the Shift key, and then press the Down Arrow key until the column is selected.

Project 1d Selecting, Moving, and Formatting Cells in a Table   Part 4 of 8

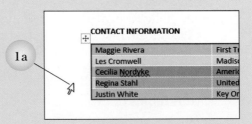

1. With **7-Tables.docx** open, move two rows in the top table by completing the following steps:
   a. Position the mouse pointer in the row selection bar at the left side of the row containing the name *Cecilia Nordyke*, click and hold down the left mouse button, and then drag down to select two rows (the *Cecilia Nordyke* row and the *Regina Stahl* row).
   b. Click the Home tab and then click the Cut button in the Clipboard group.
   c. Move the insertion point so it is positioned at the beginning of the name *Les Cromwell* and then click the Paste button in the Clipboard group.
2. Move the third column in the bottom table by completing the following steps:
   a. Position the mouse pointer on the top border of the third column in the bottom table until the pointer turns into a short black arrow that points down and then click the left mouse button. (This selects the entire column.)
   b. Click the Cut button in the Clipboard group on the Home tab.
   c. With the insertion point positioned at the beginning of the text *Basic Plan Employees*, click the Paste button in the Clipboard group. (Moving the column removed the right border.)
   d. Insert the right border by clicking the Table Tools Design tab, clicking the Border Styles button arrow, and then clicking the *Double solid lines, 1/2 pt, Accent 2* option at the drop-down list (third column, third row in the *Theme Borders* section).

e. Drag along the right border of the bottom table.

f. Click the Border Painter button to turn off the feature.

3. Apply shading to a row by completing the following steps:

a. Position the mouse pointer in the row selection bar at the left edge of the first row in the bottom table until the pointer turns into an arrow that points up and to the right and then click the left mouse button. (This selects the entire first row of the bottom table.)

b. Click the Shading button arrow in the Table Styles group and then click the *Orange, Accent 2, Lighter 80%* color option (sixth column, second row in the *Theme Colors* section).

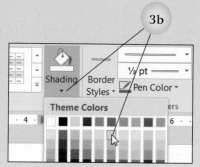

4. Apply a border line to the right sides of two columns by completing the following steps:

a. Position the mouse pointer on the top border of the first column in the bottom table until the pointer turns into a short black arrow that points down and then click the left mouse button.

b. Click the *Line Style* option box arrow and then click the top line option (a single line).

c. Click the Borders button arrow and then click *Right Border* at the drop-down list.

d. Select the second column in the bottom table.

e. Click the Borders button arrow and then click *Right Border* at the drop-down list.

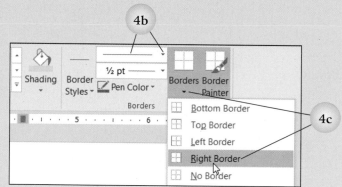

5. Apply italic formatting to a column by completing the following steps:

a. Click in the first cell of the first row in the top table.

b. Press and hold down the Shift key and then press the Down Arrow key four times. (This should select all the cells in the first column.)

c. Press Ctrl + I.

6. Save **7-Tables.docx**.

Check Your Work

Tutorial

Changing the Table Layout

Changing the Table Layout

To further customize a table, consider changing the layout by inserting or deleting columns and rows and specifying cell alignments. Change the table layout with options at the Table Tools Layout tab, shown in Figure 7.6. Use options and buttons on the tab to select specific cells, delete and insert rows and columns, merge and split cells, specify cell height and width, sort data in cells, and insert formulas.

Figure 7.6 Table Tools Layout Tab

Selecting with the Select Button

 Select

Along with selecting cells with the keyboard and mouse, specific cells can be selected with the Select button in the Table group on the Table Tools Layout tab. To select with this button, position the insertion point in the specific cell, column, or row and then click the Select button. At the drop-down list, specify what is to be selected: the entire table or a column, row, or cell.

💡 **Hint** Some table layout options are available at a shortcut menu that can be viewed by right-clicking in a table.

Viewing Gridlines

In a table, cell borders are identified by horizontal and vertical thin black gridlines. A cell border gridline can be removed but the cell border is maintained. If cell border gridlines are removed or a table style is applied that removes gridlines, the display of nonprinting gridlines can be turned on to help visually determine cell borders. These nonprinting gridlines display as dashed lines. Turn on or off the display of nonprinting dashed gridlines with the View Gridlines button in the Table group on the Table Tools Layout tab.

 View Gridlines

Inserting and Deleting Rows and Columns

Insert a row or column and delete a row or column with buttons in the Rows & Columns group on the Table Tools Layout tab. Click the button in the group that inserts the row or column in the desired location, such as above, below, to the left, or to the right. To delete a table, row, or column, click the Delete button and then click the option identifying what is to be deleted.

 Insert Above

 Insert Below

 Insert Left

 Insert Right

In addition to using options on the Table Tools Layout tab, rows or columns can be inserted using icons. Display the insert row icon by positioning the mouse pointer just outside the left border of the table at the left of the row border. When the insert row icon displays (a plus symbol in a circle and a border line), click the icon and a row is inserted below the insert icon border line. To insert a column, position the mouse pointer above the column border line until the insert column icon displays and then click the icon. This inserts a new column immediately left of the insert column icon border line.

Delete

Project 1e Selecting, Inserting, and Deleting Columns and Rows

Part 5 of 8

1. Make sure **7-Tables.docx** is open.
2. The table style applied to the bottom table removed row border gridlines. If you do not see dashed row border gridlines in the bottom table, turn on the display of nonprinting gridlines by positioning your insertion point in the table, clicking the Table Tools Layout tab, and then clicking the View Gridlines button in the Table group. (The button should display with a gray background, indicating it is active.)
3. Select a column and apply formatting by completing the following steps:
   a. Click in any cell in the first column in the top table.
   b. Make sure the Table Tools Layout tab is active, click the Select button in the Table group, and then click *Select Column* at the drop-down list.
   c. With the first column selected, press Ctrl + I to remove italic formatting and then press Ctrl + B to apply bold formatting.

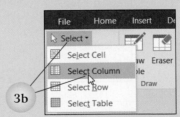

4. Select a row and apply formatting by completing the following steps:
   a. Click in any cell in the first row in the bottom table.
   b. Click the Select button in the Table group and then click *Select Row* at the drop-down list.
   c. With the first row selected in the bottom table, press Ctrl + I to apply italic formatting.
5. Insert a new row in the bottom table and type text in the new cells by completing the following steps:
   a. Click in the cell containing the text *60 days*.
   b. Click the Insert Above button in the Rows & Columns group.
   c. Type 30 days in the first cell of the new row. Press the Tab key, press Ctrl + Tab, and then type 0.85% in the second cell of the new row. Press the Tab key, press Ctrl + Tab, and then type 0.81% in the third cell of the new row.

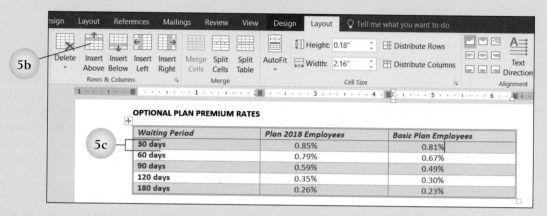

OPTIONAL PLAN PREMIUM RATES

Waiting Period	Plan 2018 Employees	Basic Plan Employees
30 days	0.85%	0.81%
60 days	0.79%	0.67%
90 days	0.59%	0.49%
120 days	0.35%	0.30%
180 days	0.26%	0.23%

6. Insert two new rows in the top table by completing the following steps:
   a. Select the two rows of cells that begin with the names *Cecilia Nordyke* and *Regina Stahl*.
   b. Click the Insert Below button in the Rows & Columns group.
   c. Click in any cell of the top table to deselect the new rows.
7. Insert a new row in the top table by positioning the mouse pointer at the left side of the table next to the border line below *Regina Stahl* until the insert row icon displays and then clicking the icon.
8. Type the following text in the new cells:

Teresa Getty	Meridian Bank	(503) 555-9800
Michael Vazquez	New Horizon Bank	(702) 555-2435
Samantha Roth	Cascade Mutual	(206) 555-6788

CONTACT INFORMATION

Maggie Rivera	First Trust Bank	(203) 555-3440
Cecilia Nordyke	American Financial	(509) 555-3995
Regina Stahl	United Fidelity	(301) 555-1201
Teresa Getty	Meridian Bank	(503) 555-9800
Michael Vazquez	New Horizon Bank	(702) 555-2435
Samantha Roth	Cascade Mutual	(206) 555-6788
Les Cromwell	Madison Trust	(602) 555-4900
Justin White	Key One Savings	(360) 555-8963

9. Delete a row by completing the following steps:
   a. Click in the cell containing the name *Les Cromwell*.
   b. Click the Delete button in the Rows & Columns group and then click *Delete Rows* at the drop-down list.
10. Insert a new column in the top table by completing the following steps:
    a. Position the mouse pointer immediately above the border line between the first and second columns in the top table until the insert column icon displays.
    b. Click the insert column icon.
11. Type the following text in the new cells:

    B1 = Vice President
    B2 = Loan Officer
    B3 = Account Manager
    B4 = Branch Manager
    B5 = President
    B6 = Vice President
    B7 = Regional Manager

12. Save **7-Tables.docx**.

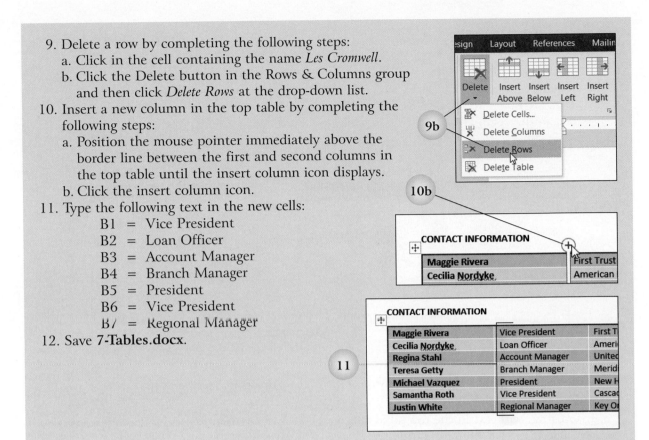

Check Your Work

Merging and Splitting Cells and Tables

Merge Cells

Split Cells

Split Table

Click the Merge Cells button in the Merge group on the Table Tools Layout tab to merge selected cells and click the Split Cells button to split the currently active cell. Click the Split Cells button and the Split Cells dialog box displays with options for specifying the number of columns or rows into which the active cell should be split. To split one table into two tables, position the insertion point in a cell in the row that will be the first row in the new table and then click the Split Table button.

Project 1f Merging and Splitting Cells and Splitting a Table   Part 6 of 8

1. With **7-Tables.docx** open, insert a new row and merge cells in the row by completing the following steps:
   a. Click in the cell containing the text *Waiting Period* (in the bottom table).

b. Click the Insert Above button in the Rows & Columns group on the Table Tools Layout tab.

c. With all of the cells in the new row selected, click the Merge Cells button in the Merge group.

d. Type OPTIONAL PLAN PREMIUM RATES and then press Ctrl + E to center-align the text in the cell. (The text you type will be italicized.)

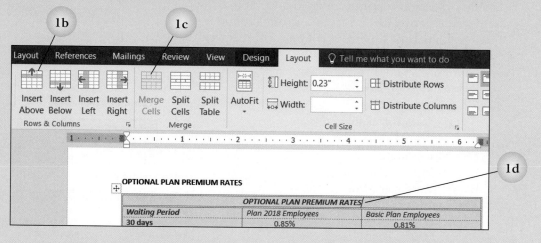

2. Select and then delete the text *OPTIONAL PLAN PREMIUM RATES* above the bottom table.

3. Insert rows and text in the top table and merge cells by completing the following steps:

   a. Click in the cell containing the text *Maggie Rivera*.

   b. Click the Table Tools Layout tab.

   c. Click the Insert Above button two times. (This inserts two rows at the top of the table.)

   d. With the cells in the top row selected, click the Merge Cells button in the Merge group.

   e. Type CONTACT INFORMATION, NORTH and then press Ctrl + E to center-align the text in the cell.

   f. Type the following text in the four cells in the new second row.

   | Name | Title | Company | Telephone |

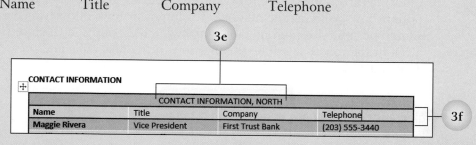

4. Apply heading formatting to the new top row by completing the following steps:

   a. Click the Table Tools Design tab.

   b. Click the *Header Row* check box in the Table Style Options group to insert a check mark.

5. Select and then delete the text *CONTACT INFORMATION* above the top table.

6. Split a cell by completing the following steps:

   a. Click in the cell containing the telephone number *(301) 555-1201*.

   b. Click the Table Tools Layout tab.

   c. Click the Split Cells button in the Merge group.

   d. At the Split Cells dialog box, click OK. (The telephone number will wrap to a new line. You will change this in the next project.)

   e. Click in the new cell.

f. Type x453 in the new cell. If AutoCorrect automatically capitalizes the *x*, hover the mouse pointer over the *X* until the AutoCorrect Options button displays. Click the AutoCorrect Options button and then click *Undo Automatic Capitalization* or click *Stop Auto-capitalizing First Letter of Table Cells*.

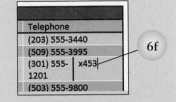

7. Split the cell containing the telephone number *(206) 555-6788* and then type x2310 in the new cell. (If necessary, make the *x* lowercase.)

8. Split the top table into two tables by completing the following steps:
   a. Click in the cell containing the name *Teresa Getty*.
   b. Click the Split Table button in the Merge group.
   c. Click in the cell containing the name *Teresa Getty* (in the first row of the new table).
   d. Click the Insert Above button in the Rows and Columns group on the Table Tools Layout tab.
   e. With the new row selected, click the Merge Cells button.
   f. Type CONTACT INFORMATION, SOUTH in the new row and then press Ctrl + E to center-align the text.

9. Save and then print **7-Tables.docx**.

10. Delete the middle table by completing the following steps:
    a. Click in any cell in the middle table.
    b. Click the Table Tools Layout tab.
    c. Click the Delete button in the Rows & Columns group and then click *Delete Table* at the drop-down list.

11. Draw a dark-orange border at the bottom of the top table by completing the following steps:
    a. Click in any cell in the top table and then click the Table Tools Design tab.
    b. Click the *Line Weight* option box arrow in the Borders group and then click *1½ pt* at the drop-down list. (This activates the Border Painter button.)
    c. Click the Pen Color button and then click the *Orange, Accent 2, Darker, 50%* color option (sixth column, bottom row in the *Theme Colors* section).
    d. Using the mouse, drag along the bottom border of the top table.
    e. Click the Border Painter button to turn off the feature.

12. Save **7-Tables.docx**.

Check Your Work

Tutorial

Customizing Cells in a Table

Distribute Rows

Distribute Columns

Customizing Cell Size

When a table is created, the column width and row height are equal. Both can be customized with buttons in the Cell Size group on the Table Tools Layout tab. Use the *Table Row Height* measurement box to increase or decrease the heights of rows and use the *Table Column Width* measurement box to increase or decrease the widths of columns. The Distribute Rows button will make all the selected rows the same height and the Distribute Columns button will make all the selected columns the same width.

Column width can also be changed using the move table column markers on the horizontal ruler or using the table gridlines. To change column width using the horizontal ruler, position the mouse pointer on a move table column marker until it turns into a left-and-right-pointing arrow and then drag the marker on the horizontal ruler to the desired position. Press and hold down the Shift key while dragging a table column marker and the horizontal ruler remains stationary while the table column marker moves. Press and hold down the Alt key while dragging a table column marker and measurements display on the horizontal ruler. To change column width using gridlines, position the arrow pointer on the gridline separating columns until the insertion point turns into a left-and-right-pointing arrow with a vertical double-line in the middle and then drag the gridline to the desired position. Press and hold down the Alt key while dragging the gridline and column measurements display on the horizontal ruler.

Adjust row height in a manner similar to adjusting column width. Drag the adjust table row marker on the vertical ruler or drag the gridline separating rows. Press and hold down the Alt key while dragging the adjust table row marker or the row gridline and measurements display on the vertical ruler.

AutoFit

Use the AutoFit button in the Cell Size group to make the column widths in a table automatically fit the contents. To do this, position the insertion point in any cell in the table, click the AutoFit button in the Cell Size group, and then click *AutoFit Contents* at the drop-down list.

Project 1g Changing Column Width and Row Height

1. With **7-Tables.docx** open, change the width of the first column in the top table by completing the following steps:
   a. Click in the cell containing the name *Maggie Rivera*.
   b. Position the mouse pointer on the move table column marker just right of the 1.5-inch mark on the horizontal ruler until the pointer turns into a left-and-right-pointing arrow.
   c. Press and hold down the Shift key and then click and hold down the left mouse button.
   d. Drag the marker to the 1.25-inch mark, release the mouse button, and then release the Shift key.

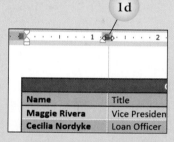

2. Complete steps similar to those in Step 1 to drag the move table column marker just right of the 3-inch mark on the horizontal ruler to the 2.75-inch mark. (Make sure the text *Account Manager* in the second column does not wrap to the next line. If it does, slightly increase the width of the column.)
3. Change the width of the third column in the top table by completing the following steps:
   a. Position the mouse pointer on the gridline separating the third and fourth columns until the pointer turns into a left-and-right-pointing arrow with a vertical double-line in the middle.
   b. Press and hold down the Alt key and then click and hold down the left mouse button, drag the gridline to the left until the measurement for the third column on the horizontal ruler displays as *1.31"*, and then release the Alt key followed by the mouse button.

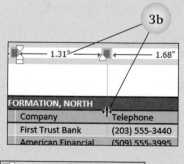

4. Position the mouse pointer on the gridline that separates the telephone number *(301) 555-1201* from the extension *x453* and then drag the gridline to the 5.25-inch mark on the horizontal ruler. (Make sure the phone number does not wrap down to the next line.)
5. Drag the right border of the top table to the 5.75-inch mark on the horizontal ruler.

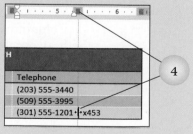

6. Automatically fit the columns in the bottom table by completing the following steps:
   a. Click in any cell in the bottom table.
   b. Click the AutoFit button in the Cell Size group on the Table Tools Layout tab and then click *AutoFit Contents* at the drop-down list.

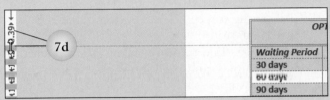

7. Increase the height of the first row in the bottom table by completing the following steps:
   a. Make sure the insertion point is positioned in one of the cells in the bottom table.
   b. Position the mouse pointer on the top adjust table row marker on the vertical ruler.
   c. Press and hold down the Alt key and then click and hold down the left mouse button.
   d. Drag the adjust table row marker down until the first row measurement on the vertical ruler displays as *0.39",* release the mouse button, and then release the Alt key.

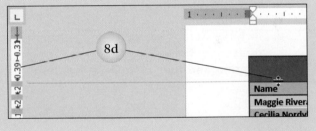

8. Increase the height of the first row in the top table by completing the following steps:
   a. Click in any cell in the top table.
   b. Position the arrow pointer on the gridline at the bottom of the top row until the arrow pointer turns into an up-and-down-pointing arrow with a vertical double-line in the middle.
   c. Click and hold down the left mouse button and then press and hold down the Alt key.
   d. Drag the gridline down until the first row measurement on the vertical ruler displays as *0.39",* release the mouse button, and then release the Alt key.
9. Save **7-Tables.docx**.

Check Your Work

Changing Cell Alignment

The Alignment group on the Table Tools Layout tab contains a number of buttons for specifying the horizontal and vertical alignment of text in cells. Each button contains a visual representation of the alignment. Hover the mouse pointer over a button to display a ScreenTip with the button name and description.

Quick Steps

Repeat a Header Row
1. Click in header row or select rows.
2. Click Table Tools Layout tab.
3. Click Repeat Header Rows button.

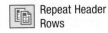
Repeat Header Rows

Repeating a Header Row

If a table is divided between two pages, consider adding the header row at the beginning of the table that continues on the second page. This helps the reader understand the data in each column. To repeat a header row, click in the first row (header row) and then click the Repeat Header Rows button in the Data group on the Table Tools Layout tab. To repeat more than one header row, select the rows and then click the Repeat Header Rows button.

1. With **7-Tables.docx** open, click in the top cell in the top table (the cell containing the title *CONTACT INFORMATION, NORTH*).
2. Click the Align Center button in the Alignment group on the Table Tools Layout tab.
3. Format and align the text in the second row in the top table by completing the following steps:

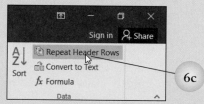

   a. Select the second row.
   b. Press Ctrl + B to turn off bold formatting for the entry in the first cell and then press Ctrl + B again to turn on bold formatting for all the entries in the second row.
   c. Click the Align Top Center button in the Alignment group.
4. Click in the top cell in the bottom table and then click the Align Center button in the Alignment group.
5. Press Ctrl + End to move the insertion point to the end of the document, press the Enter key four times, and then insert a table into the current document by completing the following steps:
   a. Click the Insert tab.
   b. Click the Object button arrow in the Text group and then click *Text from File* at the drop-down list.
   c. At the Insert File dialog box, navigate to the WL1C7 folder on your storage medium and then double-click ***ContactsWest.docx***.
6. Repeat the header row by completing the following steps:
   a. Select the first two rows in the table you just inserted.
   b. Click the Table Tools Layout tab.
   c. Click the Repeat Header Rows button in the Data group.
7. Save, print, and then close **7-Tables.docx**.

Check Your Work

Project 2 Create and Format Tables with Employee Information   **6 Parts**

You will create and format a table containing information on the names and departments of employees of Tri-State Products, a table containing additional information on employees, and a calendar quick table.

Preview Finished Project

Changing Cell Margin Measurements

Cell Margins

By default, the cells in a table contain specific margin measurements. The top and bottom margins in a cell have a default measurement of 0 inch and the left and right margins have a default measurement of 0.08 inch. Change these default measurements with options at the Table Options dialog box, shown in Figure 7.7. Display this dialog box by clicking the Cell Margins button in the Alignment group on the Table Tools Layout tab. Use the measurement boxes in the *Default cell margins* section to change the top, bottom, left, and/or right cell margin measurements.

Figure 7.7 Table Options Dialog Box

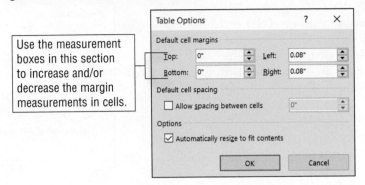

Use the measurement boxes in this section to increase and/or decrease the margin measurements in cells.

 Properties

Changes to cell margins will affect all the cells in a table. To change the cell margin measurements for one cell or selected cells, position the insertion point in the cell or select the cells and then click the Properties button in the Table group on the Table Tools Layout tab (or click the Cell Size group dialog box launcher). At the Table Properties dialog box, click the Cell tab and then the Options button in the lower right corner of the dialog box. This displays the Cell Options dialog box, shown in Figure 7.8.

Before setting the new cell margin measurements, remove the check mark from the *Same as the whole table* check box. With the check mark removed, the cell margin options become available. Specify the new cell margin measurements and then click OK to close the dialog box.

Figure 7.8 Cell Options Dialog Box

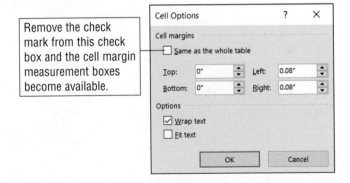

Remove the check mark from this check box and the cell margin measurement boxes become available.

Project 2a Changing Cell Margin Measurements   Part 1 of 6

1. Open **TSPTables.docx** and then save it with the name **7-TSPTables**.
2. Change the top and bottom cell margin measurements for all the cells in the table by completing the following steps:
   a. Position the insertion point in any cell in the table and then click the Table Tools Layout tab.
   b. Click the Cell Margins button in the Alignment group.

c. At the Table Options dialog box, change the *Top* and *Bottom* measurements to 0.05 inch.

d. Click OK to close the Table Options dialog box.

3. Change the top and bottom cell margin measurements for the first row of cells by completing the following steps:

a. Select the first row of cells (the cells containing *Name* and *Department*).

b. Click the Properties button in the Table group.

c. At the Table Properties dialog box, click the Cell tab.

d. Click the Options button in the lower right corner of the dialog box.

e. At the Cell Options dialog box, click the *Same as the whole table* check box to remove the check mark.

f. Change the *Top* and *Bottom* measurements to 0.1 inch.

g. Click OK to close the Cell Options dialog box.

h. Click OK to close the Table Properties dialog box.

4. Change the left cell margin measurement for specific cells by completing the following steps:

a. Select all of the rows in the table *except* the top row.

b. Click the Cell Size group dialog box launcher.

c. At the Table Properties dialog box, make sure the Cell tab is active.

d. Click the Options button.

e. At the Cell Options dialog box, remove the check mark from the *Same as the whole table* check box.

f. Change the *Left* measurement to 0.3 inch.

g. Click OK to close the Cell Options dialog box.

h. Click OK to close the Table Properties dialog box.

5. Save **7-TSPTables.docx**.

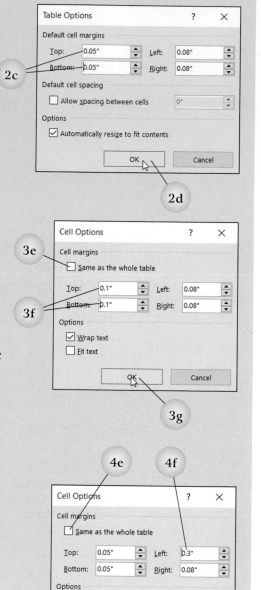

Check Your Work

Changing Cell Direction

 Text Direction

Change the direction of text in a cell using the Text Direction button in the Alignment group on the Table Tools Layout tab. Each time the Text Direction button is clicked, the text in the cell rotates 90 degrees.

Changing Table Alignment and Dimensions

By default, a table aligns at the left margin. Change this alignment with options at the Table Properties dialog box with the Table tab selected, as shown in Figure 7.9. To change the alignment, click the desired alignment option in the *Alignment* section of the dialog box. Change table dimensions by clicking the *Preferred width* check box to insert a check mark. This makes active both the width measurement box and the *Measure in* option box. Type a width measurement in the measurement box and specify whether the measurement type is inches or a percentage with the *Measurement in* option box.

Figure 7.9 Table Properties Dialog Box with Table Tab Selected

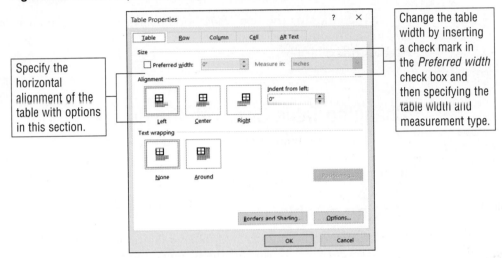

Specify the horizontal alignment of the table with options in this section.

Change the table width by inserting a check mark in the *Preferred width* check box and then specifying the table width and measurement type.

Project 2b Changing Table Alignment and Dimensions

Part 2 of 6

1. With **7-TSPTables.docx** open, insert a new column and change text direction by completing the following steps:
   a. Click in any cell in the first column.
   b. Click the Insert Left button in the Rows & Columns group.
   c. With the cells in the new column selected, click the Merge Cells button in the Merge group.
   d. Type Tri-State Products.
   e. Click the Align Center button in the Alignment group.
   f. Click two times on the Text Direction button in the Alignment group.
   g. With *Tri-State Products* selected, click the Home tab and then increase the font size to 16 points.
2. Automatically fit the contents by completing the following steps:
   a. Click in any cell in the table.
   b. Click the Table Tools Layout tab.
   c. Click the AutoFit button in the Cell Size group and then click *AutoFit Contents* at the drop-down list.

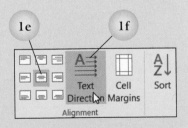

3. Change the table width and alignment by completing the following steps:
   a. Click the Properties button in the Table group on the Table Tools Layout tab.
   b. At the Table Properties dialog box, click the Table tab.
   c. Click the *Preferred width* check box to insert a check mark.
   d. Select the measurement in the measurement box and then type 4.5.
   e. Click the *Center* option in the *Alignment* section.
   f. Click OK.
4. Select the two cells containing the text *Name* and *Department* and then click the Align Center button in the Alignment group.
5. Save **7-TSPTables.docx**.

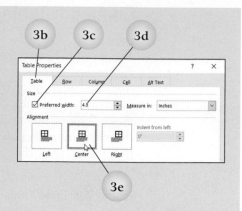

Check Your Work

Quick Steps
Move a Table
1. Position mouse pointer on table move handle until pointer displays with four-headed arrow attached.
2. Click and hold down left mouse button.
3. Drag table to new location.
4. Release mouse button.

Changing Table Size with the Resize Handle

Hover the mouse pointer over a table and a resize handle displays in the lower right corner. The resize handle displays as a small white square. Drag this resize handle to increase and/or decrease the size and proportion of the table.

Moving a Table

Position the mouse pointer in a table and a table move handle displays in the upper left corner. Use this handle to move the table in the document. To move a table, position the mouse pointer on the table move handle until the pointer displays with a four-headed arrow attached, click and hold down the left mouse button, drag the table to the new location, and then release the mouse button.

Project 2c Resizing and Moving Tables

Part 3 of 6

1. With **7-TSPTables.docx** open, insert a table into the current document by completing the following steps:
   a. Press Ctrl + End to move the insertion point to the end of the document and then press the Enter key.
   b. Click the Insert tab.
   c. Click the Object button arrow in the Text group and then click *Text from File* at the drop-down list.
   d. At the Insert File dialog box, navigate to the WL1C7 folder and then double-click **TSPEmps.docx**.
2. Automatically fit the bottom table by completing the following steps:
   a. Click in any cell in the bottom table.
   b. Click the Table Tools Layout tab.
   c. Click the AutoFit button in the Cell Size group and then click *AutoFit Contents* at the drop-down list.

3. Format the bottom table by completing the following steps:
   a. Click the Table Tools Design tab.
   b. Click the More Table Styles button in the table styles gallery and then click the *List Table 4 - Accent 6* table style (last column, fourth row in the *List Tables* section).
   c. Click the *First Column* check box in the Table Style Options group to remove the check mark.
   d. Select the first and second rows, click the Table Tools Layout tab, and then click the Align Center button in the Alignment group.
   e. Select the second row and then press Ctrl + B to turn on bold formatting.
4. Resize the bottom table by completing the following steps:
   a. Position the mouse pointer on the resize handle in the lower right corner of the bottom table.
   b. Click and hold down the left mouse button, drag down and to the right until the width and height of the table increase approximately 1 inch, and then release the mouse button.
5. Move the bottom table by completing the following steps:
   a. Move the mouse pointer over the bottom table and then position the mouse pointer on the table move handle until the pointer displays with a four-headed arrow attached.
   b. Click and hold down the left mouse button, drag the table so it is positioned equally between the left and right margins, and then release the mouse button.

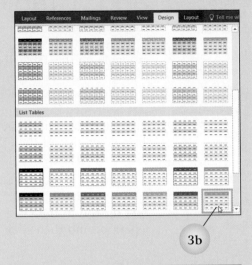

3b

TRI-STATE PRODUCTS		
Name	**Employee #**	**Department**
Whitaker, Christine	1432-323-09	Financial Services
Higgins, Dennis	1230-933-21	Public Relations
Coffey, Richard	1321-843-22	Research and Development
Lee, Yong	1411-322-76	Human Resources
Fleishmann, Jim	1246-432-90	Public Relations
Schatter, Mitchell	1388-340-44	Purchasing
Porter, Robbie	1122-361-38	Public Relations
Duchanan, Lillian	1432 857 87	Research and Development
Kensington, Jacob	1112-473-31	Human Resources

4a-4b

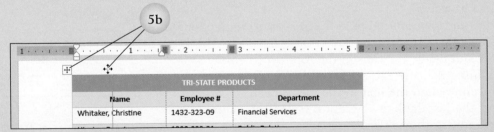

5b

6. Select the cells in the column below the heading *Employee #* and then click the Align Top Center button in the Alignment group.
7. Save **7-TSPTables.docx**.

Check Your Work

Converting Text to a Table and a Table to Text

Create a table and then enter text in the cells or create the text and then convert it to a table. Converting text to a table provides formatting and layout options available on the Table Tools Design tab and the Table Tools Layout tab. When typing the text to be converted to a table, separate units of information using separator characters, such as commas or tabs. These characters identify where the text is divided into columns. To convert text, select the text, click the Insert tab, click the Table button in the Tables group, and then click *Convert Text to Table* at the drop-down list. At the Convert Text to Table dialog box, specify the separator and then click OK.

Convert a table to text by positioning the insertion point in any cell of the table, clicking the Table Tools Layout tab, and then clicking the Convert to Text button in the Data group. At the Convert Table To dialog box, specify the separator and then click OK.

Project 2d   Converting Text to a Table

Part 4 of 6

1. With **7-TSPTables.docx** open, press Ctrl + End to move the insertion point to the end of the document. (If the insertion point does not display below the second table, press the Enter key until the insertion point displays there.)
2. Insert the document named **TSPExecs.docx** into the current document.
3. Convert the text to a table by completing the following steps:
   a. Select the text you just inserted.
   b. Make sure the Insert tab is active.
   c. Click the Table button in the Tables group and then click *Convert Text to Table* at the drop-down list.
   d. At the Convert Text to Table dialog box, type 2 in the *Number of columns* measurement box.
   e. Click the *AutoFit to contents* option in the *AutoFit behavior* section.
   f. Click the *Commas* option in the *Separate text at* section.
   g. Click OK.

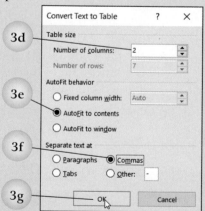

4. Select and merge the cells in the top row (the row containing the title *TRI-STATE PRODUCTS*) and then center-align the text in the merged cell.
5. Apply the List Table 4 - Accent 6 style (last column, fourth row in the *List Tables* section) and remove the check mark from the *First Column* check box in the Table Style Options group on the Table Tools Design tab.
6. Drag the table so it is centered below the table above it.
7. Apply the List Table 4 - Accent 6 style to the top table. Increase the widths of the columns so the text *Tri-State Products* is visible and the text in the second and third columns displays on one line.
8. Drag the table so it is centered above the middle table. Make sure the three tables fit on one page.

9. Click in the middle table and then convert the table to text by completing the following steps:
   a. Click the Table Tools Layout tab and then click the Convert to Text button in the Data group.
   b. At the Convert Table To dialog box, make sure *Tabs* is selected and then click OK.
10. Print **7-TSPTables.docx**.
11. Click the Undo button to return the text to a table.
12. Save **7-TSPTables.docx**.

Check Your Work

Drawing a Table

In Project 1, options in the Borders group on the Table Tools Design tab were used to draw borders around an existing table. These options can also be used to draw an entire table. To draw a table, click the Insert tab, click the Table button in the Tables group, and then click *Draw Table* at the drop-down list. Or click the Draw Table button in the Draw group on the Table Tools Layout tab; this turns the mouse pointer into a pen. Drag the pen pointer in the document to create the table. To correct an error when drawing a table, click the Eraser button in the Draw group on the Table Tools Layout tab (which changes the mouse pointer to an eraser) and then drag over any border lines to be erased. Clicking the Undo button will also undo the most recent action.

 Eraser

Project 2e Drawing and Formatting a Table

Part 5 of 6

1. With **7-TSPTables.docx** open, select and then delete three rows in the middle table from the row that begins with the name *Lee, Yong* through the row that begins with the name *Schaffer, Mitchell*.
2. Move the insertion point to the end of the document (outside any table) and then press the Enter key. (Make sure the insertion point is positioned below the third table.)
3. Click the Insert tab, click the Table button, and then click the *Draw Table* option at the drop-down list. (This turns the insertion point into a pen.)
4. Using the mouse, drag in the document (below the bottom table) to create the table shown at the right, drawing the outside border first. If you make a mistake, click the Undo button. You can also click the Eraser button in the Draw group on the Table Tools Layout tab and drag over a border line to erase it. Click the Draw Table button in the Draw group to turn off the pen feature.

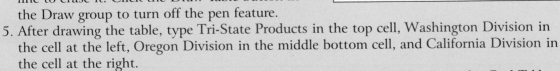

5. After drawing the table, type Tri-State Products in the top cell, Washington Division in the cell at the left, Oregon Division in the middle bottom cell, and California Division in the cell at the right.
6. Apply the Grid Table 4 - Accent 6 table style (last column, fourth row in the *Grid Tables* section).
7. Select the table, change the font size to 12 points, apply bold formatting, and then center-align the text in the cells using the Align Center button in the Alignment group.
8. Make any adjustments needed to the border lines so the text in each cell displays on one line.
9. Drag the table so it is centered and positioned below the bottom table.
10. Save **7-TSPTables.docx**.

Check Your Work

Quick Steps
Insert a Quick Table
1. Click Insert tab.
2. Click Table button.
3. Point to *Quick Tables*.
4. Click table.

Inserting a Quick Table

Word includes a Quick Tables feature for inserting predesigned tables in a document. To insert a quick table, click the Insert tab, click the Table button, point to *Quick Tables*, and then click a table at the side menu. A quick table has formatting applied but additional formatting can be applied with options on the Table Tools Design tab and the Table Tools Layout tab.

Project 2f Inserting a Quick Table

Part 6 of 6

1. With **7-TSPTables.docx** open, press Ctrl + End to move the insertion point to the end of the document and then press Ctrl + Enter to insert a page break.
2. Insert a quick table by clicking the Insert tab, clicking the Table button, pointing to *Quick Tables*, and then clicking the *Calendar 3* option at the side menu.

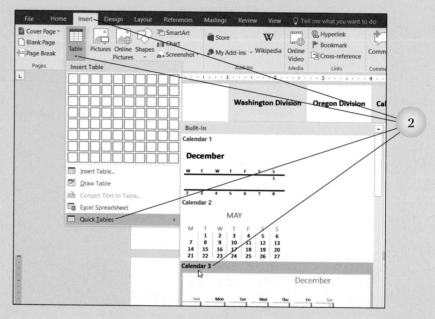

3. Edit the text in each cell so the calendar reflects the current month. (If the bottom row is empty, select and then delete the row.)
4. Select the entire table by clicking the Table Tools Layout tab, clicking the Select button in the Table group, and then clicking the *Select Table* option. With the table selected, change the font to Copperplate Gothic Light.
5. Save, print, and then close **7-TSPTables.docx**.

Check Your Work

Project 3 Calculate Sales Data

1 Part

You will insert formulas in a Tri-State Products sales table to calculate total sales, average sales, and top sales.

Preview Finished Project

Performing Calculations in a Table

Use the Formula button in the Data group on the Table Tools Layout tab to insert formulas that perform calculations on the data in a table. The numbers in cells can be added, subtracted, multiplied, and divided. In addition, other calculations can be performed, such as determining averages, counting items, and identifying minimum and maximum values. Data can be calculated in a Word table, but for complex calculations consider using an Excel worksheet.

To perform a calculation on the data in a table, position the insertion point in the cell where the result of the calculation is to be inserted and then click the Formula button in the Data group on the Table Tools Layout tab. This displays the Formula dialog box, as shown in Figure 7.10. At this dialog box, accept the default formula in the *Formula* text box or type a calculation and then click OK.

fx Formula

Quick Steps

Insert a Formula in a Table
1. Click in cell.
2. Click Table Tools Layout tab.
3. Click Formula button.
4. Type formula in Formula dialog box.
5. Click OK.

Figure 7.10 Formula Dialog Box

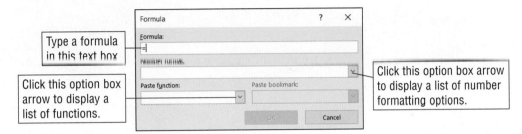

Four basic operators are available for writing a formula, including the plus symbol (+) for addition, the minus symbol (–) for subtraction, the asterisk (*) for multiplication, and the forward slash (/) for division. If a calculation contains two or more operators, Word performs the operations from left to right. To change the order of operations, put parentheses around the part of the calculation to be performed first.

In the default formula, the SUM part of the formula is called a *function*. Word also provides other functions for inserting formulas. These functions are available in the *Paste function* option box in the Formula dialog box. For example, use the AVERAGE function to average numbers in cells.

Specify the numbering format with the *Number format* option box in the Formula dialog box. For example, when calculating amounts of money, specify that the numbers display with no numbers or two numbers following the decimal point.

If changes are made to the values in a formula, the result of the formula needs to be updated. To do this, right-click the formula result and then click *Update Field* at the shortcut menu. Or click the formula result and then press the F9 function key, which is the Update Field keyboard shortcut. To update the results of all the formulas in a table, select the entire table and then press the F9 function key.

Hint Use the Update Field keyboard shortcut, F9, to update the selected field.

1. Open **TSPSalesTable.docx** and then save it with the name **7-TSPSalesTable**.
2. Insert a formula in the table by completing the following steps:
   a. Click in cell B9. (Cell B9 is the empty cell immediately below the cell containing the amount *$294,653.*)
   b. Click the Table Tools Layout tab.
   c. Click the Formula button in the Data group.
   d. At the Formula dialog box, make sure *=SUM(ABOVE)* displays in the *Formula* text box.
   e. Click the *Number format* option box arrow and then click *#,##0* at the drop-down list (the top option in the list).
   f. Click OK to close the Formula dialog box.

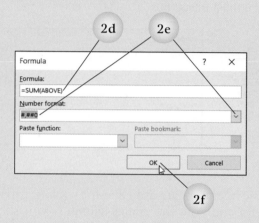

   g. In the table, type a dollar symbol ($) before the number just inserted in cell B9.
3. Complete steps similar to those in Steps 2c through 2g to insert a formula in cell C9. (Cell C9 is the empty cell immediately below the cell containing the amount *$300,211.*)
4. Insert a formula that calculates the average of amounts by completing the following steps:
   a. Click in cell B10. (Cell B10 is the empty cell immediately right of the cell containing the word *Average.*)
   b. Click the Formula button in the Data group.
   c. At the Formula dialog box, delete the formula in the *Formula* text box *except* for the equals (=) sign.
   d. With the insertion point positioned immediately right of the equals sign, click the *Paste function* option box arrow and then click *AVERAGE* at the drop-down list.
   e. With the insertion point positioned between the left and right parentheses, type B2:B8. (When typing cell designations in a formula, you can type either uppercase or lowercase letters.)
   f. Click the *Number format* option box arrow and then click *#,##0* at the drop-down list (the top option in the list).
   g. Click OK to close the Formula dialog box.
   h. Type a dollar symbol ($) before the number just inserted in cell B10.
5. Complete steps similar to those in Steps 4b through 4h to insert a formula in cell C10 that calculates the average of the amounts in cells C2 through C8.

6. Insert a formula that calculates the maximum number by completing the following steps:
   a. Click in cell B11. (Cell B11 is the empty cell immediately right of the cell containing the words *Top Sales.*)
   b. Click the Formula button in the Data group.
   c. At the Formula dialog box, delete the formula in the *Formula* text box *except* for the equals sign.
   d. With the insertion point positioned immediately right of the equals sign, click the *Paste function* option box arrow and then click *MAX* at the drop-down list. (You will need to scroll down the list to display the *MAX* option.)
   e. With the insertion point positioned between the left and right parentheses, type B2:B8.
   f. Click the *Number format* option box arrow and then click *#,##0* at the drop-down list (the top option in the list).
   g. Click OK to close the Formula dialog box.
   h. Type a dollar symbol ($) before the number just inserted in cell B11.
7. Complete steps similar to those in Steps 6b through 6h to insert the maximum number in cell C11.
8. Save and then print **7-TSPSalesTable.docx**.
9. Change the amount in cell B2 from *$543,241* to *$765,700*.
10. Recalculate all the formulas in the table by completing the following steps:
    a. Make sure the Table Tools Layout tab is active and then click the Select button in the Table group.
    b. Click the *Select Table* option.
    c. Press the F9 function key.
11. Save, print, and then close **7-TSPSalesTable.docx**.

Check Your Work

Project 4 Insert an Excel Worksheet   1 Part

You will insert an Excel worksheet in a blank document, decrease the number of rows and columns in the worksheet, insert data on sales increases in the worksheet from a Word document, and calculate data in the worksheet.

Preview Finished Project

Inserting an Excel Spreadsheet

An Excel spreadsheet (usually referred to as a *worksheet*) can be inserted into a Word document, which provides some Excel functions for modifying and formatting the data. To insert an Excel worksheet, click the Insert tab, click the Table button in the Tables group, and then click the *Excel Spreadsheet* option at the drop-down list. This inserts a worksheet in the document with seven columns and ten rows visible. Increase or decrease the number of visible cells by dragging the sizing handles that display around the worksheet. Use buttons on the Excel ribbon tabs to format the worksheet. Click outside the worksheet and the Excel ribbon tabs are removed. Double-click the table to redisplay the Excel ribbon tabs.

1. Open **SalesIncrease.docx**.
2. Press Ctrl + N to open a blank document.
3. Insert an Excel spreadsheet into the blank document by clicking the Insert tab, clicking the Table button in the Tables group, and then clicking *Excel Spreadsheet* at the drop-down list.

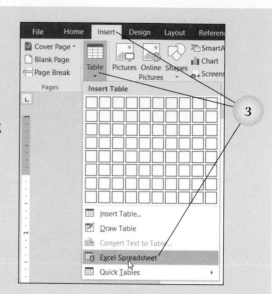

4. Decrease the size of the worksheet by completing the following steps:
   a. Position the mouse pointer on the sizing handle (small black square) located in the lower right corner of the worksheet until the pointer displays as a black, diagonal, two-headed arrow.
   b. Click and hold down the left mouse button, drag up and to the left, and release the mouse button. Continue dragging the sizing handles until columns A, B, and C and rows 1 through 7 are visible.
5. Copy a table into the Excel worksheet by completing the following steps:
   a. Position the mouse pointer on the Word button on the taskbar and then click the *SalesIncrease.docx* thumbnail.
   b. Position the mouse pointer over the table and then click the table move handle (small square containing a four-headed arrow) that displays in the upper left corner of the table. (This selects all of the cells in the table.)
   c. Click the Copy button in the Clipboard group on the Home tab.
   d. Close **SalesIncrease.docx**.
   e. With the first cell in the worksheet active, click the Paste button in the Clipboard group.
6. Format the worksheet and insert a formula by completing the following steps:
   a. Increase the width of the second column by positioning the mouse pointer on the column boundary between columns B and C and double-clicking the left mouse button.

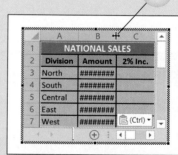

   b. Click in cell C3, type the formula =B3*102, and then press the Enter key.
7. Copy the formula in cell C3 to the range C4:C7 by completing the following steps:
   a. Position the mouse pointer (white plus symbol) in cell C3, click and hold down the left mouse button, drag down into cell C7, and then release the mouse button.
   b. Click the Fill button in the Editing group on the Home tab and then click *Down* at the drop-down list.

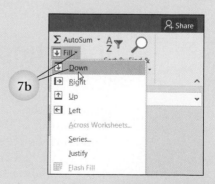

8. Click outside the worksheet to remove the Excel ribbon tabs.
9. Save the document and name it **7-Worksheet**.
10. Print and then close **7-Worksheet.docx**.

Check Your Work

Project 5 **Prepare and Format a SmartArt Graphic**   **2 Parts**

You will prepare a SmartArt process graphic that identifies steps in the production process and then apply formatting to enhance the graphic.

Preview Finished Project

Creating SmartArt

Use Word's SmartArt feature to insert graphics such as diagrams and organizational charts in a document. SmartArt offers a variety of predesigned graphics that are available at the Choose a SmartArt Graphic dialog box, as shown in Figure 7.11. At this dialog box, *All* is selected by default in the left panel and all of the available predesigned SmartArt graphics display in the middle panel.

Inserting and Formatting a SmartArt Graphic

To insert a SmartArt graphic, click the Insert tab and then click the SmartArt button in the Illustrations group to open the Choose a SmartArt Graphic dialog box. Predesigned SmartArt graphics display in the middle panel of the dialog box. Use the scroll bar at the right side of the middle panel to scroll down the list of choices. Click a graphic in the middle panel and its name displays in the right panel along with a description. SmartArt includes graphics for presenting a list of data; showing data processes, cycles, and relationships; and presenting data in a matrix or pyramid. Double-click a graphic in the middle panel of the dialog box and the graphic is inserted in the document.

When a SmartArt graphic is inserted in a document, a text pane displays at the left side of the graphic. Type text in the text pane or type directly in the graphic. Apply formatting to a graphic with options on the SmartArt Tools Design tab. This

Figure 7.11 Choose a SmartArt Graphic Dialog Box

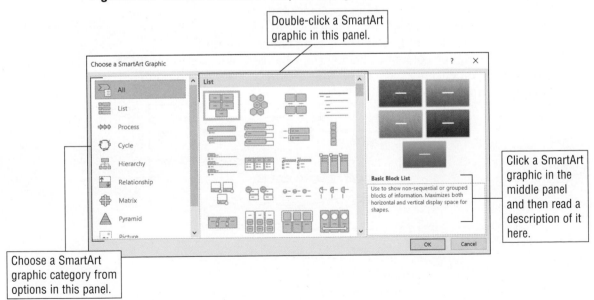

tab becomes active when the graphic is inserted in the document. Use options and buttons on this tab to add objects, change the graphic layout, apply a style to the graphic, and reset the graphic to the original formatting.

Apply formatting to a SmartArt graphic with options on the SmartArt Tools Format tab. Use options and buttons on this tab to change the sizes and shapes of objects in the graphic; apply shape styles and WordArt styles; change the shape fill, outline, and effects; and arrange and size the graphic.

Project 5a Inserting and Formatting a SmartArt Graphic

Part 1 of 2

1. At a blank document, insert the SmartArt graphic shown in Figure 7.12 by completing the following steps:
   a. Click the Insert tab.
   b. Click the SmartArt button in the Illustrations group.
   c. At the Choose a SmartArt Graphic dialog box, click *Process* in the left panel and then double-click the *Alternating Flow* graphic.
   d. If a *Type your text here* text pane does not display at the left side of the graphic, click the Text Pane button in the Create Graphic group to display it.
   e. With the insertion point positioned after the top bullet in the *Type your text here* text pane, type Design.
   f. Click the *[Text]* placeholder below *Design* and then type Mock-up.
   g. Continue clicking occurrences of the *[Text]* placeholder and typing text so the text pane displays as shown at the right.
   h. Close the text pane by clicking the Close button in the upper right corner of the pane. (You can also click the Text Pane button in the Create Graphic group.)

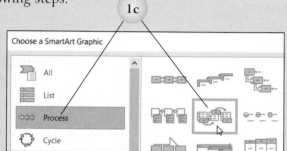

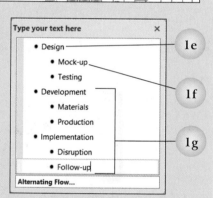

2. Change the graphic colors by clicking the Change Colors button in the SmartArt Styles group and then clicking the *Colorful Range - Accent Colors 5 to 6* option (last option in the *Colorful* section).

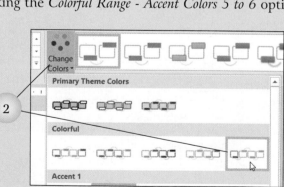

3. Apply a style by clicking the More SmartArt Styles button in the gallery in the SmartArt Styles group and then clicking the *Inset* option (second column, first row in the *3-D* section).

4. Copy the graphic and then change the layout by completing the following steps:

   a. Click inside the SmartArt graphic border but outside any shapes.

   b. Click the Home tab and then click the Copy button in the Clipboard group.

   c. Press Ctrl + End, press the Enter key, and then press Ctrl + Enter to insert a page break.

   d. Click the Paste button in the Clipboard group.

   e. Click inside the SmartArt graphic border but outside any shapes.

   f. Click the SmartArt Tools Design tab.

   g. Click the More Layouts button in the Layouts gallery and then click the *Continuous Block Process* layout (second column, second row).

   h. Click outside the graphic to deselect it.

5. Save the document and name it **7-SAGraphics**.

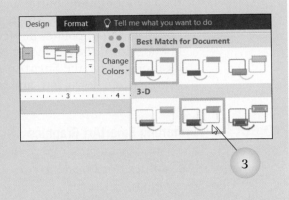

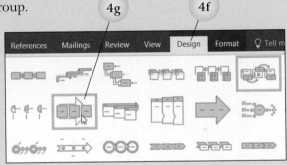

Check Your Work

Figure 7.12 Project 5a

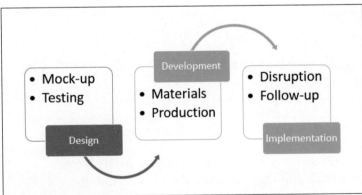

Arranging and Moving a SmartArt Graphic

Position

Arrange

Wrap Text

Position a SmartArt graphic by clicking the Arrange button on the SmartArt Tools Format tab, clicking the Position button, and then clicking the desired position option at the drop-down gallery. Along with positioning the SmartArt graphic, the options at the Position button drop-down gallery apply square text wrapping, which means text wraps around the border of an object. Text wrapping can also be applied by clicking the Arrange button, clicking the Wrap Text button, and then clicking a wrapping style at the drop-down gallery. Or it can be applied with options from the Layout Options button outside the upper right corner of the selected SmartArt graphic. Move a SmartArt graphic by positioning the arrow pointer on the graphic border until the pointer displays with a four-headed arrow attached, clicking and holding down the left mouse button, and then dragging the graphic to the new location. Nudge the SmartArt graphic or a shape or selected shapes in the graphic using the up, down, left, and right arrow keys on the keyboard.

Project 5b Formatting SmartArt Graphics

1. With **7-SAGraphics.docx** open, format shapes by completing the following steps:
    a. Click the graphic on the first page to select it (a border surrounds the graphic).
    b. Click the SmartArt Tools Format tab.
    c. In the graphic, click the rectangle shape containing the word *Design*.
    d. Press and hold down the Shift key and then click the shape containing the word *Development*.
    e. With the Shift key still held down, click the shape containing the word *Implementation*. (All three shapes should now be selected.)
    f. Click the Change Shape button in the Shapes group.
    g. Click the *Pentagon* shape (seventh column, second row in the *Block Arrows* section).

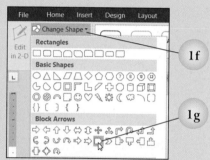

    h. With the shapes still selected, click the Larger button in the Shapes group.
    i. With the shapes still selected, click the Shape Outline button arrow in the Shape Styles group and then click the *Dark Blue* color option (ninth option in the *Standard Colors* section).

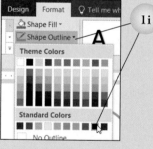

    j. Click inside the graphic border but outside any shape. (This deselects the shapes but keeps the graphic selected.)
2. Change the size of the graphic by completing the following steps:
    a. Click the Size button at the right side of the SmartArt Tools Format tab.
    b. Click in the *Shape Height* measurement box, type 4, and then press the Enter key.
3. Position the graphic by completing the following steps:
    a. Click the Arrange button on the SmartArt Tools Format tab and then click the Position button at the drop-down list.

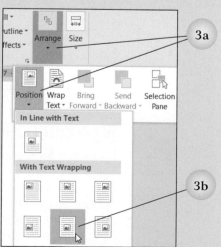

    b. Click the *Position in Middle Center with Square Text Wrapping* option (second column, second row in the *With Text Wrapping* section).
    c. Click outside the graphic to deselect it.
4. Format the bottom SmartArt graphic by completing the following steps:
    a. Press Ctrl + End to move to the end of the document and then click in the bottom SmartArt graphic to select it.

b. Press and hold down the Shift key and then click each of the three shapes.

c. Click the More WordArt Styles button in the WordArt styles gallery on the SmartArt Tools Format tab.

d. Click the *Fill - Black, Text 1, Shadow* option (first column, first row).

e. Click the Text Outline button arrow in the WordArt Styles group and then click the *Dark Blue* color option (ninth color in the *Standard Colors* section).

f. Click the Text Effects button in the WordArt Styles group, point to *Glow* at the drop-down list, and then click the *Orange, 5 pt glow, Accent color 2* option (second column, first row in the *Glow Variations* section).

g. Click inside the SmartArt graphic border but outside any shape.

5. Arrange the graphic by clicking the Arrange button, clicking the Position button, and then clicking the *Position in Middle Center with Square Text Wrapping* option (second column, second row in the *With Text Wrapping* section).

6. Click outside the graphic to deselect it.

7. Save, print, and then close **7-SAGraphics.docx**.

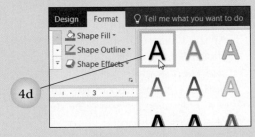

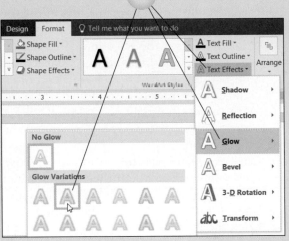

Check Your Work

Project 6 Prepare and Format a Company Organizational Chart   1 Part

You will prepare an organizational chart for a company and then apply formatting to enhance the visual appeal of the chart.

Preview Finished Project

Creating an Organizational Chart with SmartArt

Quick Steps

Insert an Organizational Chart
1. Click Insert tab.
2. Click SmartArt button.
3. Click *Hierarchy*.
4. Double-click organizational chart.

To visually illustrate hierarchical data, consider creating an organizational chart with a SmartArt option. To display organizational chart SmartArt options, click the Insert tab and then click the SmartArt button in the Illustrations group. At the Choose a SmartArt Graphic dialog box, click *Hierarchy* in the left panel. Organizational chart options display in the middle panel of the dialog box. Double-click an organizational chart and the chart is inserted in the document. Type text in a SmartArt graphic by selecting the shape and then typing text in it or type text in the *Type your text here* window at the left side of the graphic. Format a SmartArt organizational chart with options and buttons on the SmartArt Tools Design tab, the SmartArt Tools Format tab, and the Layout Options button.

1. At a blank document, create the organizational chart shown in Figure 7.13. To begin, click the Insert tab.
2. Click the SmartArt button in the Illustrations group.
3. At the Choose a SmartArt Graphic dialog box, click *Hierarchy* in the left panel of the dialog box and then double-click the *Organization Chart* option (first option in the middle panel).

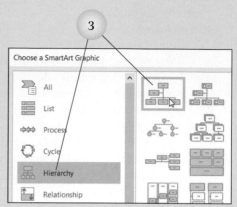

4. If a *Type your text here* pane displays at the left side of the organizational chart, close it by clicking the Text Pane button in the Create Graphic group.
5. Delete one of the boxes in the organizational chart by clicking the border of the box in the lower right corner to select it and then pressing the Delete key. (Make sure that the selection border surrounding the box is a solid line and not a dashed line. If a dashed line displays, click the box border again. This should change the border to a solid line.)
6. With the bottom right box selected, click the Add Shape button arrow in the Create Graphic group and then click the *Add Shape Below* option.

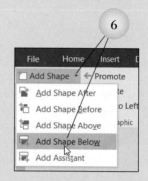

7. Click the *[Text]* placeholder in the top box, type Blaine Willis, press Shift + Enter, and then type President. Click in each of the remaining boxes and type the text as shown in Figure 7.13. (Press Shift + Enter after typing the name.)
8. Click the More SmartArt Styles button in the gallery in the SmartArt Styles group and then click the *Inset* style (second column, first row in the *3-D* section).
9. Click the Change Colors button in the SmartArt Styles group and then click the *Colorful Range - Accent Colors 4 to 5* option (fourth option in the *Colorful* section).
10. Click the SmartArt Tools Format tab.
11. Click the text pane control (displays with a left-pointing arrow) at the left side of the graphic border. (This displays the *Type your text here* window.)

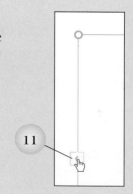

12. Using the mouse, select all the text in the *Type your text here* window.
13. Click the Change Shape button in the Shapes group and then click the *Round Same Side Corner Rectangle* option (eighth option in the *Rectangles* section).

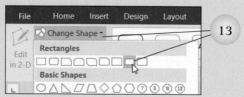

14. Click the Shape Outline button arrow in the Shape Styles group and then click the *Dark Blue* color option (ninth option in the *Standard Colors* section).
15. Close the *Type your text here* window by clicking the Close button in the upper right corner of the window.
16. Click inside the organizational chart border but outside any shape.
17. Click the Size button at the right side of the SmartArt Tools Format tab, click in the *Shape Height* measurement box, and then type 4. Click in the *Shape Width* measurement box, type 6.5, and then press the Enter key.
18. Click outside the chart to deselect it.
19. Save the document and name it **7-OrgChart**.
20. Print and then close the document.

Check Your Work

Figure 7.13 Project 6

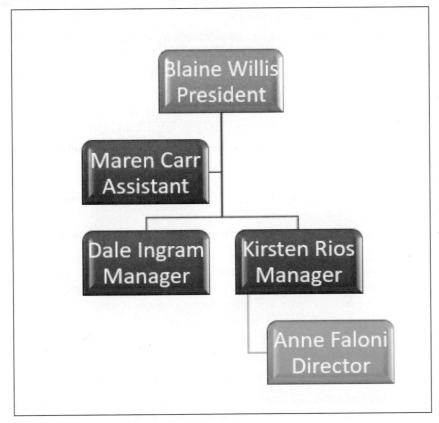

Chapter Summary

- Use the Tables feature to create columns and rows of information. Create a table with the Table button in the Tables group on the Insert tab or with options at the Insert Table dialog box.

- A cell is the intersection between a row and a column. The lines that form the cells of the table are called *gridlines*.

- Move the insertion point to cells in a table using the mouse by clicking in a cell or using the keyboard commands shown in Table 7.1.

- Change the table design with options and buttons on the Table Tools Design tab.

- Refer to Table 7.2 for a list of mouse commands for selecting specific cells in a table and Table 7.3 for a list of keyboard commands for selecting specific cells in a table.

- Change the layout of a table with options and buttons on the Table Tools Layout tab.

- Select a table, column, row, or cell using the Select button in the Table group on the Table Tools Layout tab.

- Turn on and off the display of gridlines by clicking the View Gridlines button in the Table group on the Table Tools Layout tab.

- Insert and delete columns and rows with buttons in the Rows & Columns group on the Table Tools Layout tab.

- Merge selected cells with the Merge Cells button and split cells with the Split Cells button, both in the Merge group on the Table Tools Layout tab.

- Change the column width and row height using the height and width measurement boxes in the Cell Size group on the Table Tools Layout tab; by dragging move table column markers on the horizontal ruler, adjust table row markers on the vertical ruler, or gridlines in the table; or using the AutoFit button in the Cell Size group.

- Change the alignment of text in cells with buttons in the Alignment group on the Table Tools Layout tab.

- If a table spans two pages, a header row can be inserted at the beginning of the rows that extend to the second page. To do this, click in the header row or select the header rows and then click the Repeat Header Rows button in the Data group on the Table Tools Layout tab.

- Change cell margins with options in the Table Options dialog box.

- Change text direction in a cell with the Text Direction button in the Alignment group on the Table Tools Layout tab.

- Change the table dimensions and alignment with options at the Table Properties dialog box with the Table tab selected.

- Use the resize handle to change the size of the table and the table move handle to move the table.

- Convert text to a table with the *Convert Text to Table* option at the Table button drop-down list. Convert a table to text with the Convert to Text button in the Data group on the Table Tools Layout tab.

- Draw a table in a document by clicking the Insert tab, clicking the Table button, and then clicking *Draw Table*. Using the mouse, drag in the document to create the table.

- Quick tables are predesigned tables that can be inserted in a document by clicking the Insert tab, clicking the Table button, pointing to *Quick Tables*, and then clicking a table at the side menu.
- Perform calculations on data in a table by clicking the Formula button in the Data group on the Table Tools Layout tab and then specifying the formula and number format at the Formula dialog box.
- Insert an Excel spreadsheet (worksheet) into a Word document to provide Excel functions by clicking the Insert tab, clicking the Table button in the Tables group, and then clicking Excel Spreadsheet at the drop-down list.
- Use the SmartArt feature to insert predesigned graphics and organizational charts in a document. Click the SmartArt button on the Insert tab to display the Choose a SmartArt Graphic dialog box.
- Format a SmartArt graphic with options and buttons on the SmartArt Tools Design tab and the SmartArt Tools Format tab.
- Choose a position or a text wrapping style for a SmartArt graphic with the Arrange button on the SmartArt Tools Format tab or the Layout Options button outside the upper right corner of the selected SmartArt graphic.

Commands Review

FEATURE	RIBBON TAB, GROUP	BUTTON, OPTION
AutoFit table contents	Table Tools Layout, Cell Size	
cell alignment	Table Tools Layout, Alignment	
Choose a SmartArt Graphic dialog box	Insert, Illustrations	
convert table to text	Table Tools Layout, Data	
convert text to table	Insert, Tables	, *Convert Text to Table*
delete column	Table Tools Layout, Rows & Columns	, *Delete Columns*
delete row	Table Tools Layout, Rows & Columns	, *Delete Rows*
delete table	Table Tools Layout, Rows & Columns	, *Delete Table*
draw table	Insert, Tables	, *Draw Table*
Formula dialog box	Table Tools Layout, Data	f_x
insert column left	Table Tools Layout, Rows & Columns	
insert column right	Table Tools Layout, Rows & Columns	
Insert Excel spreadsheet	Insert, Tables	, *Excel Spreadsheet*
insert row above	Table Tools Layout, Rows & Columns	

FEATURE	RIBBON TAB, GROUP	BUTTON, OPTION
insert row below	Table Tools Layout, Rows & Columns	
Insert Table dialog box	Insert, Tables	, *Insert Table*
merge cells	Table Tools Layout, Merge	
Quick Table	Insert, Tables	, *Quick Tables*
repeat header row	Table Tools Layout, Data	
Split Cells dialog box	Table Tools Layout, Merge	
table	Insert, Tables	
Table Options dialog box	Table Tools Layout, Alignment	
text direction	Table Tools Layout, Alignment	
view gridlines	Table Tools Layout, Table	

Workbook

Chapter study tools and assessment activities are available in the *Workbook* ebook. These resources are designed to help you further develop and demonstrate mastery of the skills learned in this chapter.

Microsoft®
Word

Merging Documents

Performance Objectives

Upon successful completion of Chapter 8, you will be able to:

1 Create a data source file

2 Create a main document and merge it with a data source file

3 Preview a merge and check for errors before merging

4 Create an envelope, a labels, and a directory main document and then merge it with a data source file

5 Edit a data source file

6 Select specific records for merging

7 Input text during a merge

8 Use the Mail Merge wizard to merge a letter main document with a data source file

Precheck

Check your current skills to help focus your study.

Word includes a Mail Merge feature for creating customized letters, envelopes, labels, directories, email messages, and faxes. The Mail Merge feature is useful for situations where the same letter is to be sent to a number of people and an envelope needs to be created for each letter. Use Mail Merge to create a main document that contains a letter, an envelope, or other data and then merge it with a data source file. In this chapter, you will use Mail Merge to create letters, envelopes, labels, and directories.

Data Files

Before beginning chapter work, copy the WL1C8 folder to your storage medium and then make WL1C8 the active folder.

SNAP

If you are a SNAP user, launch the Precheck and Tutorials from your Assignments page.

Project 1 Merge Letters to Customers 3 Parts

You will create a data source file and a letter main document and then merge the main document with the records in the data source file.

Preview Finished Project

Completing a Merge

Use buttons and options on the Mailings tab to complete a merge. A merge generally takes two files: the data source file and the main document. The main document contains the standard text along with fields identifying where variable information is inserted during the merge. The data source file contains the variable information that will be inserted in the main document.

Use the Start Mail Merge button on the Mailings tab to identify the type of main document to be created and use the Select Recipients button to create a data source file or specify an existing data source file. The Mail Merge Wizard is also available to provide guidance on the merge process.

Start Mail Merge

Select Recipients

Tutorial

Creating a Data Source File

Creating a Data Source File

Before creating a data source file, determine what type of correspondence will be created and what type of information is needed to insert in the correspondence. Word provides predesigned field names when creating the data source file. Use these field names if they represent the desired data. Variable information in a data source file is saved as a record. A record contains all the information for one unit (for example, a person, family, customer, client, or business). A series of fields makes one record and a series of records makes a data source file.

Quick Steps

Create a Data Source File

1. Click Mailings tab.
2. Click Select Recipients button.
3. Click *Type a New List* at drop-down list.
4. Type data in predesigned or custom fields.
5. Click OK.

Create a data source file by clicking the Select Recipients button in the Start Mail Merge group on the Mailings tab and then clicking *Type a New List* at the drop-down list. At the New Address List dialog box, shown in Figure 8.1, use the predesigned fields offered by Word or edit the fields by clicking the Customize Columns button. At the Customize Address List dialog box, insert new fields or delete existing fields and then click OK. With the fields established, type the required data. Note that fields in the main document correspond to the column headings in the data source file. When all the records have been entered, click OK.

Figure 8.1 New Address List Dialog Box

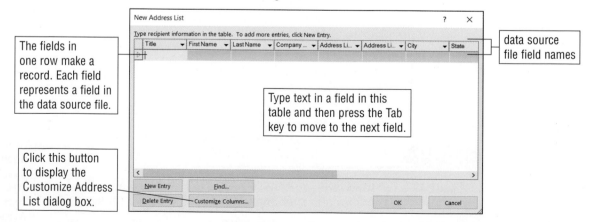

The fields in one row make a record. Each field represents a field in the data source file.

data source file field names

Type text in a field in this table and then press the Tab key to move to the next field.

Click this button to display the Customize Address List dialog box.

At the Save Address List dialog box, navigate to the desired folder, type a name for the data source file, and then click OK. Word saves a data source file as an Access database. Having Access is not required on the computer to complete a merge with a data source file.

Project 1a   Creating a Data Source File

Part 1 of 3

1. At a blank document, click the Mailings tab.
2. Click the Start Mail Merge button in the Start Mail Merge group and then click *Letters* at the drop-down list.
3. Click the Select Recipients button in the Start Mail Merge group and then click *Type a New List* at the drop-down list.

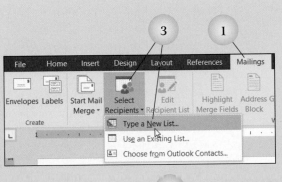

4. At the New Address List dialog box, Word provides a number of predesigned fields. Delete the fields you do not need by completing the following steps:
   a. Click the Customize Columns button.
   b. At the Customize Address List dialog box, click *Company Name* to select it and then click the Delete button.
   c. At the message that displays, click Yes.
   d. Complete steps similar to those in 4b and 4c to delete the following fields:
      Country or Region
      Home Phone
      Work Phone
      E-mail Address

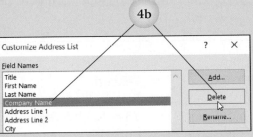

5. Insert a custom field by completing the following steps:
   a. With the *ZIP Code* field selected in the *Field Names* list in the Customize Address List dialog box, click the Add button.
   b. At the Add Field dialog box, type Fund and then click OK.
   c. Click OK to close the Customize Address List dialog box.
6. At the New Address List dialog box, enter the information for the first client shown in Figure 8.2 by completing the following steps:
   a. Type Mr. in the field in the *Title* column and then press the Tab key. (This moves the insertion point to the field in the *First Name* column. Pressing Shift + Tab will move the insertion point to the previous field. When typing text, do not press the spacebar after the last word in the field and proofread all entries to ensure that the data is accurate.)

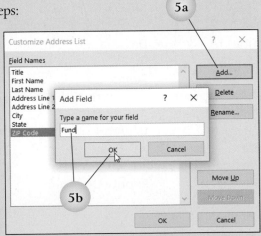

   b. Type Kenneth and then press the Tab key.
   c. Type Porter and then press the Tab key.
   d. Type 7645 Tenth Street and then press the Tab key.
   e. Type Apt. 314 and then press the Tab key.

f. Type New York and then press the Tab key.
g. Type NY and then press the Tab key.
h. Type 10192 and then press the Tab key.
i. Type Mutual Investment Fund and then press the Tab key. (This makes the field in the *Title* column active in the next row.)
j. With the insertion point positioned in the field in the *Title* column, complete steps similar to those in 6a through 6i to enter the information for the three other clients shown in Figure 8.2 (reading the records from left to right).

7. After entering all the information for the last client in Figure 8.2 (Mrs. Wanda Houston), click OK in the bottom right corner of the New Address List dialog box.

8. At the Save Address List dialog box, navigate to the WL1C8 folder on your storage medium, type 8-MFDS in the *File name* text box, and then click the Save button.

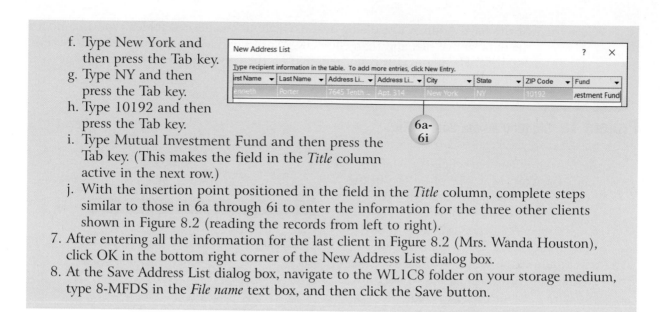

Figure 8.2 Project 1a

Title	= Mr.		Title	= Ms.
First Name	= Kenneth		First Name	= Carolyn
Last Name	= Porter		Last Name	= Renquist
Address Line 1	= 7645 Tenth Street		Address Line 1	= 13255 Meridian Street
Address Line 2	= Apt. 314		Address Line 2	= (leave this blank)
City	= New York		City	= New York
State	= NY		State	= NY
Zip Code	= 10192		Zip Code	= 10435
Fund	= Mutual Investment Fund		Fund	= Quality Care Fund
Title	= Dr.		Title	= Mrs.
First Name	= Amil		First Name	= Wanda
Last Name	= Ranna		Last Name	= Houston
Address Line 1	= 433 South 17th Street		Address Line 1	= 566 North 22nd Avenue
Address Line 2	= Apt. 17-D		Address Line 2	= (leave this blank)
City	= New York		City	= New York
State	= NY		State	= NY
Zip Code	= 10322		Zip Code	= 10634
Fund	= Priority One Fund		Fund	= Quality Care Fund

Tutorial

Creating a Main Document

Creating a Main Document

After creating and typing the records in the data source file, type the main document. Insert in the main document fields that identify where variable information is to be inserted when the document is merged with the data source file. Use buttons in the Write & Insert Fields group to insert fields in the main document.

Quick Steps

Create a Main Document
1. Click Mailings tab.
2. Click Start Mail Merge button.
3. Click document type at drop-down list.
4. Type main document text and insert fields as needed.

Insert all of the fields required for the inside address of a letter with the Address Block button in the Write & Insert Fields group. Click this button and the Insert Address Block dialog box displays with a preview of how the fields will be inserted in the document to create the inside address; the dialog box also contains buttons and options for customizing the fields. Click OK and the «AddressBlock» field is inserted in the document. The «AddressBlock» field is an example of a composite field, which groups a number of fields (such as *Title, First Name, Last Name, Address Line 1*, and so on).

Click the Greeting Line button and the Insert Greeting Line dialog box displays with options for customizing how the fields are inserted in the document to create the greeting line. Click OK at the dialog box and the «GreetingLine» composite field is inserted in the document.

To insert an individual field from the data source file, click the Insert Merge Field button. This displays the Insert Merge Field dialog box with a list of fields from the data source file. Click the Insert Merge Field button arrow and a drop-down list displays containing the fields in the data source file.

A field or composite field is inserted in the main document surrounded by chevrons (« and »). The chevrons distinguish fields in the main document and do not display in the merged document. Formatting can be applied to merged data by formatting the merge field in the main document.

 Address Block

 Greeting Line

 Insert Merge Field

Project 1b Creating a Main Document

Part 2 of 3

1. At a blank document, create the letter shown in Figure 8.3. Begin by clicking the *No Spacing* style in the styles gallery on the Home tab.
2. Press the Enter key six times and then type February 23, 2018.
3. Press the Enter key four times and then insert the «AddressBlock» composite field by completing the following steps:
   a. Click the Mailings tab and then click the Address Block button in the Write & Insert Fields group.
   b. At the Insert Address Block dialog box, click OK.
   c. Press the Enter key two times.
4. Insert the «GreetingLine» composite field by completing the following steps:
   a. Click the Greeting Line button in the Write & Insert Fields group.
   b. At the Insert Greeting Line dialog box, click the option box arrow for the option box containing the comma (the box to the right of the box containing *Mr. Randall*).
   c. At the drop-down list, click the colon.
   d. Click OK to close the Insert Greeting Line dialog box.
   e. Press the Enter key two times.

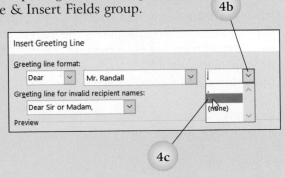

5. Type the letter shown in Figure 8.3 to the point where «Fund» displays and then insert the «Fund» field by clicking the Insert Merge Field button arrow and then clicking *Fund* at the drop-down list.
6. Type the letter to the point where the «Title» field displays and then insert the «Title» field by clicking the Insert Merge Field button arrow and then clicking *Title* at the drop-down list.
7. Press the spacebar and then insert the «Last_Name» field by clicking the Insert Merge Field button arrow and then clicking *Last_Name* at the drop-down list.
8. Type the remainder of the letter shown in Figure 8.3. (Insert your initials instead of *XX* at the end of the letter.)
9. Save the document and name it **8-MFMD**.

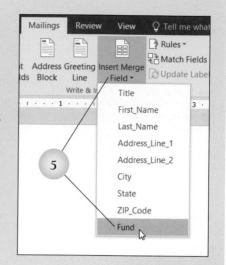

Check Your Work

Figure 8.3 Project 1b

February 23, 2018

«AddressBlock»

«GreetingLine»

McCormack Funds is lowering its expense charges beginning May 1, 2018. The reduction in expense charges means that more of your account investment performance in the «Fund» is returned to you, «Title» «Last_Name». The reductions are worth your attention because most of our competitors' fees have gone up.

Lowering expense charges is noteworthy because before the reduction, McCormack expense deductions were already among the lowest, far below most mutual funds and variable annuity accounts with similar objectives. At the same time, services for you, our client, will continue to expand. If you would like to discuss this change, please call us at (212) 555-2277. Your financial future is our main concern at McCormack.

Sincerely,

Jodie Langstrom
Director, Financial Services

XX
8-MFMD.docx

Preview
Results

First
Record

Previous
Record

Next
Record

Last
Record

Find
Recipient

Previewing a Merge

To view how the main document will appear when merged with the first record in the data source file, click the Preview Results button on the Mailings tab. View the main document merged with other records by using the navigation buttons in the Preview Results group. This group contains the First Record, Previous Record, Next Record, and Last Record buttons and the *Go to Record* text box. Click the button that will display the main document merged with the desired record. Viewing the merged document before printing is helpful to ensure that the merged data is correct. To use the *Go to Record* text box, click in the text box, type the number of the record, and then press the Enter key. Turn off the preview feature by clicking the Preview Results button.

The Preview Results group on the Mailings tab also includes a Find Recipient button. To search for and preview merged documents with specific entries, click the Preview Results button and then click the Find Recipient button. At the Find Entry dialog box, type the specific field entry in the *Find* text box and then click the Find Next button. Continue clicking the Find Next button until Word displays a message indicating that there are no more entries that contain the typed text.

Checking for Errors

Check for
Errors

Before merging documents, check for errors using the Check for Errors button in the Preview Results group on the Mailings tab. Click this button and the Checking and Reporting Errors dialog box, shown in Figure 8.4, displays containing three options. Click the first option, *Simulate the merge and report errors in a new document,* and Word will test the merge, not make any changes, and report errors in a new document. Choose the second option, *Complete the merge, pausing to report each error as it occurs,* and Word will merge the documents and display errors as they occur during the merge. Choose the third option, *Complete the merge without pausing. Report errors in a new document,* and Word will complete the merge without pausing and insert any errors in a new document.

Merging Documents

Finish &
Merge

To complete the merge, click the Finish & Merge button in the Finish group on the Mailings tab. At the drop-down list, merge the records and create a new document, send the merged documents directly to the printer, or send the merged documents by email.

Figure 8.4 Checking and Reporting Errors Dialog Box

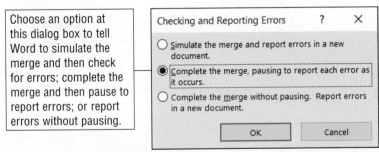

Choose an option at this dialog box to tell Word to simulate the merge and then check for errors; complete the merge and then pause to report errors; or report errors without pausing.

Quick Steps

Merge Documents
1. Click Finish & Merge button.
2. Click *Edit Individual Documents* at drop-down list.
3. Make sure *All* is selected in Merge to New Document dialog box.
4. Click OK.

Hint Press Alt + Shift + N to display the Merge to New Document dialog box and press Alt + Shift + M to display the Merge to Printer dialog box.

To merge the documents and create a new document with the merged records, click the Finish & Merge button and then click *Edit Individual Documents* at the drop-down list. At the Merge to New Document dialog box, make sure *All* is selected in the *Merge records* section and then click OK. This merges the records in the data source file with the main document and inserts the merged documents in a new document.

Identify specific records to be merged with options at the Merge to New Document dialog box. Display this dialog box by clicking the Finish & Merge button on the Mailings tab and then clicking the *Edit Individual Documents* option at the drop-down list. Click the *All* option in the Merge to New Document dialog box to merge all the records in the data source file and click the *Current record* option to merge only the current record. To merge specific adjacent records, click in the *From* text box, type the beginning record number, press the Tab key, and then type the ending record number in the *To* text box.

Project 1c Merging the Main Document with the Data Source File

Part 3 of 3

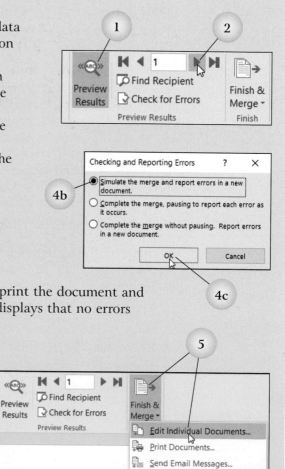

1. With **8-MFMD.docx** open, preview the main document merged with the first record in the data source file by clicking the Preview Results button on the Mailings tab.
2. Click the Next Record button to view the main document merged with the second record in the data source file.
3. Click the Preview Results button to turn off the preview feature.
4. Automatically check for errors by completing the following steps:
   a. Click the Check for Errors button in the Preview Results group on the Mailings tab.
   b. At the Checking and Reporting Errors dialog box, click the first option, *Simulate the merge and report errors in a new document*.
   c. Click OK.
   d. If a new document displays with any errors, print the document and then close it without saving it. If a message displays that no errors were found, click OK.
5. Click the Finish & Merge button in the Finish group and then click *Edit Individual Documents* at the drop-down list.
6. At the Merge to New Document dialog box, make sure *All* is selected and then click OK.
7. Save the merged letters and name the document **8-MFLtrs**.
8. Print **8-MFLtrs.docx**. (This document will print four letters.)
9. Close **8-MFLtrs.docx**.
10. Save and then close **8-MFMD.docx**.

Check Your Work

You will use Mail Merge to prepare envelopes with customer names and addresses.

Preview Finished Project

Tutorial

Merging Labels

Merging with Other Main Documents

In addition to merging letters, a data source file can be merged with an envelope, label, or directory main document. Create an envelope main document with the *Envelopes* option at the Start Mail Merge button drop-down list and create a label main document with the *Labels* option. Create a directory, which merges fields to the same page, with the *Directory* option at the Start Mail Merge button drop-down list.

Tutorial

Merging Envelopes

Merging Envelopes

A letter created as a main document and then merged with a data source file will more than likely need properly addressed envelopes in which to send the letters. To prepare an envelope main document that is merged with a data source file, click the Mailings tab, click the Start Mail Merge button, and then click *Envelopes* at the drop-down list. This displays the Envelope Options dialog box, as shown in Figure 8.5. At this dialog box, specify the envelope size, make any other changes, and then click OK.

The next step in the envelope merge process is to create the data source file or identify an existing data source file. To identify an existing data source file, click the Select Recipients button in the Start Mail Merge group and then click *Use an Existing List* at the drop-down list. At the Select Data Source dialog box, navigate to the folder containing the data source file and then double-click the file.

With the data source file attached to the envelope main document, the next step is to insert the appropriate fields. Click in the envelope in the approximate location the recipient's address will appear and a box with a dashed gray border displays. Click the Address Block button in the Write & Insert Fields group and then click OK at the Insert Address Block dialog box.

Figure 8.5 Envelope Options Dialog Box

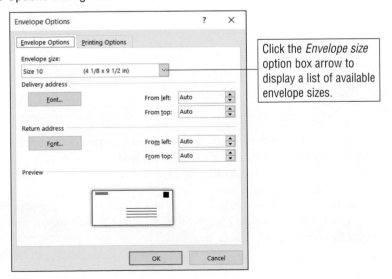

Click the *Envelope size* option box arrow to display a list of available envelope sizes.

Project 2 Merging Envelopes

Part 1 of 1

1. At a blank document, click the Mailings tab.
2. Click the Start Mail Merge button in the Start Mail Merge group and then click *Envelopes* at the drop-down list.

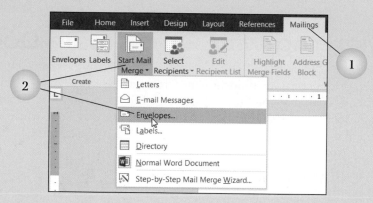

3. At the Envelope Options dialog box, make sure the envelope size is Size 10 and then click OK.
4. Click the Select Recipients button in the Start Mail Merge group and then click *Use an Existing List* at the drop-down list.

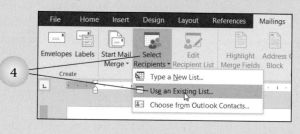

5. At the Select Data Source dialog box, navigate to the WL1C8 folder on your storage medium and then double-click the data source file named *8-MFDS.mdb*.
6. Click in the approximate location in the envelope document where the recipient's address will appear. (This causes a box with a dashed gray border to display. If you do not see this box, try clicking in a different location on the envelope.)

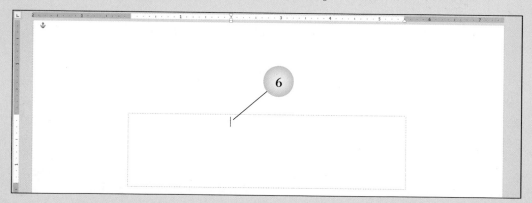

7. Click the Address Block button in the Write & Insert Fields group.
8. At the Insert Address Block dialog box, click OK.
9. Click the Preview Results button to see how the envelope appears merged with the first record in the data source file.
10. Click the Preview Results button to turn off the preview feature.
11. Click the Finish & Merge button in the Finish group and then click *Edit Individual Documents* at the drop-down list.

12. At the Merge to New Document dialog box, specify that you want only the first two records to merge by completing the following steps:
    a. Click in the *From* text box and then type 1.
    b. Click in the *To* text box and then type 2.
    c. Click OK. (This merges only the first two records and opens a document with two merged envelopes.)
13. Save the merged envelopes and name the document **8-MFEnvs**.
14. Print **8-MFEnvs.docx**. (This document will print two envelopes. Manual feeding of the envelopes may be required. Please check with your instructor.)
15. Close **8-MFEnvs.docx**.
16. Save the envelope main document and name it **8-EnvMD**.
17. Close **8-EnvMD.docx**.

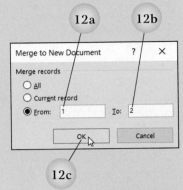

Check Your Work

Project 3 Merge Mailing Labels   1 Part

You will use Mail Merge to prepare mailing labels with customer names and addresses.

Preview Finished Project

Merging Labels

Mailing labels for records in a data source file are created in much the same way that envelopes are created. Click the Start Mail Merge button and then click *Labels* at the drop-down list. This displays the Label Options dialog box, as shown in Figure 8.6. Make sure the desired label is selected and then click OK to close the dialog box. The next step is to create the data source file or identify an existing data source file. With the data source file attached to the label main document, insert the appropriate fields and then complete the merge.

Figure 8.6 Label Options Dialog Box

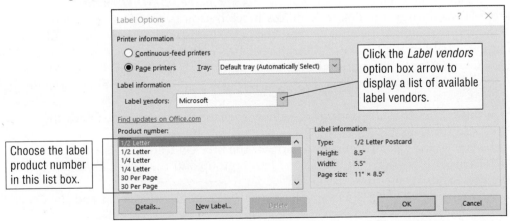

1. At a blank document, change the document zoom to 100% and then click the Mailings tab.
2. Click the Start Mail Merge button in the Start Mail Merge group and then click *Labels* at the drop-down list.
3. At the Label Options dialog box, complete the following steps:
   a. If necessary, click the *Label vendors* option box arrow and then click *Avery US Letter* at the drop-down list. (If this option is not available, choose a vendor that offers labels that print on a full page.)
   b. Scroll in the *Product number* list box and then, if necessary, click *5160 Easy Peel Address Labels*. (If this option is not available, choose a label number that prints labels in two or three columns down a full page.)
   c. Click OK to close the dialog box.

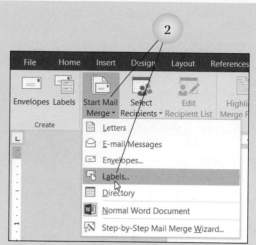

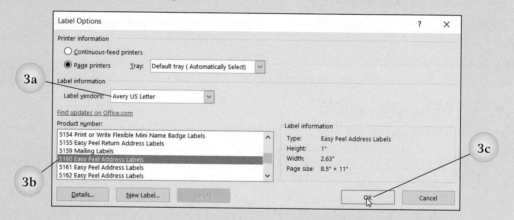

4. Click the Select Recipients button in the Start Mail Merge group and then click *Use an Existing List* at the drop-down list.
5. At the Select Data Source dialog box, navigate to the WL1C8 folder on your storage medium and then double-click the data source file named *8-MFDS.mdb*.
6. At the labels document, click the Address Block button in the Write & Insert Fields group.
7. At the Insert Address Block dialog box, click OK. (This inserts the «AddressBlock» composite field in the first label. The other labels contain the «Next Record» field.)
8. Click the Update Labels button in the Write & Insert Fields group. (This adds the «AddressBlock» composite field after each «Next Record» field in the second and subsequent labels.)
9. Click the Preview Results button to see how the labels appear merged with the records in the data source file.
10. Click the Preview Results button to turn off the preview feature.
11. Click the Finish & Merge button in the Finish group and then click *Edit Individual Documents* at the drop-down list.
12. At the Merge to New Document dialog box, make sure *All* is selected and then click OK.

13. Format the labels by completing the following steps:
   a. Click the Table Tools Layout tab.
   b. Click the Select button in the Table group and then click the *Select Table* option.
   c. Click the Align Center Left button in the Alignment group.
   d. Click the Home tab and then click the Paragraph group dialog box launcher.
   e. At the Paragraph dialog box, click the *Before* measurement box up arrow to change the measurement to 0 points.
   f. Click the *After* measurement box up arrow to change the measurement to 0 points.
   g. Click the *Inside* measurement box up arrow three times to change the measurement to 0.3 inch.
   h. Click OK.

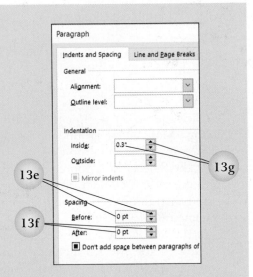

14. Save the merged labels and name the document **8-MFLabels**.
15. Print and then close **8-MFLabels.docx**.
16. Save the label main document and name it **8-LabelsMD**.
17. Close **8-LabelsMD.docx**.

Check Your Work

Project 4 Merge a Directory
1 Part

You will use Mail Merge to prepare a directory list containing customer names and types of financial investment funds.

Preview Finished Project

Tutorial

Merging a Directory

Merging a Directory

When merging letters, envelopes, or mailing labels, a new form is created for each record. For example, if the data source file merged with the letter contains eight records, eight letters are created, each on a separate page. If the data source file merged with a mailing label contains 20 records, 20 labels are created. In some situations, merged information should remain on the same page. This is useful, for example, when creating a list such as a directory or address list.

Begin creating a merged directory by clicking the Start Mail Merge button and then clicking *Directory* at the drop-down list. Create or identify an existing data source file and then insert the desired fields in the directory document. To display the merged data in columns, set tabs for all of the columns.

1. At a blank document, click the Mailings tab.
2. Click the Start Mail Merge button in the Start Mail Merge group and then click *Directory* at the drop-down list.
3. Click the Select Recipients button in the Start Mail Merge group and then click *Use an Existing List* at the drop-down list.
4. At the Select Data Source dialog box, navigate to the WL1C8 folder on your storage medium and then double-click the data source file named **8-MFDS.mdb**.

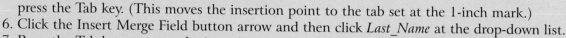

5. At the document screen, set left tabs at the 1-inch mark, the 2.5-inch mark, and the 4-inch mark on the horizontal ruler and then press the Tab key. (This moves the insertion point to the tab set at the 1-inch mark.)
6. Click the Insert Merge Field button arrow and then click *Last_Name* at the drop-down list.
7. Press the Tab key to move the insertion point to the tab set at the 2.5-inch mark.
8. Click the Insert Merge Field button arrow and then click *First_Name* at the drop-down list.
9. Press the Tab key to move the insertion point to the tab set at the 4-inch mark.
10. Click the Insert Merge Field button arrow and then click *Fund* at the drop-down list.
11. Press the Enter key.
12. Click the Finish & Merge button in the Finish group and then click *Edit Individual Documents* at the drop-down list.
13. At the Merge to New Document dialog box, make sure *All* is selected and then click OK. (This merges the fields in the document.)
14. Press Ctrl + Home, press the Enter key, and then press the Up Arrow key.
15. Press the Tab key, turn on bold formatting, and then type Last Name.
16. Press the Tab key and then type First Name.
17. Press the Tab key and then type Fund.

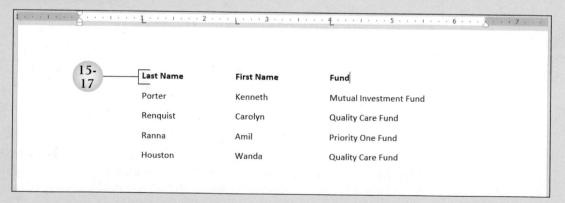

Last Name	First Name	Fund
Porter	Kenneth	Mutual Investment Fund
Renquist	Carolyn	Quality Care Fund
Ranna	Amil	Priority One Fund
Houston	Wanda	Quality Care Fund

18. Save the directory document and name it **8-Directory**.
19. Print and then close the document.
20. Close the directory main document without saving it.

Check Your Work

You will use Mail Merge to prepare mailing labels with the names and addresses of customers living in Baltimore.

Preview Finished Project

Tutorial

Editing a Data
Source File

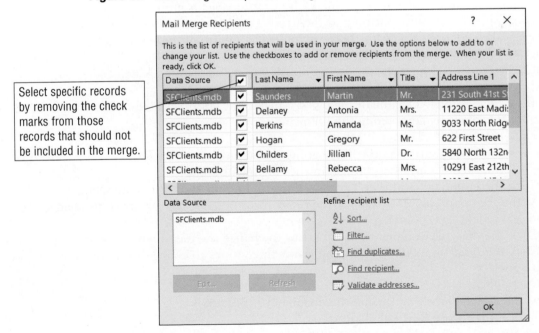

Edit Recipient
List

Editing a Data Source File

Edit a main document in the normal manner. Open the document, make the required changes, and then save the document. Since a data source file is actually an Access database file, it cannot be opened in the normal manner. Open a data source file for editing using the Edit Recipient List button in the Start Mail Merge group on the Mailings tab. Click the Edit Recipient List button and the Mail Merge Recipients dialog box displays, as shown in Figure 8.7. Select or edit records at this dialog box.

Selecting Specific Records

Each record in the Mail Merge Recipients dialog box contains a check mark before the first field. To select specific records, remove the check marks from those records that should not be included in a merge. This way, only certain records in the data source file will be merged with the main document.

Figure 8.7 Mail Merge Recipients Dialog Box

Select specific records by removing the check marks from those records that should not be included in the merge.

Data Source	☑	Last Name	First Name	Title	Address Line 1
SFClients.mdb	☑	Saunders	Martin	Mr.	231 South 41st St
SFClients.mdb	☑	Delaney	Antonia	Mrs.	11220 East Madi:
SFClients.mdb	☑	Perkins	Amanda	Ms.	9033 North Ridg
SFClients.mdb	☑	Hogan	Gregory	Mr.	622 First Street
SFClients.mdb	☑	Childers	Jillian	Dr.	5840 North 132n
SFClients.mdb	☑	Bellamy	Rebecca	Mrs.	10291 East 212th

1. At a blank document, create mailing labels for customers living in Baltimore. Begin by clicking the Mailings tab.
2. Click the Start Mail Merge button in the Start Mail Merge group and then click *Labels* at the drop-down list.
3. At the Label Options dialog box, make sure *Avery US Letter* displays in the *Label vendors* option box and *5160 Easy Peel Address Labels* displays in the *Product number* list box and then click OK.
4. Click the Select Recipients button in the Start Mail Merge group and then click *Use an Existing List* at the drop-down list.
5. At the Select Data Source dialog box, navigate to the WL1C8 folder on your storage medium and then double-click the data source file named **SFClients.mdb**.
6. Click the Edit Recipient List button in the Start Mail Merge group.
7. At the Mail Merge Recipients dialog box, complete the following steps:
   a. Click the check box immediately left of the *Last Name* field column heading to remove the check mark. (This removes all the check marks from the check boxes.)
   b. Click the check box immediately left of each of the following last names: *Saunders, Perkins, Dutton, Fernandez,* and *Stahl.* (These are the customers who live in Baltimore.)
   c. Click OK to close the dialog box.

7a

Mail Merge Recipients		
This is the list of recipients that will be used in your merge. Use the change your list. Use the checkboxes to add or remove recipients fr ready, click OK.

Data Source		Last Name ▼	First Name ▼
SFClients.mdb		Saunders	Martin
SFClients.mdb		Delaney	Antonia

8. At the labels document, click the Address Block button in the Write & Insert Fields group.
9. At the Insert Address Block dialog box, click OK.
10. Click the Update Labels button in the Write & Insert Fields group.
11. Click the Preview Results button and then click the Previous Record button to display each label. Make sure only labels for those customers living in Baltimore display.
12. Click the Preview Results button to turn off the preview feature.
13. Click the Finish & Merge button in the Finish group and then click *Edit Individual Documents* at the drop-down list.
14. At the Merge to New Document dialog box, make sure *All* is selected and then click OK.
15. Format the labels by completing the following steps:
   a. Click the Table Tools Layout tab.
   b. Click the Select button in the Table group and then click *Select Table*.
   c. Click the Align Center Left button in the Alignment group.
   d. Click the Home tab and then click the Paragraph group dialog box launcher.
   e. At the Paragraph dialog box, click the *Before* measurement box up arrow to change the measurement to 0 points.
   f. Click the *After* measurement box up arrow to change the measurement to 0 points.
   g. Click the *Inside* measurement box up arrow three times to change the measurement to 0.3 inch.
   h. Click OK.
16. Save the merged labels and name the document **8-SFLabels**.
17. Print and then close **8-SFLabels.docx**.
18. Close the main labels document without saving it.

Check Your Work

You will edit records in a data source file and then use Mail Merge to prepare a directory with the edited records that contains customer names, telephone numbers, and cell phone numbers.

Preview Finished Project

Editing Records

Quick Steps

Edit a Data Source File
1. Open main document.
2. Click Mailings tab.
3. Click Edit Recipient List button.
4. Click data source file name in *Data Source* list box.
5. Click Edit button.
6. Make changes at Edit Data Source dialog box.
7. Click OK.
8. Click OK.

A data source file may need editing on a periodic basis to add or delete customer names, update fields, insert new fields, or delete existing fields. To edit a data source file, click the Edit Recipient List button in the Start Mail Merge group. At the Mail Merge Recipients dialog box, click the data source file name in the *Data Source* list box and then click the Edit button below the list box. This displays the Edit Data Source dialog box, as shown in Figure 8.8. At this dialog box, add a new entry, delete an entry, find a particular entry, and customize columns.

Figure 8.8 Edit Data Source Dialog Box

Edit text in fields in columns in the data source file at this dialog box.

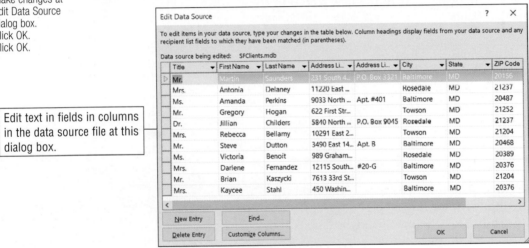

Project 6 **Editing Records in a Data Source File** Part 1 of 1

1. Make a copy of the **SFClients.mdb** file by completing the following steps:
   a. Display the Open dialog box and make WL1C8 the active folder.
   b. If necessary, change the file type option to *All Files (*.*)*.
   c. Right-click **SFClients.mdb** and then click *Copy* at the shortcut menu.
   d. Position the mouse pointer in a white portion of the Open dialog box Content pane (outside any file name), click the right mouse button, and then click *Paste* at the shortcut menu. (This inserts a copy of the file in the dialog box Content pane and names the file **SFClients - Copy.mdb**.)
   e. Right-click **SFClients - Copy.mdb** and then click *Rename* at the shortcut menu.
   f. Type 8-DS and then press the Enter key.
   g. Close the Open dialog box.

2. At a blank document, click the Mailings tab.
3. Click the Select Recipients button and then click *Use an Existing List* from the drop-down list.
4. At the Select Data Source dialog box, navigate to the WL1C8 folder on your storage medium and then double-click the data source file named ***8-DS.mdb***.
5. Click the Edit Recipient List button in the Start Mail Merge group.
6. At the Mail Merge Recipients dialog box, click *8-DS.mdb* in the *Data Source* list box and then click the Edit button.
7. Delete the record for Steve Dutton by completing the following steps:
   a. Click the square at the beginning of the row for *Mr. Steve Dutton*.
   b. Click the Delete Entry button.
   c. At the message asking if you want to delete the entry, click Yes.
8. Insert a new record by completing the following steps:
   a. Click the New Entry button in the dialog box.
   b. Type the following text in the new record in the specified fields:

Title	Ms.
First Name	Jennae
Last Name	Davis
Address Line 1	3120 South 21st
Address Line 2	(none)
City	Rosedale
State	MD
ZIP Code	20389
Home Phone	410-555-5774

9. Insert a new field and type text in the field by completing the following steps:
   a. At the Edit Data Source dialog box, click the Customize Columns button.
   b. At the message asking if you want to save the changes made to the data source file, click Yes.
   c. At the Customize Address List dialog box, click *ZIP Code* in the *Field Names* list box. (A new field is inserted below the selected field.)
   d. Click the Add button.
   e. At the Add Field dialog box, type Cell Phone and then click OK.
   f. You decide that you want the *Cell Phone* field to display after the *Home Phone* field. To move the *Cell Phone* field, make sure it is selected and then click the Move Down button.
   g. Click OK to close the Customize Address List dialog box.

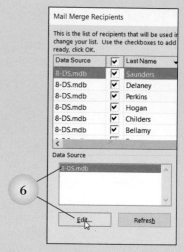

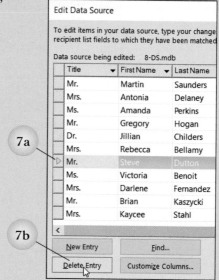

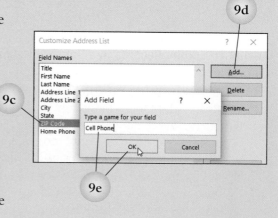

h. At the Edit Data Source dialog box, scroll to the right to display the *Cell Phone* field (last field in the file) and then type the following cell phone numbers (after typing each cell phone number except the last number, press the Down Arrow key to make the next field below active):

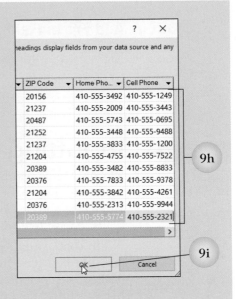

	ZIP Code	Home Pho...	Cell Phone
	20156	410-555-3492	410-555-1249
	21237	410-555-2009	410-555-3443
	20487	410-555-5743	410-555-0695
	21252	410-555-3448	410-555-9488
	21237	410-555-3833	410-555-1200
	21204	410-555-4755	410-555-7522
	20389	410-555-3482	410-555-8833
	20376	410-555-7833	410-555-9378
	21204	410-555-3842	410-555-4261
	20376	410-555-2313	410-555-9944
	20389	410-555-5774	410-555-2321

9h

9i

Record 1   410-555-1249
Record 2   410-555-3443
Record 3   410-555-0695
Record 4   410-555-9488
Record 5   410-555-1200
Record 6   410-555-7522
Record 7   410-555-8833
Record 8   410-555-9378
Record 9   410-555-4261
Record 10   410-555-9944
Record 11   410-555-2321

  i. Click OK to close the Edit Data Source dialog box.
  j. At the message asking if you want to update the recipient list and save changes, click Yes.
  k. At the Mail Merge Recipients dialog box, click OK.
10. Create a directory by completing the following steps:
  a. Click the Start Mail Merge button and then click *Directory* at the drop-down list.
  b. At the blank document, set left tabs on the horizontal ruler at the 1-inch mark, the 3-inch mark, and the 4.5-inch mark.
  c. Press the Tab key. (This moves the insertion point to the first tab set at the 1-inch mark.)
  d. Click the Insert Merge Field button arrow and then click *Last_Name* at the drop-down list.
  e. Type a comma and then press the spacebar.
  f. Click the Insert Merge Field button arrow and then click *First_Name* at the drop-down list.
  g. Press the Tab key, click the Insert Merge Field button arrow, and then click *Home_Phone* at the drop-down list.
  h. Press the Tab key, click the Insert Merge Field button arrow, and then click *Cell_Phone* at the drop-down list.
  i. Press the Enter key.
  j. Click the Finish & Merge button in the Finish group and then click *Edit Individual Documents* at the drop-down list.
  k. At the Merge to New Document dialog box, make sure *All* is selected and then click OK. (This merges the fields in the document.)
11. Press Ctrl + Home, press the Enter key, and then press the Up Arrow key.
12. Press the Tab key, turn on bold formatting, and then type Name.
13. Press the Tab key and then type Home Phone.
14. Press the Tab key and then type Cell Phone.

12-14

Name	**Home Phone**	**Cell Phone**
Saunders	Martin	410-555-1249
Delaney	Antonia	410-555-3443

15. Save the directory document and name it **8-Directory-P6**.
16. Print and then close the document.
17. Close the directory main document without saving it.

Check Your Work

You will edit a form letter and insert sales representative contact information during a merge.

Preview Finished Project

Tutorial

Inputting Text during a Merge

Inputting Text during a Merge

Word's Merge feature contains a large number of merge fields that can be inserted in a main document. The fill-in field is used to identify information that will be entered at the keyboard during a merge. For more information on the other merge fields, please refer to the on-screen help.

In some situations, keeping all the variable information in a data source file may not be necessary. For example, variable information that changes on a regular basis might include a customer's monthly balance, a product price, and so on. Insert a fill-in field in the main document and when the main document is merged with the data source file, variable information can be inserted in the document using the keyboard. Insert a fill-in field in a main document by clicking the Rules button in the Write & Insert Fields group on the Mailings tab and then clicking *Fill-in* at the drop-down list. This displays the Insert Word Field: fill-in dialog box, shown in Figure 8.9. At this dialog box, type a short message indicating what should be entered at the keyboard and then click OK. At the Microsoft Word dialog box with the message entered displayed in the upper left corner, type the text to display in the document and then click OK. When the fill-in field or fields are added, save the main document in the normal manner. A document can contain any number of fill-in fields.

 Rules

When the main document is merged with the data source file, the first record is merged with the main document and the Microsoft Word dialog box displays with the message entered displayed in the upper left corner. Type the required information for the first record in the data source file and then click OK. Word displays the dialog box again. Type the required information for the second record in the data source file and then click OK. Continue in this manner until the required information has been entered for each record in the data source file. Word then completes the merge.

Quick Steps

Insert a Fill-in Field in a Main Document
1. Click Mailings tab.
2. Click Rules button.
3. Click *Fill-in*.
4. Type prompt text.
5. Click OK.
6. Type text to be inserted.
7. Click OK.

Figure 8.9 Insert Word Field: Fill-in Dialog Box

In this text box, type a short message indicating what should be entered at the keyboard.

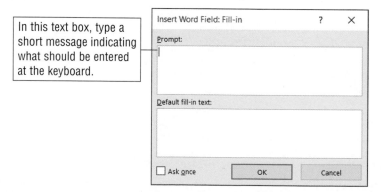

1. Open the document **8-MFMD.docx**. (At the message asking if you want to continue, click Yes.) Save the document with the name **8-MFMD-P7**.
2. Edit the second paragraph in the body of the letter to the paragraph shown in Figure 8.10. Insert the first fill-in field (representative's name) by completing the following steps:
   a. Click the Mailings tab.
   b. Click the Rules button in the Write & Insert Fields group and then click *Fill-in* at the drop-down list.
   c. At the Insert Word Field: Fill-in dialog box, type Insert rep name in the *Prompt* text box and then click OK.
   d. At the Microsoft Word dialog box with *Insert rep name* displayed in the upper left corner, type (representative's name) and then click OK.

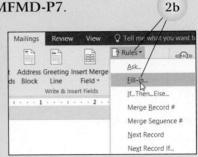

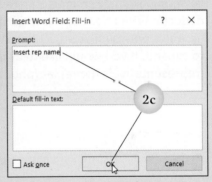

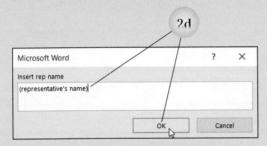

3. Complete steps similar to those in Step 2 to insert the second fill-in field (phone number), except type Insert phone number in the *Prompt* text box at the Insert Word Field: Fill-in dialog box and type (phone number) at the Microsoft Word dialog box.
4. Save **8-MFMD-P7.docx**.
5. Merge the main document with the data source file by completing the following steps:
   a. Click the Finish & Merge button and then click *Edit Individual Documents* at the drop-down list.
   b. At the Merge to New Document dialog box, make sure *All* is selected and then click OK.
   c. When Word merges the main document with the first record, a dialog box displays with the message *Insert rep name* and the text *(representative's name)* selected. At this dialog box, type Marilyn Smythe and then click OK.

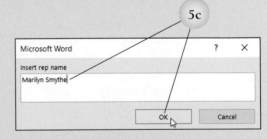

   d. At the dialog box with the message *Insert phone number* and *(phone number)* selected, type (646) 555-8944 and then click OK.
   e. At the dialog box with the message *Insert rep name*, type Anthony Mason (over *Marilyn Smythe*) and then click OK.
   f. At the dialog box with the message *Insert phone number*, type (646) 555-8901 (over the previous number) and then click OK.
   g. At the dialog box with the message *Insert rep name*, type Faith Ostrom (over *Anthony Mason*) and then click OK.
   h. At the dialog box with the message *Insert phone number*, type (646) 555-8967 (over the previous number) and then click OK.

i. At the dialog box with the message *Insert rep name*, type Thomas Rivers (over *Faith Ostrom*) and then click OK.

j. At the dialog box with the message *Insert phone number*, type (646) 555-0793 (over the previous number) and then click OK.

6. Save the merged document and name it **8-MFLtrs**.
7. Print and then close **8-MFLtrs.docx**.
8. Save and then close **8-MFMD-P7.docx**.

Check Your Work

Figure 8.10 Project 7

Lowering expense charges is noteworthy because before the reduction, McCormack expense deductions were already among the lowest, far below most mutual funds and variable annuity accounts with similar objectives. At the same time, services for you, our client, will continue to expand. If you would like to discuss this change, please call our service representative, **(representative's name)**, at **(phone number)**.

Project 8 Use Mail Merge Wizard   1 Part

You will use the Mail Merge wizard to merge a main document with a data source file and create letters for clients of Sorenson Funds.

Preview Finished Project

Tutorial

Using the Mail Merge Wizard

Merging Using the Mail Merge Wizard

The Mail Merge feature includes a Mail Merge wizard with steps for completing the merge process. To access the wizard, click the Mailings tab, click the Start Mail Merge button, and then click the *Step-by-Step Mail Merge Wizard* option at the drop-down list. The first of six Mail Merge task panes displays at the right side of the screen. The options in each task pane may vary depending on the type of merge being performed. Generally, one of the following steps is completed at each task pane:

- Step 1: Select the type of document to be created, such as a letter, email message, envelope, label, or directory.
- Step 2: Specify whether the current document is to be used to create the main document, a template, or an existing document.
- Step 3: Specify whether a new list will be created or an existing list or Outlook contacts list will be used.
- Step 4: Use the items in this task pane to help prepare the main document by performing tasks such as inserting fields.
- Step 5: Preview the merged documents.
- Step 6: Complete the merge.

1. At a blank document, click the Mailings tab, click the Start Mail Merge button in the Start Mail Merge group, and then click *Step-by-Step Mail Merge Wizard* at the drop-down list.

2. At the first Mail Merge task pane, make sure *Letters* is selected in the *Select document type* section and then click the <u>Next: Starting document</u> hyperlink at the bottom of the task pane.

3. At the second Mail Merge task pane, click the *Start from existing document* option in the *Select starting document* section.

4. Click the Open button in the *Start from existing* section of the task pane.

5. At the Open dialog box, navigate to the WL1C8 folder on your storage medium and then double-click *SFLtrMD.docx*.

6. Click the <u>Next: Select recipients</u> hyperlink at the bottom of the task pane.

7. At the third Mail Merge task pane, click the <u>Browse</u> hyperlink in the *Use an existing list* section of the task pane.

8. At the Select Data Source dialog box, navigate to the WL1C8 folder on your storage medium and then double-click *SFClients.mdb*.

9. At the Mail Merge Recipients dialog box, click OK.

10. Click the <u>Next: Write your letter</u> hyperlink at the bottom of the task pane.

11. At the fourth Mail Merge task pane, enter fields in the form letter by completing the following steps:
    a. Position the insertion point a double space above the first paragraph of text in the letter.
    b. Click the <u>Address block</u> hyperlink in the *Write your letter* section of the task pane.
    c. At the Insert Address Block dialog box, click OK.
    d. Press the Enter key two times and then click the <u>Greeting line</u> hyperlink in the *Write your letter* section of the task pane.
    e. At the Insert Greeting Line dialog box, click the option box arrow at the right of the option box containing the comma (the box to the right of the box containing *Mr. Randall*).
    f. At the drop-down list, click the colon.
    g. Click OK to close the Insert Greeting Line dialog box.

12. Click the <u>Next: Preview your letters</u> hyperlink at the bottom of the task pane.

13. At the fifth Mail Merge task pane, look over the letter in the document window and make sure the information merged properly. If you want to see the letters for the other recipients, click the Next button (button containing two right-pointing arrows) in the Mail Merge task pane.

14. Click the Preview Results button in the Preview Results group to turn off the preview feature.

15. Click the <u>Next: Complete the merge</u> hyperlink at the bottom of the task pane.

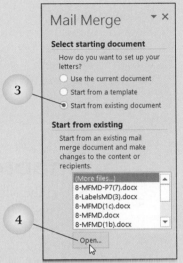

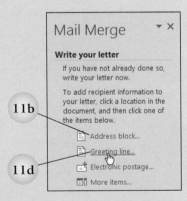

16. At the sixth Mail Merge task pane, click the <u>Edit individual letters</u> hyperlink in the *Merge* section of the task pane.
17. At the Merge to New Document dialog box, make sure *All* is selected and then click OK.
18. Save the merged letters document with the name **8-SFLtrs**.
19. Print only the first two pages of **8-SFLtrs.docx**.
20. Close the document.
21. Close the letter main document without saving it.

Check Your Work

Chapter Summary

- Use the Mail Merge feature to create documents such as letters, envelopes, labels, and directories with personalized information.
- Generally, a merge takes two documents: the data source file containing the variable information and the main document containing standard text along with fields identifying where variable information is inserted during the merge process.
- Variable information in a data source file is saved as a record. A record contains all the information for one unit. A series of fields makes a record and a series of records makes a data source file.
- A data source file is saved as an Access database but having Access on the computer is not required to complete a merge with a data source file.
- Use predesigned fields when creating a data source file or create custom fields at the Customize Address List dialog box.
- Use the Address Block button in the Write & Insert Fields group on the Mailings tab to insert all of the fields required for the inside address of a letter. This inserts the «AddressBlock» field, which is considered a composite field because it groups together a number of fields.
- Click the Greeting Line button in the Write & Insert Fields group on the Mailings tab to insert the «GreetingLine» composite field in the document.
- Click the Insert Merge Field button arrow in the Write & Insert Fields group on the Mailings tab to display a drop-down list of the fields contained in the data source file.
- Click the Preview Results button on the Mailings tab to view the main document merged with the first record in the data source file. Use the navigation buttons in the Preview Results group on the Mailings tab to display the main document merged with the desired record.
- Before merging documents, check for errors by clicking the Check for Errors button in the Preview Results group on the Mailings tab. This displays the Checking and Reporting Errors dialog box with three options for checking errors.
- Click the Finish & Merge button on the Mailings tab to complete the merge.
- Select specific records for merging by inserting or removing check marks from the records in the Mail Merge Recipients dialog box. Display this dialog box by clicking the Edit Recipient List button on the Mailings tab.
- Edit specific records in a data source file at the Edit Data Source dialog box. Display this dialog box by clicking the Edit Recipient List button on the Mailings tab, clicking the data source file name in the *Data Source* list box, and then clicking the Edit button.

- Use the fill-in field in a main document to insert variable information at the keyboard during a merge.
- Word includes a Mail Merge wizard that provides guidance through the process of creating letters, envelopes, labels, directories, and email messages with personalized information.

Commands Review

FEATURE	RIBBON TAB, GROUP	BUTTON, OPTION
Address Block field	Mailings, Write & Insert Fields	
Checking and Reporting Errors dialog box	Mailings, Preview Results	
directory main document	Mailings, Start Mail Merge	, *Directory*
envelopes main document	Mailings, Start Mail Merge	, *Envelopes*
fill-in merge field	Mailings, Write & Insert Fields	, *Fill-in*
Greeting Line field	Mailings, Write & Insert Fields	
insert merge fields	Mailings, Write & Insert Fields	
labels main document	Mailings, Start Mail Merge	, *Labels*
letter main document	Mailings, Start Mail Merge	, *Letters*
Mail Merge Recipients dialog box	Mailings, Start Mail Merge	
Mail Merge wizard	Mailings, Start Mail Merge	, *Step-by-Step Mail Merge Wizard*
New Address List dialog box	Mailings, Start Mail Merge	, *Type a New List*
preview merge results	Mailings, Preview Results	

Index

A

active document, 163
addition formula, 209
Address Block button, 227
Align Left button, 46, 72
alignment
   changing
      cell alignment, 199–200
      table alignment, 203–204
      vertical, of text, 131–132
Alignment button, 49, 72
Align Objects button, 134
Align Right button, 46, 72
Arrange All button, 163
arrow shape, drawing, 142–143
asterisk, 209
AutoComplete, 6
AutoCorrect, 4
AutoCorrect dialog box, 63
AutoCorrect Options button, 62
AutoFit button, 198
AVERAGE function, 209

B

background
   inserting page border, 104–106
   inserting watermark, 103
Backstage area
   Help button, 26
   Open document, 10–11
   Print button, 8–9
   Save As, 7
   Save option, 13
Bing Image Search feature, 137
blank document, 4, 5
blank page, inserting, 96–97
Blank Page button, 96
Bold button, 35
bold typeface, 33, 34–35
Border and Shading Options dialog box, 104–106
Border Painter button, 188
borders
   customizing, 67–68

inserting and changing page border, 104–106
   paragraph borders, 66–68
Borders and Shading dialog box, 67–68
Borders button, 66–67
Border Styles button, 188
Breaks button, 120
bulleted lists, 65
Bullets button, 62

C

calculations, performing in table, 209–211
Calibri, 6
Cell Margins button, 200
Cell Options dialog box, 201
cells
   cell designation, 184
   changing
      cell alignment, 199–200
      cell margin measurements, 200–202
      column width and row height, 198–199
      text direction, 202
   customizing size of, 197–199
   defined, 184
   entering text in, 185
   merging and splitting, 195–197
   selecting
      with keyboard, 191–192
      with mouse, 190
cell selection bar, 190
Center button, 46, 72
centering, vertical, of text, 132
Change Case button, 36
Change your view button, 157
charts, creating organizational chart with SmartArt, 217–219
Check for Error button, 229
Checking and Reporting Errors dialog box, 229

Clear All Formatting button, 32, 36
Click and Type feature, 130–131
Clipboard
   in cutting and pasting text, 77–78
   defined, 77
   in deleting selected text, 77
   using, 81–82
Clipboard task pane, 81–82
closing
   documents, 9
   Word, 9
Collapse the Ribbon button, 5
color, changing
   page color, 103
   theme color, 44–45
Colors button, 44
columns
   balancing on page, 124
   changing width in table, 198–199
   creating
      with Column button, 121–122
      with Columns dialog box, 122–124
   formatting text into, 121–124
   inserting and deleting in tables, 193–195
   inserting column break, 123
   newspaper, 121
   removing formatting, 123
Columns button, 121
Columns dialog box, 122–124
Compact option, 44
continuous section break, 120–121
Convert to Text button, 206
Copy button, 80
copying
   documents, 156–157
   shapes, 142–143
copying and pasting text, 80
cover page, inserting, 96–97
Cover Page button, 96

Crop button, 133
customizing
    borders, 66–67
    cell size, 197–199
    images, 133–138
    picture, 133–137
    shading, 68–69
Cut button, 77
cutting and pasting text, 77–78

D

data source file
    creating, 224–226
    defined, 224
    editing, 237–241
date, inserting, 129–130
Date and Time dialog box,
    129–130
deleting
    documents, 154–155
    folder, 157–158
    hard page break, 95
    rows and columns, 193–195
    section break, 120
    tabs, 74
    text, 17, 77
    undo and redo, 20–21
Design tab, 42
directory, merging, 235–236
Distribute Columns button, 197
Distribute Rows button, 197
division formula, 209
Document Formatting group, 44
documents
    active, 163
    blank, 4, 5
    closing, 9
    copying, 156–157
    creating new, 6, 10–11
    deleting, 154–155
    editing, 14–21
    indenting text in, 49–50
    inserting
        Excel spreadsheet, 211–212
        file into, 167
    maintaining, 152–162
    moving, 156–157

moving insertion point in,
    15–16
naming, 8
navigating, 89–90
opening, 10–11
    multiple, 157, 163–164
pinning and unpinning,
    11–12
previewing pages in, 168–169
printing, 8–9, 169–172
renaming, 157–158
saving, 7–8, 13
    in different formats,
        158–162
scrolling in, 13
selecting, 154–155
template to create, 178–180
view
    changing, 86–87, 157-158
    side by side, 165–166
Draft view, 86
drawing
    arrow shape, 142–143
    enclosed object, 142
    line drawing, 142
    shapes, 142–143
    table, 207
    text box, 141
drop cap, 125–126

E

Edit Data Source dialog box,
    239
editing
    data source file, 237–241
    documents, 14–21
    predesigned header and
        footer, 101–102
Edit Recipient List button, 237
enclosed object, 142
end-of-cell marker, 184
end-of-row marker, 184
Envelope Options dialog box,
    231
envelopes
    creating and printing,
        172–175

general guidelines for
    addressing, 173–174
mailing labels, 175–178
merging, 231–233
Envelopes and Labels dialog
    box, 173, 174, 176
Eraser button, 207
Excel spreadsheet
    inserting into document,
        211–212
Export backstage area, 158–160

F

file, inserting, 167
File tab, 5
Fill-in dialog box, 242–243
Find and Replace dialog box,
    109–112
    options in expanded, 110–111
Find button, 107
finding and replacing
    formatting, 112–113
    text, 112–113
Find option, find and highlight
    text, 107–109
Find Recipient button, 229
Finish & Merge button, 229
First Record button, 229
folder
    change view of, 157-158
    copying and moving
        documents from, 156–157
    creating, 152–153
    deleting, 157–158
    pinning, 12
    renaming, 153–154
    root folder, 152
Font Color button, 36
Font dialog box, 40–41
fonts
    change theme fonts, 44–45
    changing
        with Font dialog box, 40–41
        with Font group buttons,
            33–34
        with Mini toolbar, 37
    choosing font effects, 36,
        38–39